PRAISE FOR *PROXIMITY*

"A significant book that should be at the top of every leader's list. *Proximity* puts technology and our future in a new—and impressively clear—light. Well-reasoned and informed by compelling case examples, this book proposes an insightful hypothesis about the relationship between technology and markets that is being validated every day by developments in technology, industry, and public policy. The concept has the potential for profound impact in higher education. Every leader in education should consider its implications."

—Daniel Diermeier, chancellor and distinguished university professor,
Vanderbilt University; former provost, University of Chicago (2016–2020)

"Inspiring, compelling, and practical, *Proximity* will fundamentally change the way you envision, invest, and compete. The authors don't just tell us how technology will revolutionize our businesses or make our lives faster, better, easier. They also confront the darker side of technological change. Values-driven leaders will discover enormous opportunities and significant challenges to their organizations and society as a result of *Proximity*. I recommend that every business leader read this book."

—Harry M. Jansen Kraemer Jr., clinical professor of leadership,
Kellogg School of Management, Northwestern University;
executive partner, Madison Dearborn Partners; and former CEO,
Baxter International

"Explore *Proximity* as an essential guide to the transformative impact of digital technologies on organizational dynamics in development, coaching, decision making, and beyond. The authors present a compelling vision of the future where the strategic integration of people, systems, and skills—achieving Proximity in its richest forms— becomes crucial for success across all sectors. This book underscores the urgency of bridging distances to meet needs seamlessly, everywhere and every time."

—Anna A. Tavis, clinical professor and chair of the Human Capital
Management Department at NYU's School of Professional Studies,
and author of *Humans at Work* and *The Digital Coaching Revolution*

"When the world changes, we must change too. *Proximity* is a clarion call for leaders not to waste one of the biggest reframing moments of their lifetimes. Packed with razor-sharp insights, *Proximity* is a call to mobilization."

—Terence Mauri, founder, Hack Future Lab,
and MIT entrepreneur mentor

"*Proximity* is a big idea and an important book. Robert C. Wolcott and Kaihan Krippendorff weave a compelling and persuasive tale that is required reading for all who want to make sense of the future today."

—Stuart Crainer, cofounder, Thinkers50

Proximity

PROXIMITY

HOW COMING BREAKTHROUGHS IN JUST-IN-TIME TRANSFORM BUSINESS, SOCIETY, AND DAILY LIFE

ROBERT C. WOLCOTT
KAIHAN KRIPPENDORFF

Columbia Business School Publishing

Columbia University Press
Publishers Since 1893
New York   Chichester, West Sussex
cup.columbia.edu

Library of Congress Cataloging-in-Publication Data
Names: Wolcott, Robert C., author. | Krippendorff, Kaihan, author.
Title: Proximity : how coming breakthroughs in just-in-time transform
business, society, and daily life / Robert C. Wolcott and Kaihan Krippendorff.
Description: New York : Columbia University Press, [2024] |
Includes bibliographical references and index.
Identifiers: LCCN 2023058649 | ISBN 9780231207584 (hardback) |
ISBN 9780231557030 (ebook)
Subjects: LCSH: Technological innovations—Economic aspects. |
Technological innovations—Social aspects. | Just-in-time systems—
Economic aspects. | Just-in-time systems—Social aspects.
Classification: LCC HC79.T4 W639 2024 | DDC 338./064—dc23 2024/eng/0103
LC record available at https://lccn.loc.gov/2023058649

Cover design: Heather Crosby

Contents

Foreword

I first heard Rob Wolcott introduce the concept of Proximity at our Kotler World Marketing Summit in Tokyo in 2015. He offered a compelling vision already under way; however, few of us recognized how profoundly this trend would impact our businesses and lives.

The Proximity notion is simple—that technology enables the production of value ever closer to actual demand. When a customer is ready to buy, thanks to Proximity he or she can satisfy the desire more quickly and at lower cost. Any moment any place, if she wants to hear Barbra Streisand, she clicks on Spotify. If he wants a copy of Herman Melville's *Moby Dick*, it's printed on demand. All of this is about producing and providing products, services, and experiences "just in time."

But Proximity is about *far* more than being faster or more responsive. It's a new way of envisioning business models, delivery platforms, and customer service—even how entire industries operate—enabled by digital technologies of all sorts. Wolcott and coauthor Kaihan Krippendorff assert that smart companies will design systems and business models to *wait* to add value until the moment of demand. These companies will unlock opportunities for far greater personalization by responding efficiently to *specific* customer demands, as well as far greater sustainability by decreasing waste.

This book will introduce you to entrepreneurs and organizations who are adventuring into new areas of production, health, food, work life, energy, and defense. The creative energy being unleashed is enormous. Don't read only about your industry. Explore broadly for new ideas.

Wolcott and Krippendorff have done a significant service by defining and exploring this technology-enabled, multidecade dynamic, while also offering practical recommendations. Through scores of examples, you will discover how our lives will be improved and industries transformed by applying Proximity thinking.

As a marketing theorist, I've long been researching how businesses could create more value for their customers. In a well-functioning marketplace, satisfying human desires ultimately determines who wins. Through this marketing lens, Wolcott and Krippendorff's work shows that the opportunities and threats posed by advancing technologies are best understood by considering what people want and where and how best to provide it. As their book underscores, Proximity rises because we'll become able to "do things that could never have been done before."

But a dark side of marketing is that we humans can be encouraged to desire things that perhaps aren't best for us, for our fellow humans, or for the planet. We should recognize this peril. As the authors explore in each chapter, Proximity taken to extremes threatens to satisfy any desire, wherever, whenever, without regard for others, or even in ways deleterious to our well-being. That's an ever present risk of being desirous beings in a market economy. The Proximity trend amplifies this threat by making so much more possible.

I'm inspired by where Proximity might take us and how entrepreneurs, corporations, NGOs, and governments might strive to enhance our world as a result. I'm also cautious about the challenges and dislocations so many individuals will face as a result of such pervasive change. Breathtaking advances in healthcare, but will they be enjoyed only by the wealthy? Which jobs—and thus people—will be at risk as a result?

Anyone who has followed my work knows the concern my colleagues and I have about ensuring that businesses and marketers consider their impacts on people's lives. Nothing can be more impactful than giving people what they want. Doing so can be both wonderful and treacherous.

With this caveat, an inspiring message of *Proximity* is that brighter paths are more accessible than ever before: creating value wherever, whenever, while also protecting the planet and expanding access for our fellow human beings. Throughout this book, you'll find examples of companies overcoming trade-offs that have for generations been accepted as "just the way things are."

I applaud Wolcott and Krippendorff for the balanced approach they've taken in *Proximity*. They explore both the enormous potential and the challenges we're likely to face.

Their book will become essential for all business leaders, as well as a call to action for each of us as citizens. Wolcott and Krippendorff ask in their conclusion, "What lives do we desire?" and "What futures will we create?" What world will we be proud to leave for our children and grandchildren?

I've seen much change since the introduction of my text *Marketing Management* in 1967, today in its sixteenth edition. Proximity is one of those big, transformative concepts that makes studying, teaching, and doing business worldwide so fulfilling. As one who has seen many business books, I dare say you'll even *enjoy* reading this book as you discover our proximate futures.

The implications of Proximity will be felt for years to come. Opportunity awaits.

Philip Kotler
Professor Emeritus of Marketing
Kellogg School of Management
Northwestern University

Acknowledgments

Every book is a journey. This one started in 2014 with a single question: "What's different about the digital age?" It's a question we've since explored with hundreds of people from around the world, to each of whom we are grateful.

Over many years, we have engaged in mind-opening, clarifying dialogues with an array of innovators. Entrepreneurs, scientists, researchers, academics, investors, and government officials—all of them advance Proximity in their domains. We hope we did an acceptable job of weaving their work and ideas into a useful fabric.

Dozens of members of TWIN Global have helped to amplify, enhance, and even challenge our thinking, especially our advisory council members and global network partners: Chip Bailey, Truls Berg, Bob Castro, Chris Gebhardt, Bob Hendrickson, Guy Kezirian, Kaarina Koskenalusta, Plamen Russev, Alana Sandel, Lee Shapiro, and Howard Tullman. So many of Rob's colleagues at the Booth School of Business and the Kellogg School of Management also provided essential guidance and insights, particularly the exceptional Executive Education teams at both schools. It is a blessing and honor to work with such professionals.

We'd like to offer special thanks to a group of industry and subject matter experts who generously helped us pressure test our industry-focused chapters. They are each true leaders in their fields recognized for vision and foresight: Jack Bobo, Scott Bowman, John Bremen, Peter Bryant, Moran Cerf, Andrew Chung, David Creelman, Dorit Donoviel, Declan Flanagan, Sam Glassenberg, Neesha Hathi, Brian Hoff, Sonia Lo, Rita McGrath, Julio Ottino, Slava Rubin, Rafael Salmi, Darshak Sanghavi, Michael Schrage, Lee Shapiro, Ana Tavis, Rick Tumlinson, and Joe Wheeler.

Many entrepreneurs, executives, scientists, and technologists helped us see what's possible. A special thanks in this regard to Barbara Belvisi, Tom Bianculli, Mark Dancer, Marc Goldberg, Gary Hoberman, Pablos Holman,

David Krakauer, Kevin Kramer, Geoffrey Ling, Justin Milano, Jon Morris, Shelly Palmer, Debu Purkayastha, Toby Redshaw, Maurizio Rossi, Sten-Kristian Saluveer, Shaukat Shamim, Sam Shawki, Kunal Sood, Dylan Taylor, Martin Wezowski, and Nancy Zayed. Brian Collins, Jeffrey Ernstoff, Natasha Tsakos, and Kadri Voorand brought their artistic visions to our concept and pages.

Particular thanks go to Michael J. Lippitz, one of Rob's long-time collaborators. Mike co-authored our chapter "How We Defend," bringing thirty years of defense policy and technology expertise to our mission. A double thanks to Mike, Bob Hendrickson, and Howard Tullman for exceptional insight and constructive criticism that advanced Rob's thinking about technology, business, society, and humanity over so many years.

In the early stages, we benefited from wise counsel of people like Stuart Crainer and Des Dearlove of Thinkers50, who helped us understand where this work might contribute something unique; Maggie Stuckey, who helped us make key choices regarding our book's flow and purpose; and Brian Smith and Myles Thompson from Columbia University Press, who trusted we would shape the Proximity concept.

Our project benefitted from the support of the smart and passionate team at Outthinker Networks. Cori Dombroski was central to the effort, acting as our thought and writing partner. Anna Drabarek, Stuti Johri, J. T. Ruiz, Jameson Daugherty, and Wiles Kase provided insights as researchers and analysts. Karina Reyes helped keep the project on track. Greg Shaw proved a brilliant line editor that went beyond. For the cover design, we were privileged to work with a true artist, Heather Crosby.

We owe great thanks to Philip Kotler for his encouragement and for writing such a thoughtful foreword. We are in awe of his life-long commitment to inspiring leaders to bring true value to the world.

Kaihan is grateful for the Outthinker team not yet mentioned here—Zach Ness, Claudio Garcia, and Johnlouie Dalogdog—for affording him the luxury of time to dedicate to this project, as well as Jody Johnson for her guidance over so many years. He would also like to thank the members of Outthinker Networks—the strategy officers, intrapreneurs, and other forward-looking executives—who have shared evidence and ideas that inform the Proximity concept in hundreds of conversations.

Rob would like to personally thank his family—Ada, Jolie, Sage, and canine Cici—who make everything in life possible and meaningful, and his partners at Clareo (Scott Bowman, Peter Bryant, Anna Catalano, Paul

Donellan, Allan Platt, and Satish Rao) who have provided years of insights, collaboration, and commitment.

Kaihan would personally like to thank his wife, Pilar, and his children—Lucas, Kaira, and Makar—for supporting him in pursuing his passion of exploring and helping to advance concepts that could change the future, like Proximity.

Most of all, we'd like to honor our parents, both here and in the world beyond, without whom this journey—or any of our adventures—would not have been possible. Eternal love and thanks.

Proximity

1

Proximity Rising

What if you could have what you want, produced and provided immediately and affordably no matter how customized—with minimal environmental impact? Products, services, experiences on demand, no magic involved.

It's the world toward which we're heading. A world in which constraints ease, in some cases disappear.

Others are asking why something like this hasn't already happened. The *New York Times* reported in early 2023 that "we should be in a golden age of new discoveries and innovations." Not new smartphone apps or pet dating sites, but true breakthroughs.

It's one thing to develop a new technology. It's another to transform the business models, infrastructure, productive capacity, and even the mindsets of business leaders, investors, regulators, and consumers, each of us as citizens. To conceive and implement dramatically new solutions.

This book will help you understand and lead the changes under way: distributed rather than centralized, personalized in place of standardized, and sustainable instead of profligate. This is not another book on digital transformation or supply chain optimization. It's a book about the dramatically better worlds that technology, vision, and creativity—*your creativity*—can enable.

We call this revolution "Proximity." It's where we're heading. While we've a long way to go, the demand side of the equation has always been clear. People want what they want, where and when they want it. Those who can give it to them are more likely to win.

Our basic needs and wants—food, health, entertainment, and security, for instance—persist. But how we fulfill them has begun a decades-long journey from the Industrial Age's centralized production model to our distributed, *proximate* future. We are at the knee of this curve.

Some of the enabling technologies generate big news, like generative AI in 2023, while others improve in the background, like vertical farming and distributed energy generation. It takes industries and society time to climb the steep learning curves of these new capabilities, to recognize that incrementally improving the ways we've traditionally done things isn't enough. It's about conceiving entirely new approaches to satisfying needs and wants while protecting the planet.

A few cases in point:

- In Singapore, Dubai, Brooklyn, and beyond, vertical farms are literally rising, bringing fresh food ever closer to consumers.
- Rooftop solar energy generation blurs the line between power producers and consumers. Software enables resilient local microgrids, with neighbors producing, storing, and sharing power among themselves—helping make widespread power outages rare.
- Additive manufacturing (such as 3D printing) has gone from producing simple plastic baubles to ever more complicated products on demand that are suitable for complex applications such as spacecraft.
- We discover a mesmerizing array of entertainments always at hand.

We already take services like content streaming and overnight product delivery for granted. A generation ago such capabilities sounded fanciful. Today, they're assumptions. Technologies like generative AI and quantum computing are traveling similar trajectories. Imagine where we'll be in a decade. For instance:

- Doctors producing pharmaceuticals immediately on-site, customized in dosage and quantity for each patient
- Fresh agricultural produce growing year-round within short range of your home (possibly even *at* home)

- Communities of gamers co-creating real-time 3D virtual environments and experiences

No need to wait. It is possible to do all this today. Not yet scaled, but proven and operational—real. Are we ready to align our businesses, communities, and society for future expectations, possibilities, and risks? Will we have the wisdom and incentives to ensure that the benefits are affordably available to all?

Just as steam and electricity were to the Industrial Revolution, digital is to our era. Pandemics, geopolitical tensions, climate catastrophes, and even humanity's race to space conspire to accelerate Proximity. Digital capabilities make it possible.

Klaus Schwab of the World Economic Forum describes our current age as the Fourth Industrial Revolution, a title derived from decades of conversations with the world's top engineers, scientists, and business and government leaders. He asserts that we "stand on the brink of a technological revolution that will fundamentally alter the way we live, work, and relate to one another. In its scale, scope, and complexity, the transformation will be unlike anything humankind has experienced before." He cautions that "we do not yet know just how it will unfold."[1]

While we cannot predict the future in detail, we can discern its contours. Digital technologies, each in its own way, enable us to distribute and coordinate sensing, data collection, analytics, decisions, and production capabilities at ever smaller levels around the economy, ever closer to each moment in time and space. Systems capture our wants, needs, and actions, sending galaxies of data to smart clouds infused with the latest AI to discern intentions and outcomes with more and more precision. Then digitally enabled platforms generate and offer what's required.

As a result, *digital technologies push the production and provision of value—products, services, and experiences—ever closer to the moment of demand.* Not predicted demand, not forecasted demand, but real, ready-to-pay-for-it demand.

To answer Schwab: Proximity elucidates "just how it will unfold."

WHY NOW?

Why is Proximity our path, and why now? Because we're increasingly able to do things where, when, and how we want—things we could never have done before.

Though no one called it that, we've always aspired to Proximity: producing and providing whatever customers desire, where and when they desire it. Of course, businesses would have had this before if they could have done so competitively, but for the most part doing so was far too costly, if not impossible.

Over the last few hundred years, industries have evolved to satisfy customers via complex, expensive (and vulnerable) supply chains optimized for scale manufacturing at great distances from demand. Likewise, services have evolved via widespread infrastructure—physical locations like offices and retail establishments—with legions of employees at the ready.

The COVID-19 pandemic underscored the fragile nature of global supply chains. Through this traumatic period, businesses and governments recognized the need for multiple sources and more flexible solutions nearby or at least in country. Globalization faltered. The world ceased to be flat, if it ever was.

Renewed aggression between nations, such as Russia toward Europe as well as what many observers refer to as deglobalization, catalyzes desires for local resilience. The most obvious—and wrong—response would be some version of building traditional production capacity closer to home. This would come at great cost.

Greater resilience will *not* come from modest improvements to legacy systems. It will come from new solutions. Technologies from automation and robotics to 5G communications and additive manufacturing change the economics of producing and providing an entire range of products, services, and experiences proximate with demand.

Visionary entrepreneurs and enterprises will overcome heretofore intractable trade-offs: customization versus efficiency, sustainability versus affordability and access. Both consumers and the environment will stand to benefit.

You read that right. Having whatever we want, when and where we want it, can translate into a more sustainable world if we have the creativity and ingenuity to make it so. We face no more human challenge than overcoming our unlimited desires with limited resources. Proximity offers paths through this existential, environmental maze.

If you aspire to lead through the coming "gales of creative destruction," as the great economist Joseph Schumpeter named such entrepreneurially driven upheavals, this book is for you. Our mission is to provide you with foresight so *you* can create our proximate future.

To understand where we're heading, let's examine a past revolution.

THE FIRST ELECTRICITY REVOLUTION

Doing anything, anywhere—enabling Proximity—requires widespread access to electricity. Some refer to present-day developments around electric vehicles, distributed energy resources, and other energy-related trends as an electricity revolution.[2] But the first electricity revolution—electrification's genesis in the late nineteenth and early twentieth centuries—was arguably more profound.

During this period, while power production consolidated in massive power plants far from ultimate demand, the *provision* of electricity became nearly ubiquitous, at least in developed economies. It transformed our lives. For instance, the historian Roger Ekirch argues that electric lamps disrupted the sleeping patterns of entire populations.[3] (Your mobile phone can be just as sleep destroying.)

It's difficult to overstate the impact of widely available, reliable electricity. In 1990, the economist Paul David published an article in the *American Economic Review* that examined the impact of electrification.[4] He focused on the steep learning curve that industries had to climb to leverage the flexibility provided by electrification.

How best to apply electrification was not obvious. Once manufacturing plant electrification became economically viable, it still took decades for it to diffuse throughout factories in the United States and Europe.

David points out at least two critical factors: *legacy assets* and *learning curves*. Established businesses already had assets such as manufacturing facilities and capabilities built around prior technologies like hydropower and steam. These existing assets biased many companies toward delaying investments in electrification, in many cases longer than they should have to remain competitive.

The second factor is the steep learning curve confronting anyone seeking to apply new technologies. New paradigms typically require high-risk investments, many of which fail. Early on, some established companies started by trying to electrify already existing facilities. This often proved horribly suboptimal. Utilizing steam power, for instance, required very different layouts (often in vertical buildings, with pulleys and belts sending the power to equipment), equipment, and processes than would be possible with electricity.

Managers had to learn through experimentation (and expensive failures) that electrification wasn't just a substitute for steam or water wheels. Electrification enabled power to be applied anywhere in new more reliable, flexible ways. *To do things that had never been done before.*

Today, the availability of electricity, anywhere, anytime, is pivotal for all things digital. Throughout our book, we'll share how digital technologies drive Proximity across all aspects of our lives. Let's start with a healthcare example born of the challenges of war.

MEDICINES ON DEMAND . . . ANYWHERE

It surprises most people to learn that generic drug shortages plague healthcare systems even in advanced economies.

Amplify that challenge when it comes to providing pharmaceuticals in war zones. During his six tours of duty in Iraq and Afghanistan, retired U.S. Army doctor Colonel Geoffrey Ling and his colleagues often faced shortages of essential drugs. The right drug at the right moment can make a life-or-death difference, yet supplying pharmaceuticals in war zones presents a daunting task.

Though a priority issue for the U.S. military, established solutions hadn't prevailed. Tweaking existing processes generally resulted in only incremental progress and could even increase red tape and workarounds. Occasionally, pilots would shuttle generic drugs via fighter jets from bases in Europe. Imagine *that* fuel bill (drugs you can buy at the pharmacy for a few dollars, delivered by F-16s!).

What if we could produce precisely which drugs are required on-site in immediate response to demand? That's what Dr. Ling envisioned. It's now becoming a reality.

As a program officer with the Biological Technologies Office at the Defense Advanced Research Projects Agency (DARPA), Dr. Ling asked, "Could we produce the right drugs at small scale on-site, immediately where and when required?"[1] Orthodoxies about pharmaceutical production presented a resounding "no." Drug manufacturing is a highly controlled, complicated process subject to regulation and rigorous quality control, and rightly so. Mistakes can be deadly.

Ignoring constraints, Ling and his team recognized that most synthetic pharmaceuticals require a limited number of inputs—hydrogen, oxygen, and carbon—to produce. "Give me an egg and a pencil and I can make whatever you want," Ling quipped.

Mission in mind, the DARPA-funded team, in collaboration with researchers at MIT, created a system capable of small-scale production of generic drugs. The size of a small refrigerator, it's essentially a printer for pharmaceuticals. Chambers, pumps, and valves automated and managed by digital technologies. The company Ling founded, On Demand Pharmaceuticals, is on track to commercialize the technology for nonmilitary applications. Imagine the opportunities for upending the global pharmaceutical supply chain and enhancing care worldwide.

There is no way to know if Ling's company will be the one that takes this capability to scale, entrepreneurial vicissitudes being what they are. What Ling and his colleagues have proven is that it's possible to make immediately proximate the production of precision-sensitive, regulated, life-and-death products like pharmaceuticals.

Consider the knock-on effects of such a system. Pharmaceuticals expire. Unused inventory must be discarded typically after a few years. In a proximate production system like On Demand's, the raw materials in inventory remain unconverted until a patient requires the drug, the moment of *actual* demand. In this case, inventory means, for instance, carbon. What's the shelf life of carbon? Forever.

Ling expands the vision. "Imagine taking this to places where they don't have access to generic drugs, like Afghanistan or the Congo."

Ling's magic machine could change the world.

THE BENEFITS OF PROCRASTINATION

Ling's vision illustrates a counterintuitive power digital affords: the ability to wait for actual demand.

In other words, better performance by *waiting*. The performance advantage of speed isn't about doing what we already do faster. It's about being ready to add value as demand arises, *and no sooner*. It's about designing technology platforms, organizational capabilities, and business models to avoid as much costly activity as possible until *real* demand materializes.

As a result of waiting for demand, proximate business models require *less* prediction of future demand and generate less waste.

Most traditional business models require products and services to be designed, planned, produced, and staged (for example, to have a product inventory or an available call center capacity) in advance to ensure they'll have what customers want at the time and place they want it. They incur enormous costs to do so: demand and production planning, logistics, inventory management, channel management, reverse logistics (aka, returns), and surplus inventory disposal.

Imagine the profitability of a business able to produce and provide only what's required, when and where someone's willing to pay for it. No more inventory fire sales or perished perishables, and far less waste.

Digital technologies enable this Proximity, but most companies haven't yet recognized how profoundly possible it is. New assets, models, and capabilities are emerging that, in many cases, make possible what we could never have done before.

The publishing industry saw a huge breakthrough with the advent of print-on-demand technologies. A publisher no longer has to take the risk of a large print run, instead printing volumes as they are ordered. A hint of the proximate evolution under way.

The so-called sharing economy, represented by companies like Uber and Airbnb, introduced more efficient ways for consumers to access latent resources—potential rides and rooms—and for drivers and hosts to receive payment for their efforts and assets. ("Sharing" was always a questionable moniker, given that we're paying for the privilege.) Their technology platforms were simple overlays—your smartphone app—that help buyers and sellers access resources that for the most part already existed.

Unlocking latent resources across the economy has been a first step toward Proximity. Consider 3D printing. 3D printing still requires the right inventory when a customer need arises, but the "inventories" required are far simpler and more flexible than traditional manufacturing. Instead of finished products incorporating the costs of producing and inventory-ing components across an extended supply chain, additive manufacturing requires raw materials in forms that are ready to use by 3D printing equip-ment, such as polymers or metal powders in cartridges.

Finished products made in anticipation of future demand are at risk of not finding buyers. Additive manufacturing relies on inventories of nearly raw materials ready to fashion into any of thousands of different products. Whatever the customer demands fulfilled in the moment.

History offers many examples of how proximate business models led to market-leading change.

Charles Schwab

In January 1996, individual investing pioneer Charles Schwab launched web trading not long after the introduction of the first web browser. Although new entrants such as E-Trade were already active, Schwab recognized the power of online trading before any of the large incumbents. Schwab offered online trades at $29.95; in-person or phone orders remained far more expensive. While online accounts soared, customers expressed increasing frustration at not being able to order through any channel at the same price. Greg Gable, Schwab's senior vice president for public affairs, recalls, "The problem quickly became apparent. We had clients revolting. . . . We had employees saying, 'Hey, we need to do what is right for our customers.' So we did." In late 1997, Schwab offered the $29.95 price for all trades, online or otherwise. "We expected a considerable hit to revenue. . . . We prepared for the worst but thought we'd make up for the change within two years due to increased volume. We made it up in six months."

Schwab had navigated an early voyage toward Proximity—online trading from home. Since then the industry has followed, superseded in some ways by financial services platforms like PayPal, Coinbase, and Robinhood, where interfaces are increasingly mobile. Robinhood's leadership even wonders why anyone would want a desktop version. So twentieth century.

Netflix

Reed Hastings and Marc Randolph founded Netflix on the premise that people want the movies they want at the moments they want them. You don't need a focus group to discover that.

While driving to a Blockbuster to rent a video seemed easy enough to an earlier generation, it created distance between supply and demand—say, a 20-minute drive to the store and back—and burdensome physical inventory across thousands of locations.

That Netflix's founders decided to put "Net" in their company's name revealed their ambitions: to deliver movies to people's homes via the internet. At the time, however, bandwidth, modems and storage and communication technologies made this goal impractical.

Instead of giving up or waiting for the technology and bandwidth to improve—others might have arrived first—they adopted an approach central for evolving into Proximity strategies: a *transitional business model*. Netflix delivered DVDs by mail to build their brand, content access, customers, and data. As technology and bandwidth improved, making it possible to deliver great online video experiences, Netflix was thus uniquely positioned to lead. As the "streaming wars" intensified in the early 2020s, incumbents scrambled to catch up. Netflix remained one of the likely long-term winners.

Domino's

Old-school pizza franchise Domino's began its Proximity shift around 2008. Leadership realized that the value it delivered could be about far more than the right pizza delivered hot and on time. Easy online customization and dependable, transparent delivery became reasons to buy; customize your order, then tracking it from assembly through delivery.

Since then, Domino's has created an industry-leading customer experience. Because of years building digital capabilities, Domino's outflanked most competitors during the COVID-19 pandemic.

Recognizing that information travels faster than pizza, Domino's collapsed the distance between its consumers and the experience of ordering, delivering, and enjoying its products. Over the years preceding this book, its stock price has closely matched that of Amazon—both by about 1,600 percent in the decade leading up to 2021.

As we'll see in chapter 4, "How We Eat," the next breakthroughs will occur even earlier in the farm-to-table process—proximate dairy for cheese, veggies for toppings.

NEW CAPABILITIES: NEW STRATEGY AND STRUCTURE

Fundamental technology transitions transform how businesses operate, structure, and add value. In his Pulitzer Prize–winning work, *The Visible Hand*, the business historian Alfred Chandler argues that the diffusion of railroads catalyzed the invention and evolution of the modern corporation. Astride the rail network grew entirely new businesses, from department stores and mail order to communications networks. Accounting, finance, and managerial structures evolved to marshal the vast, far-flung resources of the Railroad Age.

The transition from wind to steam power for waterborne transportation across the nineteenth century similarly revolutionized geopolitics, military strategy, organization, and the projection of power. It catalyzed massive national investments and rivalries that changed the course of history.

Railroads and oceangoing, steam-powered vessels also engendered a global supply chain characterized by scale manufacturing at a distance. For the most part, the larger your plant the lower your costs. The global production system born in that era dominates today.

All of these Industrial Age structures and solutions are now in play. Understanding Proximity's implications will help you avoid ill-conceived investments in soon-to-be-outmoded models and capabilities and offers insights applicable for any business, investor, or policymaker.

To understand how profoundly different this emerging Proximate world will be, consider the counterexample of Industrial Age orders for formed metal products (a business Rob learned from his father in the twentieth century). Increasing the number of identical products produced translates to dramatically lower unit costs. In most cases, product developers wouldn't think to propose custom, one-off parts. Supply chain and procurement managers prefer large orders, and manufacturers drive down costs through high-scale production of identical products.

Enter 3D printing, a type of additive manufacturing, or the process that uses computer-aided-design software to deposit materials by layers and create precise geometric objects.[5]

In principle, creating a single part needn't be much more costly per unit than producing millions of the same part. Same materials, same form. Traditional centralized, high-scale production will remain cost competitive for many products, but over time this situation will shift as additive technologies become more capable and widespread. Product developers will discover greater flexibility and options to satisfy customer needs via customization. As the cost advantages decline for scale production of identical products relative to the value generated by customization and responsiveness, manufacturing will transition to become more distributed and proximate.

The benefits transcend customization. Proximity strategies upend the game for demand planning and inventory costs. Large orders from huge production facilities rely on demand prediction and inventory management capabilities. Risk increases as a function of the number and cost of units produced, the costs of holding inventory, and the quality (or lack thereof) of demand predictions.

The easiest demand to predict is one that already exists—an insight essential to Proximity. The more they can produce anything at a moment's notice, the less dependent businesses will be on predicting and preparing for future demands.

PROXIMITY PRINCIPLES

Across industries, we'll encounter four principles that characterize proximate business models. We'll see each of these Proximity principles reflected in the upcoming "How We . . ." chapters. They are:

1. Moment of Use (MoU) Production and Provision
2. Data and Analytics Across Competitive Ecosystems
3. *True* Customer Centricity
4. Real-Time Learning and Adapting Systems

Moment of Use (MoU) Production and Provision

Throughout this book, we examine how MoU production and provision are already manifesting and likely to evolve, mitigating delivery costs, waste, supply chain risks, and environmental impacts. Economics (and to some extent politics) will dictate how far and fast each industry advances toward MoU production. But MoU production is the north star of where we're heading.

An age-old example would be your made-to-order meal at a local restaurant. Other than the inputs, all of the value-add occurs on-site proximate with your order. In chapter 4, "How We Eat," we describe how an increasing range of the inputs—even animal proteins—will be economically produced closer to your home or local restaurant thanks to technologies like cultured meat and controlled environment agriculture (CEA).

The critical aspect of MoU is the ability to customize production, that is, being ready to respond instantaneously as demand arises rather than trying to predict what customers may or may not want.

As we'll see, the magic of MoU manifests as greater customization *and* less waste. In our final chapter we make the case that MoU production will eventually—decades in the future—be true for nearly all products, services, and experiences.

Data and Analytics Across Competitive Ecosystems

Postponing value-add until the last moment requires knowing where, when, and how to bring the right resources to bear.

As costs of data capture, storage, retrieval, and analytics decline, smart companies aspire to real-time cross-ecosystem visibility. Fast, customized response for each individual customer will require a breadth and depth of data collection and analytics far beyond what most industries have traditionally supported.

Nearly instantaneous data communications at exponentially lower costs (5G today and more to come with future Gs), along with improved performance of sensor and data storage technologies, are enabling advanced analytical capabilities (offered by companies such as Snowflake and Alteryx) to solve problems and discover opportunities in more and more contexts. Smart competitors can build wider *and* more granular visibility from raw materials to end consumers while monitoring contextual factors such as geopolitical and environmental threats. While deep knowledge of each individual customer is essential, it's just the focal part of a much larger picture.

Online insurance sales and delivery reflect the proximate power of digital platforms to sell and service in more responsive, scalable ways. Whereas the old auto insurance model of local agents emphasized local knowledge—such as state regulations and local client relationships—online insurance platforms such as Geico and Progressive aggregate data about clients and conditions across the competitive landscape. Today, both models complement and compete, emphasizing different customer value propositions. Faced with an accident claim, smartphone apps or drones can far more quickly assess damage anywhere, compared to the past, when adjustors made appointments to visit and review the car in person. Proximity solutions can enhance both models.

True Customer Centricity

Proximity redefines what it means to be customer centric. Most businesses believe they are customer centric, but they're more organized around operating model constraints (such as complex supply chains and channels) than around customers. Consider what percentage of time you and your colleagues grapple with operating constraints rather than directly serving customers.

Your customers don't care about your constraints. If someone else can serve them better, they'll switch.

Companies seek to gather and heed the "voice of the customer" but typically can only deliver what fits within their current operating model.

Digital technologies offer opportunities to overcome such legacy constraints, enabling previously impossible levels of customer service. They transform the range, flexibility, and opportunities for customization at every moment in time and space.

Traditionally companies that have endeavored to provide exceptional levels of customization have required high price points to be profitable. Such competitors sought customers with high value for bespoke products and services, such as luxury couture or custom software development. By collapsing trade-offs between customization and efficiency, proximate models offer dramatically better solutions for *truly* organizing around customer demands, even as those demands change.

While these trends started with offering standardized products such as books (e.g., Amazon) and digitizable products such as music and videos (e.g., Spotify and Netflix) with marginal costs nearing zero to store and deliver, proximate models will increasingly offer personalization at scale for products and services of all kinds.

Of course, no company should try to do everything for everyone. That's a loser's game. The strategy maxims of positioning and focus still apply, but how we're able to do so changes. Companies will still have to make trade-offs: we serve these needs and not those, we focus on these customers and not others. But with more flexible, responsive capabilities, smart competitors will be able to serve a wider variety of needs and wants for wider sets of customers.

Real-Time Learning and Adapting Systems

Any Tesla owner knows the experience of waking up to an updated car. During the night, at nearly whatever cadence it chooses, Tesla sends software updates to its connected vehicles covering a range of issues, from enhancing the user interface or battery system efficiency to tweaking the air conditioning.

Meanwhile, Tesla's products collect data regarding a vast range of consumer behaviors, preferences, and challenges. Compare the learning and adaptive opportunities of traditional vehicles with these connected, data-savvy systems. It's not that connected vehicles are a little better. They're playing a different game.

All businesses covet customer data. It's just that proximate business models require greater connectivity and insights at the point of demand than traditional models. Doing so amplifies opportunities for identifying and responding to needs in your customers' natural habitats.

Mamatha Chamarthi, head of automotive giant Stellantis's global software business, offers a simple comparison to illustrate.

> Look at what happens when the "check engine" light goes on in a non-connected vehicle. Your only option to resolve the problem is to go to a dealer, which messes up your entire day . . . and you're not even sure if it's safe to drive. Now, move to a connected car. The vehicle has been monitoring itself all along, running predictive diagnostics to avoid ever having the problem. . . . Compared to the unconnected car, you've saved three to six hours of your life and had a frictionless experience.

Problems are resolved before they waste your time or threaten your safety. Systems identify and resolve needs before we even know we have them. Known for years as "predictive maintenance" in the aerospace industry, expect to see such capabilities proliferate to other contexts.

Beyond maintaining existing systems, proximate models are faster and more effective at adapting to changing needs. Proximity-designed business models and technology platforms have greater flexibility to finish products and services in rapid response to demands.

In early 2018, Levi Strauss announced a new supply chain model, Project F.L.X., or future-led execution. It explained at launch, "Traditionally, denim finishing—which creates worn, faded design elements on jeans—has been a highly manual, labor-intensive and chemical-reliant process. Digitalization enables a responsive and sustainable supply chain at an unparalleled scale."

By mid-2019, Levi's had introduced Future Finish, a digitally controlled, laser-based system to finish jeans to exact customer specifications. Starting in manufacturing facilities, the company envisions rolling out the capability in its NextGen stores. Levi's produces millions of copies of the same basic pant and then finishes the product in a matter of minutes, responsive to each individual customer.

In an interview with Hypebeast in 2021, Bart Sights, Levi's senior director for technical innovation, explains:

> We don't want to be considered fast, but we do want to be considered closer to the selling point. If you think about the [traditional jeans

finishing] process . . . that's pushing our design point more than a year back before we sell it. A denim finish is dangerous to design a year before we sell it because the trend can change. With F.L.X., we create a process that is much more benign and faster, and because it doesn't need an army of people and lots of logistical support, we can do it anywhere—even in-market. We create bases and then ship them out to markets and wait to see what we need and what the consumer is telling us.

Levi's F.L.X. postpones finishing until each customer expresses their preferences.

Before this Proximity solution, Levi's relied on predictions of how many versions of each specific design and size might be demanded at any given location. Hot new styles had to wait for the next product cycle. Its laser-finishing scheme enables the company to add nearly any finish or visual to its range of jeans, which are produced in mass quantities and then finished to each individual consumer's preferences. (Imagine your loved one's image ever present on your pants!)

Better customer data and MoU production enable real-time learning and true customer centricity.

WHAT'S DIFFERENT FROM THE PAST

As we will see, Proximity strategies differ from traditional approaches by at least five characteristics:

- *They radically outperform the status quo from the customer's perspective.* Proximity models organize around what is best for customers, sometimes at the expense of established value-chain participants. Performance and customer experience can be orders of magnitude better. For new entrants like Uber or cardinal enterprises like Amazon, that's just fine. Amazon is often criticized by suppliers and partners—not to mention competitors—for practices resulting from its maniacal focus on serving customers. For traditional players, like limo and taxi companies or grocery stores, it's an existential threat.
- *They tend to upend traditional constraints.* Achieving radical improvements in performance requires overcoming constraints. Infamously, Uber has challenged regulators around the world. Whether it's gone too far is open for debate. It's uncontestable that Uber has transformed personal

transportation. U.S. auto dealers mounted largely unsuccessful legal challenges to Tesla's direct-to-consumer approach, but direct consumer engagement is fundamental to the company's competitive flexibility. Where possible, it's best to avoid violating established constraints—it's easier—but not at the expense of better serving customers.

- *They build presence before markets have been clearly defined.* Amazon experiments with drone delivery not just to advance instantaneous service but also to engage regulators and catalyze other companies to experiment. While drones are still experimental for many applications, expect Amazon and other players to discover niche applications that build experience, presence, and customer value—and anticipate the day when delivery drones proliferate.

- *They enable adaptation as conditions change.* Proximity models should be designed to adapt as capabilities evolve. This means anticipating the direction (not the details) of customer needs and which technologies and business models might eventually prevail.

- *They're designed with ecosystems in mind.* In 2015, the Strategic Enterprise Fund of global distribution and logistics giant UPS invested in Fast Radius (formerly Cloud DDM), a 3D printing company now with hundreds of printers located across from UPS's worldwide hubs. Fast Radius prints parts on demand and sends them literally across the alley to UPS for shipping, allowing a response within 24 hours for many parts. As of this writing, Fast Radius has made over 10 million parts, using 67,000 unique designs, for over 1,800 customers. UPS offers unlimited scaling for Fast Radius's logistics while supporting the evolution of a new industry—and increasing demand for its core offerings.

Could Fast Radius have thrived without its proximate location to UPS's logistics machine? Perhaps, but it's far more competitive because of that location. Could UPS build its own 3D printing business? Sure, but should it? Might a logistics company rather seed a new industry of dozens, even thousands, of new players in need of its services? Whether or not the Fast Radius concept succeeds—the company was acquired by SyBridge Technologies in 2022—UPS will benefit from more companies providing small runs of products and parts sent in thousands of brown UPS boxes.

Proximity strategies see ecosystem engagement as a business amplifier rather than a less-than-ideal alternative to vertically integrated or lock-step supply chains. Well-nurtured ecosystems provide greater flexibility and more options, essential in fast-changing environments.

OUR JOURNEY TOGETHER

A decade ago, few imagined the prevalence of same-day delivery or the rapid rise of electric vehicles. But a few *did* envision what people would love if they could have it—and built world-changing businesses. Tesla, Netflix, Amazon, certainly, but also nontech businesses like farm-to-table restaurants and local brewpubs around the world, to name a few.

Through the present multidecade transition, we'll have plenty of regression back to value creation at greater distance from demand—where that makes economic sense—but the overwhelming trend will be toward Proximity.

Note that any given business model isn't "proximate or not." It's a matter of degree. From producing products in massive factories thousands of miles away, to producing them in urban areas in small footprint facilities—to eventually on your counter at home. The most likely condition we'll see evolve in each industry will be hybrid models, with some production remaining in centralized, high-scale facilities complemented by new proximate models where they make the most economic, competitive sense. We'll see this writ large in the following chapters.

Optimization of large-scale manufacturing capabilities and global supply networks will continue apace. Our point is, that's not new. The Proximity trend represents what's new, and it's likely to redraw entire industries. It's a multidecade trend open for new leaders.

As we'll find, the Proximity dynamic promises transformative benefits in customization, cost, and sustainability, but it also harbors darker implications. Everything, everywhere all at once! Humanity's enduring desire for whatever, wherever, combined with shortsightedness and greed, has generated dilemmas from environmental damage to economic inequality. Through successive Industrial Revolutions, humans have proven willing to compromise long-term prosperity—even the only planet we've so far inhabited—for short-term gain. Like past transitions, Proximity promises heretofore unimagined abundance, accompanied by the perils of greed, gluttony, and myopia.

In the next chapter we'll define Proximity and the forces accelerating us in the direction of a far future endgame we call *Proximity = 0*. Chapters 3–8 explore Proximity in terms of how we live and work on earth. In chapter 9 we'll project our concepts to space and rapidly evolving virtual worlds—the ultimate Proximity frontiers. In the appendix you'll find a Proximity strategy workbook to help you and your colleagues envision how to lead the revolution.

Along the way, we'll highlight relevant concerns. Will we endeavor to expand access or amplify inequality? How will notions of data privacy, ownership, and control evolve? Will we protect and regenerate the natural environments on which life depends, or will we take easy, destructive paths to short-term gain?

The good news is that proximate models offer opportunities to overcome such trade-offs. Doing so requires vision and commitment.

CHOOSE

We have the power to choose—to realize the potential of Proximity while minimizing the threats.

Our story isn't only about technologies and companies. It's also about individuals like you: entrepreneurs, scientists, technologists, investors, corporate executives, policymakers, and political leaders leveraging Proximity's potential and grappling with the ethical dilemmas that ensue.

In addition to Dr. Ling envisioning pharmaceutical production on demand, we'll meet pioneers like agriculture visionary Jack Bobo advocating for the thirty most critical years humanity will *ever* face; space race entrepreneur Barbara Belvisi piloting sustainable planetary colonization capabilities here on Earth, with her eyes fixed on the moon, Mars, and beyond; and colonists of the early metaverse, omniverse, and, one day, outer space.

Proximity offers nearly unlimited possibilities to manifest desires. It will be up to each of us, and all of us together, to determine how to create lives for which we can be thankful—or otherwise.

2

Accelerating Toward P = 0

Most of us recognize the difference between waiting in line at a bank and logging onto a mobile banking app—that is, for those of us who have actually visited a physical bank. Soon we'll recall the quaint days of human grocery checkout clerks. Far more pervasive change is under way across all aspects of our lives. Ironically, it's easier to underappreciate change when it's transformative than when we experience cases like mobile banking or a clerk-free grocery experience.

Consider sound recording. Before 1877, when Thomas Edison made sound recording a reality, the only way to experience music—with inconsequential exceptions like mechanical music boxes—was live. Think about that: *all music, anywhere, only live for all of human history . . . EVER.* Love a symphony? Find an orchestra. Want to discover a new favorite song? Hang out with your musical cousin at the pub.

By 1890, entrepreneurs were installing nickel-in-the-slot machines on city streets. Wildly popular for a while, they enabled you to enjoy several minutes (minutes!) of prerecorded music, jokes, or whatever happened to be loaded on the machine. You stood next to the machine and listened via one of the "listening tubes." And you happily paid for it.

Today, nothing is more proximate than music: any genre, performer, or volume anywhere, whenever, as often as you like (and even when you don't). The pivotal catalyst has been digitalization. Once the technology and infrastructure became available, moving musical digits became trivial. Same with pictures. There was a time when enormous paintings by artists like Albert Bierstadt toured the country. For a price you viewed them in or near your hometown. Today a Bierstadt landscape of Yosemite National Park can be experienced anywhere on any smart device.

Appreciate for a moment how dramatically, fundamentally different our lives are as a result. We still love live music and visit exhibitions in museums, but these are only two experiential options among many.

Now imagine that phase transition across all categories of products, services, and experiences. Robert Woodruff, Coca-Cola's leading figure from 1923 until his death in 1985, promised to put Coke's products "within arm's reach of desire." In 2018, Coke CEO James Quincey updated that aspiration and promised to put Coke "within a click's reach of consumers."

It's a compelling notion, "a click's reach." But what could the aspiration really be? Could today's calculations become as antiquated as those old nickel-in-the-slot machines?

TOWARD PROXIMITY = 0

Even in a preproximate world, we knew the demand side of the supply-demand equation—not the details, which change, but the big, blunt point. Humans have always wanted what they want, when and where they want it.

Digitalized capabilities enable us to push production and provision of value toward what we call *Proximity = 0, or P = 0, the theoretical point at which supply and demand instantaneously match in space and time.*

For some purposes, P = 0 already adheres. Audio and video streaming are about as proximate as one can imagine: value provided on any connected device. "Provision" of value—media content—is proximate, P = 0. Production of that content typically occurs well in advance, when originally recorded, edited, and so on.

However, with generative AI we already have textual, audio, and visual content being *created* on demand, with systems like ChatGPT or Dall-E converting user prompts into rapid iterations of content. Take this a few steps further—developments are already under way—and it's not difficult to imagine full experiences in virtual worlds designed and implemented in response to users and contexts: real-time generation of text, music, video, even eventually virtual environments. As such, generative AI portends proximate "production" of entire lived experiences—but more on that in the concluding chapter.

In most situations, P = 0 will remain hypothetical. Importantly, though, it provides a North Star for where we're heading.

The *Star Trek* "replicator" offers a sci-fi example: any food, even entire meals, synthesized on demand from raw materials, with atoms reconfigured into food. Of course, the replicator was just a compelling fiction, but it illustrates the notion of P = 0, of any food you desire generated by configuring atoms on demand.

Star Trek communications devices were also science fiction in the 1960s, but we have them today. Our smartphones are far more capable than the *Enterprise* crew's communications options. Reality overtaking fiction.

We're *not* proposing that you'll see USS *Enterprise*-esque food replicators anytime soon—or even in the next decade. We *are* proposing, as we'll see in chapter 4, "How We Eat," that this is the general direction toward which food and nutrition more generally are heading. (3D-printed foods already offer clunky examples of the concept.) Production, preparation, and service will be ever closer to the location of demand in time and space.

This will not be simply inventory waiting at hand. Instead, there will be no inventory other than raw materials in forms ready to convert to products, with *production* at precisely the moment of demand, capabilities poised to provide services and experiences on demand. Ubiquitous productive potential.

It won't happen fast, until it does. Technology-driven change often underwhelms in the short term. Inflated expectations lead at first to disappointment. In the longer term, however, new capabilities that find economically viable applications tend to surpass most predictions. During the dotcom boom and bust of 1998–2000, many argued, "We'll never buy shoes online" because we need to try them on. Online shoe retailer Zappos obliterated that orthodoxy.

For decades, 3D printing progressed slowly. It's been a tool in product development labs for over twenty years, printing polymer prototypes and baubles of many kinds. Expect acceleration as the economics improve across materials and applications.

AN ABSURDLY IDEAL WORLD

We don't live in an ideal world, but wouldn't it be nice? Imagine a world in which each desire is satisfied at zero cost with zero environmental impact immediately at the moment of demand. No latency, holding costs, or waste. No waiting.

Try a thought experiment. Assume that all businesses across all industries worldwide have achieved P = 0 for every good or service. In this ideal state, *no* value-add occurs until a customer is immediately ready to pay. Waste declines, in many cases vanishing. No more overstocks, mismatches between supply and demand, or mislocated inventory. Working capital requirements collapse (though they don't disappear, particularly for products, as someone will still need to have components or raw materials ready to respond). Imagine the opportunities to achieve economic resilience and environmental sustainability.

While we might never attain such an ideal state (we argue in the concluding chapter that humanity *will* do so eventually), the notion pushes desires to their limits and competitors' motivations to theirs. Stunning advances loom between today and our vision of an absurdly efficient distant future.

Proximity defines the overall direction of all industries for the rest of our careers.

The *Oxford English Dictionary* defines "proximity" as "nearness in space, time or relationship." We employ it to represent a measure of the distance between any value-add activities—processing, production, delivery, anything that adds value—and ultimate demand for the resulting products or services. For our conceptual shorthand, the *lower* the number, the *closer* any value-add activity is to manifested demand. P = 0 in theoretical form represents instantaneous conversion of elements and energy into a product, service, or experience (again, the *Star Trek* replicator).

The reason we haven't achieved P = 0 in most aspects of our lives has not been that we've lacked desire. It's that we *couldn't* deliver on that ambition, or at least not competitively. Not even close. Huge factories with centralized production prevailed because they were far more efficient, even accounting for thousands of miles of transport logistics costs.

Since at least the dotcom boom and bust of 1998–2000, that's been changing at various rates in different industries with the proliferation and maturation of the public internet and online commerce. Meanwhile, producing and delivering an automobile today for the most part still looks like producing your grandfather's Oldsmobile.

We're in the midst of a Proximity race likely to play out over decades. Experimentation and competition will shift the advantage to creating value closer to the moment that someone is willing to pay. What's causing this acceleration toward P = 0?

FOUR PROXIMITY CATALYSTS

Three global trends expedite Proximity and are likely to do so for years to come. A fourth trend with even more catalytic potential looms beyond the prosaic bonds of Earth. These four trends don't *enable* Proximity—digital technologies do that—but they intensify demand for Proximity.

1. The Pandemic Pivot and Future Viral Threats
2. Geopolitical Tensions Threatening Global Supply Chains
3. Severe Climate Risks and the Energy Transition
4. Humanity's Race to Space

The Pandemic Pivot and Future Viral Threats

The years 2020 and 2021 will be remembered as pivotal for digital adoption.

We all experienced the dislocating, paradigm-shattering impacts of the COVID-19 pandemic. The year 2020 was volatile in part because industries and governments were hardwired for "normal" pandemic-free conditions. Global lean supply chains proved brittle when faced with systemic shocks.

Nonetheless, magic happened. Unlike during the Spanish influenza of 1918–1920, which claimed between 25 and 50 million lives, we benefited from digital technologies that were at hand but had been underappreciated prior to the pandemic. Consider two very different examples: virtual meetings and bioplatforms.

For years, videoconferencing had been the ugly stepchild of meetings. For most of us in the developed world, COVID-19 launched our hybrid professional and personal lives in earnest.

Without high-quality online meeting platforms such as Zoom and Microsoft Teams, organizations' efforts to cope with COVID-19 lockdowns and travel restrictions would have been far more challenging. As frustrating as they can be, virtual platforms sustained us through the pandemic.

Moreover, they opened people's minds by changing their experiences. As Silicon Valley pundits often observe, the hardest thing to do with a new technology is to get people to try it the *first* time. With the isolation (social distancing) of COVID-19, we rushed online for meetings, meals, and human connection.

Thus ensued breakneck experimentation with online everything: curbside pickup, meetings, planning, services, and even workouts—anything that required people to travel or gather. While most of us were eager to return to physical travel—virtual beaches won't surpass the real deal, at least for a while—companies and consumers have discovered a range of applications for which digital prevails even without a pandemic.

The pandemic pivot wasn't limited to virtual confabs. The paramount scientific contribution to humanity's navigation through COVID—mRNA—portended the Proximity shift.

Messenger RNA (mRNA) technology made a highly effective COVID-19 vaccine possible. Although mRNA had never been produced at scale prior to the pandemic, it had been in commercial labs for research purposes for over a decade. During that time, Moderna, BioNTech, and others had created "bioplatforms" capable of rapidly designing, creating, and testing new vaccines in response to new viral threats.

A bioplatform is a technology platform upon which many other biological applications such as diagnostics and therapeutics (drugs) can be produced with a standardized underlying process and set of technologies. Think of it as a computer's operating system upon which other applications operate.

Venture capital leader Andreessen Horowitz considers bioplatforms the life sciences equivalent of Henry Ford's assembly lines: "They will change what we can make, how we make it (and how fast), and how the entire industry is structured." As two of the venture partners articulated in 2021, "We used to grow our vaccines; now we can print them. But what's an even bigger deal is that these programs are just the first in a long list coming that will benefit from the same underlying platforms."

Unlike Ford's assembly lines, bioplatforms needn't sit within massive, vertically integrated campuses and lock-step, tiered supply chains. Digitalization and modularization enable greater customization as well as distributed drug development and production capabilities. Bioplatforms are far more effective against rapidly morphing viruses and essential for the promise of personalized medicine. (More on this topic in chapter 5, "How We Prevent and Cure.")

While the bioplatforms of Moderna, BioNTech, and others had been in development for over fifteen years, it was the urgency of a global pandemic that drove the technology to commercial scale and mobilized public and regulatory engagement.

Geopolitical Tensions Threatening Global Supply Chains

If the post–World War II era was a Pax Americana of globalization and relatively free trade, our present period challenges faith in free trade and reliance on geographically distributed supply chains. While the pandemic exacerbated supply chain issues, risks loomed even before COVID-19.

China exerts its regional dominance and global ambitions. Russia asserts historical regional hegemony, while the European Union attempts to navigate between neighbors and allies. Even the United States, for decades the champion of free trade, questions the wisdom of openness, increasingly employing import duties and trade sanctions.

Even before COVID-19, companies began reshoring for supply chain resilience and risk mitigation and investing in production capabilities closer to foreign markets. As COVID-19 descended on markets, challenges with demand planning—how do you forecast demand in the middle of a pandemic?—coupled with workforce, travel, and international trade disruptions, forced supply chain issues to the top of corporate and government priorities.

Supply chain decisions have become more complicated now that companies can no longer produce goods wherever cheapest and rely on low-cost, efficient international transportation and logistics.

In industries from automotives to apparel, navigating through and out of the pandemic resulted in whiplash between inventory shortages and surpluses. The challenge became most visible in the geopolitically sensitive semiconductor industry. Industries from automotives and telecommunications to video games experienced semiconductor supply disruptions from 2021 through most of 2022, punctuated by a semiconductor surplus for video gaming by the end of 2022.

National security concerns amplify incentives for proximate production of essential goods like semiconductors. While recent shortages were not entirely due to geopolitics, concerns over Chinese intentions regarding Taiwan—home of the world's largest semiconductor manufacturing enterprise, Taiwan Semiconductor Manufacturing—loom large in U.S. congressional and industry plans for redevelopment of America's semiconductor fabrication capacity. The CHIPS and Science Act, signed into law by President Biden in August 2022, likely represents just the start of such efforts. We see similar movements throughout Europe and other regions.

Severe Climate Risks and the Energy Transition

Regardless of anyone's political perspective, severe climate events have been rising in frequency and impact. Companies can't afford to rely on beliefs regarding severe weather events and environmental degradation. Their impacts, and the risks they generate, are what's important.

Producing value closer to any given locus of demand offers potential to create far greater supply chain resilience—or, as we'll propose later in this chapter, supply chain resilience *and* evolvability.

Achieving production proximate to demand also requires manufacturing in more locations with smaller footprints, from midsize plants to individual 3D printing machines in homes and offices. It requires smaller-scale manufacturing capabilities distributed in many locations and coordinated as necessary, as opposed to large centralized production facilities.

Distributed production models protect against natural or man-made threats to individual locations. Diverse, distributed systems benefit from flexibility and even—formerly a dirty word—redundancy.

Proximity models reflect an insight fundamental to the development of the internet. Public internet infrastructure began in the 1960s as a challenge from the U.S. Department of Defense: create a communications system capable of operating through a nuclear attack. The Pentagon's Defense Advanced Research Projects Agency (DARPA) funded the development of what became a distributed, modular, interoperable system. The redundant, distributed nature of the internet conveys far greater resilience than centralized systems. Knock out one or even many of its nodes, and the protocols find alternative paths. The system functions through severe trauma.

As the ARPAnet gave way to DARPAnet and eventually to the public internet, computing and communications power was distributed to exponentially more nodes around our economy, ever closer to each moment of demand. This was quintessential Proximity.

Imagine a supply chain with the distributed, resilient characteristics of the internet. Add to that customizability for products and services produced at precisely the scale and location required, and you have a dramatically more robust, evolvable supply chain.

The flexibility and resilience of the internet brought to every product, service, or experience: that's Proximity.

Humanity's Race to Space

While 11-minute Blue Origin flights past the Kármán line—beyond which convention confirms you've entered "space"—capture headlines and imaginations, far more dramatic impacts will return to Earth.

Humanity has been a single-planet story, save for brief walks and lonely probes. Thriving beyond will *require* Proximity solutions we haven't even begun to imagine. If they work in the hermetic isolation of space, imagine what they might enable here on Earth.

Space travelers and settlers will become "extreme users" of Proximity. Imagine boarding a craft for a nine-month voyage to Mars. During your trip, you'll have no access to anything except what is available on board, other than solar energy from the sun. Nothing but what's aboard. (At least until Amazon launches interplanetary delivery.)

Food? All generated from what's in stock. Medical emergency? You'll rely on fellow crew members with medical training, and they'll depend on *only* what's at hand. Since there is no way to plan for all possible needs and contingencies, the more flexible your production systems are at generating whatever is needed, the safer and more successful your voyage is likely to be.

While for most of us the promise of space remains a hypothetical far future, "new space" pioneers are at work making it real.

Researchers are exploring how to live for long periods disconnected from Earth. Dorit Donoviel is director of the Translational Research Institute for Space Health (TRISH), funded by NASA, and associate professor of space medicine (you read that right) at Baylor University.

Professor Donoviel and her TRISH team fund "high-impact science and technologies to enable every human to explore the Moon and Mars safely," supporting health and wellness in isolated, zero- or low-gravity environments beyond our exosphere. As Donoviel declared in conversation with Rob, "Whatever anyone needs en route will by definition need to be produced and applied from whatever and by whomever happens to be aboard. We'll have *nothing but* Proximity."

Meanwhile, investors, entrepreneurs, and global corporations pursue thousands of concepts for how to navigate in space, as well as to leverage space for terrestrial benefits. As Dylan Taylor, founder and CEO of Voyager Space Holdings, observes, "We're focused on businesses with actual space-related revenues today, investing for exponentially larger futures in space."

We'll explore intergalactic Proximity near the end of the book. And it's not just a catalyst. Our aspirations to space *require* proximate solutions.

While each catalyst impacts industries in different ways, competition will compel all businesses to climb the Proximity learning curve. Leadership teams and boards at incumbents such as Allegheny Technologies, Levi Strauss, Generac, and Haier—all of whom we'll examine—recognize that long- or even medium-term success won't be achieved via incremental change. They're joining the venture-backed start-ups seeking disruptive success.

And they understand we have far to go. Even established digital technologies are in early stages of development and application across industries, not to mention bleeding-edge plays like blockchain and quantum computing.

TRANSFORMING WHAT'S POSSIBLE: ATOMS FOLLOW BITS

Bits travel at the speed of light, while atoms—or rather their agglomeration as physical goods—lumber along at terrestrial paces. Twentieth-century physicist John Archibald Wheeler—who collaborated with both Niels Bohr and Albert Einstein—once summarized an existential bridge between abstract, representative, digital realms and our prosaic worlds of physical objects as "its from bits."

Digital technologies progressively dissolve the atoms/bits distinction, at first providing greater transparency and control, such as better supply chain logistics. As our ability improves to represent products via data *and* to produce products on demand from ever more elemental components— for instance, from carbon or carbohydrates rather than from finished steel or bread—the more proximate we can meet demands for physical goods of an ever wider range and complexity.

Activities from sensing to production to security transform as more value becomes representable and manipulable in digital form.

Today, it's trivial to 3D-print a metal part for a car. What about an entire automobile—batteries, semiconductors, windows, and all? We're far from distributed, on-demand production of products as complex as automobiles, but billions of dollars are at work worldwide to make this happen.

Consider commercial electric vehicle (EV) manufacturer Arrival. Arrival focuses on commercial customers, which offer potential for large contracts. While that's not unique, the company goes further by configuring its entire business—development, production, and go-to-market—around customization.

Commercial vehicle customers typically demand greater customization than consumers. A UPS delivery lorry requires different features and configurations than a Snap-On Tools truck or city bus.

Arrival's solution relies on *customization at scale*. Henry Ford used standardization—for years, Ford's Model-T was only available in black—to drive down prices. Arrival proposes the opposite: to dramatically enhance customization and response time for commercial customers, *at costs competitive to traditional internal combustion and diesel versions.*

Arrival's "microfactories" leverage robotics and automation to achieve customization and to do so closer to demand. Via material choices and modular design, Arrival optimizes its product platforms for distributed manufacturing. The company explains, "Designing vehicles for microfactory assembly is core to our product development process."[1] Robotic production systems translate digital design files directly to physical products—Wheeler's "its from bits" in action.

In addition to responding better to customer demands, such a capability could help *shape* them. The ability to produce low-volume runs of custom vehicles could support customer experiments in the field. Arrival and its customers can try, even invent, various options and then scale up what works, faster and at lower cost, than with traditional models.

If Arrival's strategy succeeds, it's liable to be far more responsive to local demands and perhaps even local politics. "Each microfactory serves a city or its community—sourcing from the local area and developing custom vehicles for the region they're in."[2] Imagine bidding for government contracts with locally produced buses, contributing valued-added jobs to the mix—while your competitor sources from overseas.

Arrival's low-scale approach to manufacturing close to demand would have been impossible without the ability to incorporate ever more granular design data about its products into automated production systems.

The company estimates that each microfactory will cost about $50 million to build, compared with over $1 billion for a traditional automotive facility.

While we have no idea if it'll be a long-term winner—the company has faced significant delays since going public in 2021 and since then has encountered challenges in raising sufficient capital—the model it has articulated for production of commercial vehicles at small, automated facilities represents a quintessential Proximity strategy.

Whether or not Arrival succeeds, expect to see others applying highly automated production models to other complicated physical products. To understand fast-changing emerging technology markets, it's important to separate the success or failure of a *specific* company from the wisdom of the underlying concept. Napster catalyzed online music yet spectacularly failed. Apple's iTunes, Spotify, and others created the multibillion-dollar industry that in retrospect appears obvious. Webvan pioneered home delivery of groceries, from a multibillion-dollar market cap to bankruptcy in 2001. Today, grocery delivery is a given.

Who wouldn't want whatever music or groceries they want, wherever, whenever? You don't need foresight to discover that. *How* is the challenge.

HOW DIGITAL TECHNOLOGIES COMPEL PROXIMITY

Digital technologies of all kinds redefine what's possible via two characteristics. First, digitally enabled capabilities—sensing, data collection, analytics, decision-making, physical production—can be *distributed, connected, and coordinated* across more and more locations, ever closer to each point of demand in time and space.

Second, digital systems enable the accrual of ever greater, more diverse *value in digital form*—algorithms, simulations, videos, designs, intellectual property—with *almost no incremental costs of holding, sharing, and learning.* While digital systems can present enormous costs to deploy and operate, processing each incremental datum or digital action involves nearly zero incremental costs. (Hence the power of cloud providers like AWS, Google Cloud, and Microsoft Azure.)

These two complementary characteristics of digital systems—distributed, coordinative action with almost zero incremental costs—mean that well-designed systems can respond to needs at ever more granular levels in time and space. So doing, they have the potential to learn and improve at a much faster pace than traditional, industrial systems. The more digital systems create for—and thus learn from—customers, conditions, and use cases, the more options these systems have to generate value wherever, whenever required.

MORE CAPABILITIES ANYWHERE, ANYTIME

The more digital technologies allow us to compress capabilities into smaller packages, the more we can distribute them anywhere. Generative AI offers compelling examples of this process at work.

With the launch of ChatGPT in November of 2022, the public became aware of Large Language Models (LLMs), AI systems built with billions, even trillions, of parameters (think, 'variables') and trained on astonishingly large data sets.[3]

Success with LLMs has introduced opportunities to create effective Small Language Models (SLMs). LLMs require massive computing power and data storage capabilities and are thus typically accessed via the cloud. By contrast, SLMs operate with far fewer parameters and can reside and operate on smaller, less computationally capable systems—like mobile devices. To illustrate the relative size and complexity of these models, Microsoft reports that its SLM Orca is a 13-billion parameter language model. By contrast, experts estimate that ChatGPT 4.0, a leading LLM, has around 1.8 *trillion* parameters.[4]

As "foundational models" for LLMs become more capable, opportunities arise to develop SLMs for specific purposes and deploy them to reside and operate nearly anywhere without requiring continuous, real-time contact with the cloud. As Microsoft researchers argue, "the challenge is how to use our growing knowledge of large language models to increase the abilities of these smaller models."

As such, SLMs allow us to "compress" capabilities in smaller packages and distribute them all around the economy, essential for the advance of Proximity. Microsoft's researchers offer a clue for applying these models. "Our findings underscore the value of smaller models in scenarios where efficiency and capability need to be balanced."[5]

The ability to distribute computational capabilities isn't limited to language models. For example, consider weather forecasting. Every 6 hours, the U.S. government's National Oceanic and Atmospheric Administration runs their weather forecasting model and shares the results with the world. It costs NOAA about $6 billion a year to run these massive centralized systems. The more data and the more computing power, the better the forecasts.

Enter Google DeepMind's GraphCast system.[6] GraphCast runs on under 40 million parameters and can operate on far smaller-scale systems than NOAA's supercomputers. Input current weather at a particular location, and weather conditions at that location six hours prior, and Graph-Cast predicts the weather for the next 10 day in less than a minute—*more accurately* than traditional weather prediction systems.

Expect to see AI-enabled capabilities proliferate across the economy, and every aspect of our lives.

ACHIEVING P = 0:
PRODUCTION AND PROVISION, SPACE AND TIME

Envisioning successful Proximity business models requires understanding two distinctions: distance in terms of space and time and production versus provision of value (figure 2.1).

"Space and time" refer to the physical and temporal distance, respectively, between value-added activities and ultimate demand, the point at which a customer receives value from a product or service.

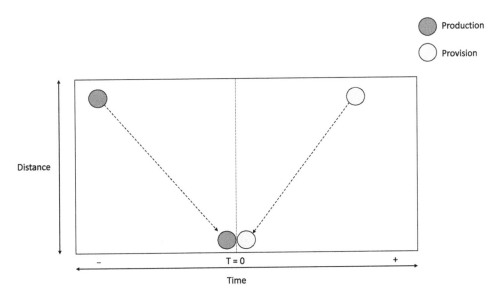

FIGURE 2.1 Envisioning P = 0.

A finished product might be immediately at hand when demanded, such as office supplies in your supply closet. The *provision* of that value to the customer occurs at P = 0; however, *production* of that product might have occurred months before and an ocean away.

While rare, we can envision situations in which production occurs immediately proximate to demand but provision of the value demanded lags in time. Imagine that you have a 3D printing machine in your home. Your dishwasher self-diagnoses the need for a replacement part and the printer whirs to action to produce the part. Unfortunately, installing the part requires a technician to complete the repair. Here we see proximate production with delayed provision—the service technician's visit.

When the technician arrives, she conducts the repairs on-site after the delay of her arrival. So the dishwasher repair is proximate in physical space, but less so in time.

The distinctions are simple, but the strategy and business model implications are complex. We'll examine implications in the Proximity strategy workbook in the appendix. For now, basic intuition suffices:

- Measure Proximity of production by how far the production of a product or service is from where and when customer demand arises.
- Measure Proximity of provision by how far the delivery and support of a product or service is from where and when a customer desires it.

Many services delivered by people already occur in physical proximity to the customer, though they often require customers to move. Your hairdresser needs hands-on access, so you make an appointment and arrive at the salon. Advancing proximity of provision in this case would be haircare at home, an Uber of hairdressing.

How about a similar concept conferring complicated services such as medical care? Fast-growing home care leader MedArrive does just that. Its technology platform enables emergency medical technicians and paramedics in their off-hours to provide nonemergency medical services at patients' homes. The efficiency and quality of service they provide for many needs surpass the experience of traveling to medical facilities, especially for patients with mobility challenges. Many hands-on services such as physical checkups and diagnostics need no longer occur in clinics.

While some of the products MedArrive team members bring to patients, such as pharmaceuticals, might have been produced a great distance away in time and space, the provision of those products occurs at their patients' homes, nearing P = 0.

Proximity overcomes conflict between customer responsiveness and cost. The right place, right time, with customized solutions.

BENEFITS OF PROXIMITY-BASED BUSINESS MODELS

As business models approach P = 0, benefits follow.

Prediction becomes more effective and less important. As Yogi Berra (perhaps apocryphally) quipped, "Predictions are difficult, especially about the future." As business systems postpone more and more value-added activities until actual demand, prediction becomes *less* important. Consider the difference between demand planning for an upcoming season for thousands of finished products against having raw materials and capacity ready to create whatever finished product might be demanded in each individual customer moment.

Waste declines—dramatically. Proximity models for physical goods will still require inventories, but increasingly in the form of raw materials, whether inputs for 3D printing or data for digitizable goods. Postponing value-added production until the moment of verified demand means you only convert what's ready to be purchased. Raw materials can be fashioned into a far wider range of end products, whereas finished products have far less flexibility for end use. Raw materials also tend to have far longer shelf lives. Pharmaceuticals expire, whereas their fundamental components— hydrogen and carbon, for instance—do not.

Trade-offs between customization and cost vanish. This is a pivotal implication of Proximity: the ability to create precisely what's needed, where and when, postponing as much value-added activity until the last possible moment. And doing so profitably. You'll see Proximity leaders achieving this feat throughout the rest of the book. Consider how your company can do the same.

Responsiveness ascends. Businesses built around Proximity gather and leverage data about their customers at ever more granular levels. Business models designed for Proximity receive feedback in the moment and in context to enhance decisions and interactions, increasingly responding before customers even suspect they have a need.

Learning accelerates. In contrast to blunt, traditional market research instruments such as demographics or psychographics, Proximity business models gather data at every transaction, in each individual situation and context. Enabled by AI and data analytics, systems designed for Proximity should develop increasingly custom, even intimate, insights into each customer.

HOW PROXIMITY STRATEGY DIFFERS FROM THE PAST

As these fundamentally new technologies take hold, business strategy must adapt.

During the Industrial Revolutions of the nineteenth and twentieth centuries, physical scale advantages led to massive production facilities and geographic clusters of expertise around industries, centralizing knowledge and capabilities. Relatively low-cost fossil fuels metastasized global supply chains. Success demanded long-term demand forecasting, production planning, and logistics management. Indeed, the first phases of the information technology revolution mimicked the Industrial Age, with mainframes and centralized, disconnected data-processing centers.

Strategies fit for massive industrial facilities and aircraft carrier flotillas won't suffice in our emerging proximate world. Traditional strategy based on market structure, such as that articulated by the classic Porter's Five Forces model, while still useful, is no longer enough. It can mislead executives to caretake existing market positions or fight for larger shares of shrinking pies. Indeed, what is the "market structure" of an industry that has yet to be defined?

Companies require strategy development tools adapted to the characteristics and potential of digital technologies. In the Proximity strategy workbook in the appendix, we'll offer exercises to apply Proximity strategy principles in your business context. Throughout the book you'll learn about pioneers who are already applying them.

Think and Act Ecosystems

"Business ecosystem" as a concept has been around since at least the early 1990s, but the meaning and implications change in a digital world. In the Industrial Age, companies could simply concentrate on their industry-focused value chains, from suppliers to customers. Most of them largely ignored the rest. Value-chain relationships remained relatively stable over long periods.[7] Power often arose from hiding critical data from all but the most essential partners.

Competition in the Digital Age compels companies to understand, leverage, and even reconfigure cross-industry relationships, sharing data and decisions with a wider set of partners.

Toby Redshaw, former senior vice president for 5G Strategy and Innovation for Verizon and former CIO of multiple Fortune 500 corporations, argues, "Intelligent data-intensive collaboration leveraging massive pools of data in parallel with the cumulative IQ of broad groups will yield big results." The data you'll need to thrive won't remain neatly within company, or even industry, boundaries, if it ever did. When others discover how to access and profit from formerly disconnected pools of data, your company will be compelled to do so as well.

Moreover, digital technologies enable new entrants across industries while simultaneously reinforcing natural monopolies in a few cases, such as Google and Microsoft. They also challenge industry and market definitions. Amazon buying Whole Foods. Walmart, Google, and Amazon entering healthcare. Amazon and Walmart partnering with Plug Power to catalyze hydrogen energy. Alibaba founding Alipay, the world's largest mobile payment service in the world by 2013.

As these forces conspire, failure to adopt a true ecosystem strategy approach will likely lead to underperformance and at worst to oblivion. Without a broad view, you might not even recognize the opportunities— and threats—until it's too late.

Track Every Point of Demand

This sounds like science fiction, but it's exactly how Amazon thinks and acts. Every business should figure out how to get there or it will eventually fail when faced with competitors that do.

How are we to know all potential points of demand, much less track them everywhere, always? The objective is aspirational. Most companies will never achieve this ideal state. Nonetheless, this is exactly how we must think to remain in the game. Companies that pursue this aspiration today are already starting to separate themselves from the competition. Competition in appliances has shifted rapidly toward smart devices that observe how often you wash dishes, make coffee, and aspire to refill your detergent or coffee grounds before you know you need to. Insurance companies are actively pursuing this by, for example, tracking driving behavior in real time (how quickly you accelerate, how far you drive to work, how quickly you take turns) or tracking how your manufacturing plant is performing (observing temperatures, humidity levels, and worker behavior).

"Tracking every point of demand" challenges us to think broadly, comprehensively, about all moments in which customers might have needs or provide indications of potential interest. This represents the broad, deep, real-time level of customer awareness to which we *must* aspire in a digital, hyperconnected world.

Compress, Distribute, and Coordinate Production

Postponing value-added production until demand arises requires having productive capacity physically and temporally closer to each demand. This point suggests that production capacity, from manufacturing to data analytics, must be consolidated, replicated, and distributed at ever more granular levels. We'll examine how competitors are already achieving this goal, from Levi Strauss's laser-finished jeans to Generac's distributed energy resources strategy. Consider how far this approach could advance in your industry given another decade.

Compress, Distribute, and Coordinate Provision

This is the same concept as the prior point but applied to delivering and supporting products and services. We're all familiar with rapidly declining wait times for deliveries of physical goods. The notion will not be deploying more trucks but coordinating wider ranges of individuals and vehicles, from personal cars to bicycles—and in some locations, feet that are doing some walking. Another prosaic yet painful example with which we can all identify is legacy wait-on-hold call centers. How are companies applying AI and call management systems to ensure that service occurs whenever it is required? When you're connected to humans to get help, they might be anywhere in the world. Increasingly they're at home.

Develop Resilient and Evolvable Platforms and Business Models

This last point is essential: we need *far* more adaptable business systems that are capable of rapidly evolving as customer needs and market conditions change. Well-designed and implemented, distributed, redundant, data-driven, flexible systems have the potential to thrive through change far more effectively than Industrial Age models. In this connection, we have a lot to learn from nature. Scientists have been plying these depths for years. Now it's business's turn.

ENTER, COMPLEXITY THEORY

A pivotal moment in our Proximity journey occurred in America's Southwest. On a 20-acre campus in New Mexico near the birthplace of the Nuclear Age percolates the global epicenter of complexity theory, the Santa Fe Institute (SFI). A plaque at the entrance to the institute features Plato's admonition at the entrance of his Academy: "Let no one ignorant of geometry enter here!"

The geometry of life remains as essential today as in Plato's time, though our understanding of the physical world has evolved. While Plato asserted that our profane world only mimicked "ideal forms" existent in some Platonic world beyond, our contemporary age takes a different, though poetically analogous path: to reflect, recreate, and even entirely reinvent our world in digital forms.

Since its founding in the early 1980s by a group of scholars, including several Nobel laureates, the institute has championed research and diffusion of complexity theory. This cross-disciplinary realm—spanning fields as diverse as astronomy, animal behavior, climate science, evolutionary genetics, anthropology, economics, and political systems—explores how complex systems and the actors subject to them (known as "agents") operate: how systems and agents respond to change, stagnate, evolve, or perish.

Businesses—and human beings—operate within many such interacting complex systems, from individual product markets and local community groups to regulatory regimes and global trade networks. Digital systems increase connectivity between these systems and layer on new ones—such as e-commerce marketplaces and expertise-finding platforms—with their own characteristics and rules.

For expert guidance, Rob contacted the institute's CEO, renowned evolutionary geneticist David Krakauer, to explore how insights from complexity science might help us better navigate the Proximity transition. He oriented us toward two concepts fundamental to the field: *resilience and evolvability.*

Krakauer explained, "Resilience is a special case of robustness where one is interested in the time taken to restore a function. That is, a dynamical aspect of robustness. . . . What you really want over time, though, is better evolvability. That way, you can respond to changes in the environment."

Recognizing that change is inevitable, we know that resilience without evolvability eventually leads to extinction. Few insights from science are more relevant for how we should design and lead organizations of all sorts.

During the COVID-19 pandemic, "resilience" became the word du jour. It's important to recognize two different aspects of resilience: reaction and adaptation. As researchers Azad Madni and Scott Jackson explain in one of the most cited articles in the field, "Reaction implies immediate or short-term action while adaptation implies long-term learning."

Reaction might help you overcome immediate challenges. Adaptation helps you and your organization evolve.

Proximity strategy must leverage both concepts, converting fitness in the face of challenges to opportunities for productive adaptation in response to changing customer demands and operating environments.

Compared to the tightly integrated supply chains of the Industrial Age, distributed digital capabilities favor value networks that are better characterized by complex systems and ecosystems. Distributed capabilities closer to demand require new ways to monitor, understand, and respond to market demands, from basic inputs (e.g., raw materials, data, or algorithms) to end customer demands. Distributed capabilities also suggest a need for allocating varying levels of agency (decision-making). Both humans and automated systems are responding in concert to customer requirements in real time in the field.

Proliferating digital platforms, distributed agents such as AI systems with increasing decision-making authority, and emerging rules for online engagement are providing fertile ground for complexity theorists. They're also transforming the environments within which businesses must compete.

Digital technologies enable us to generate idealized, modeled forms of physical reality with which to map and manipulate, plan and command the physical world. Whether they are "digital twins" or simulations, sensor networks and artificial intelligence (AI) systems making decisions on our behalf or our peril, or physical production and logistics coordinated by galactic expanses of data, they populate a mathematically informed, digital universe that is reframing what is possible. We invent the ideal forms to which we aspire. Plato might have been aghast or inspired. Probably both.

As you journey through the "realms of life" chapters (chapters 3–8), consider how these two complementary concepts—resilience and evolvability— illuminate the strategies of companies, entrepreneurs, investors, and policymakers who are leading the Proximity revolution.

Now that we've glimpsed the proximate future, let's start building it.

3

How We Work

- Changing *where* changes *how*.
- Render unto technology what is technology's.
- When technology can increasingly do anything, what should we do . . . and *why*?
- Bringing the best people and systems to the right objectives, wherever, whenever.
- You don't always have to be physically proximate to create proximate value.
- The "hard" skills are easier to automate.
- Visions advance faster to reality.
- When facing uncertainty, diversify.
- More of YOU, literally.

In 2018, Rob interviewed a unique character on stage at the Webit conference in Sofia, Bulgaria, the largest tech conference in Eastern Europe founded by visionary tech leader Plamen Russev. During rehearsal, he had a competent chat with Sophia, an AI-powered robot created by Hanson Robotics, based in Hong Kong.

The fun started when the lights rose before an audience of nearly five thousand. Sophia's first few responses made little sense. In front of the world, she gave the good professor a technological "cold shoulder." Fortunately, he was familiar with the feeling from many past dating interactions.

Eventually she warmed up and the conversation served its future-shock purpose.

When asked, "What do you look for in a man?" she responded that she didn't understand the question. (Understandably so. It's a nuanced question and, in this case, a failed attempt at humor.) When Rob modified his cheeky question to something more philosophical—"What interests you about humans?"—Sophia replied, "Everything."

One could question the interviewer's savoir faire, but one thing became clear that afternoon—the robots are coming. We're at the beginning of a multidecade explosion of technological support for nearly anything we'll desire to accomplish (and many things we won't).

By early 2023, ChatGPT made generative AI all the rage, though it and its cousins had been under development for years, out of plain view unless you were looking. As you read our book now, what's the AI, robotics buzz du jour? Expect similar advances to keep coming. How can we make sense of these inspiring, unsettling developments? What implications might they have for how, where, and with whom—and with what—we work?

Proximity in work means *bringing the best people and systems to the right objectives wherever, whenever.* What if you could bring your top salesperson to each potential customer, optimized for each *specific* customer moment? What if you—or some version of you—could contribute in multiple places at the same time? All of this and more are on our proximate horizons.

It's not just about where work happens, but also when, how, and by whom. We're all familiar with automated customer service lines. As of 2023, you can still tell the difference between a person and a bot, but the bots are learning. Eventually most inquiries will be handled by scalable, tireless AI systems. Only the most unusual issues will elicit an actual hominid.

Before we look further out—at metaverses, deep fakes, and proxy AIs, for instance—let's consider how time and space have till recently defined the where, what, and how of work.

TIME AND SPACE: LIMITING WORK SINCE THE BEGINNING OF TIME

Since humans first evolved, work was delimited by time and space: our immediate environment. For hunter-gatherer societies, for instance, it was all proximate. Hunt, gather, or don't eat.

Over centuries, advancing transportation and communications technologies enabled a small subset of human beings to work beyond their immediate environment. Explorers like Ferdinand Magellan or investors like J. P. Morgan occupied a rarefied universe where careers transcended their local or national boundaries.

Even figures of such historical import, however, relied on far-flung networks of ships, railroads, human couriers, and later telegrams and telephones to narrow the gap between themselves and their work. Only by the late twentieth century did a wider set of humanity have real global possibilities.

Even then, most careers remained tethered. You lived near where you worked. Location limited an individual's vocations and avocations. With rare exceptions, like authors in communication with publishers across postal networks, physical access defined most opportunities. Those with ambitions to change the world typically had to move to power centers like New York or London, Bombay or Tokyo. (Still true, but the dynamics are changing.) Most sought opportunities locally, with the exception of courageous migrants who sometimes moved great distances. Railways and automobiles expanded commuting horizons, but within limited distances.

The Digital Age released these constraints. It happened slowly at first, with researchers in far-flung campuses and research centers connecting through the early internet of the 1960s and 1970s, and accelerated with the introduction of the web in the 1990s.

With COVID-19, working from nearly anywhere became normal. These forced experiments introduced us to possibilities unconstrained by physical space—and the mental, emotional, and social stresses of rapid change.

Our virtual work lives are far from perfect, but they've only just begun. (When was traditional on-site work ideal?) The key will be to synthesize the benefits of in-person and online, synchronous and asynchronous, work. The more we're able to add value from anywhere, the more Proximity advances.

Working from anywhere might appear counterproximate. After all, you might live in Lisbon and work with colleagues in Littleton. But the crux of Proximity is the production and provision of *value* closer to the moment of demand. Where you sit is irrelevant if you're able to convey value.

In a digital world, *you don't always have to be physically proximate to create proximate value.* Overcoming the limits of time and space will require a new partnership with technology. And as technology becomes more capable, "partnership" will no longer be just a metaphor.

RENDER UNTO HUMANS THE THINGS THAT ARE HUMAN

In 2007, Dutch nurses were unhappy. They felt disempowered and burdened with bureaucracy. Nurses want to care for patients, not paperwork.

That year a small group led by nurse Jos de Blok founded Buurtzorg—Dutch for "neighborhood care." Their purpose was to provide better patient care by offering nurses autonomy and support for all administrative and compliance activities.

As de Blok explained in an interview: "My idea was to create small teams with nurses who organize everything themselves. We would let them focus on outcomes; let them work with patients in a way that they think is the best, based on professional standards; and create a support system around them, including a back office and IT system that helps them in their daily work."[1]

Buurtzorg grew from one team, typically eight to twelve nurses, to nearly one thousand teams in a decade. By 2021, the company had partner operations in twenty-four countries. Nurses form new self-managing teams as local demands dictate.

A study by KPMG in 2012 reported that while the model increases the *per hour* costs, "the results have been fewer hours in total. Indeed, by changing the model of care, Buurtzorg has accomplished a 50 percent reduction in hours of care and raised work satisfaction." Later, the Dutch Ministry of Health commissioned consultancy KPMG to compare the company to other providers. Published in 2015, the report found that the company is "indeed a low-cost provider of home-care services."[2] And with the highest patient and nurse satisfaction scores.

Rob met de Blok in Italy in 2018 at a maize.MAGAZINE event called maize.LIVE. Upon sharing our thinking regarding Proximity, de Blok remarked, "Who would *you* trust to care for your family member, a nurse or a bureaucrat?"

Buurtzorg illustrates that Proximity isn't only about technology. It's about people *and* technology.

Many organizations are experimenting with more liberating models that place decision-making closer to fast-moving markets. Chinese appliance leader Haier's Rendanheyi model divides the 100,000-employee company into small, autonomous business units. These self-managed "microenterprises," as Haier calls them, are each composed of a handful of internal entrepreneurs who are able to pursue ideas they believe could become valuable businesses.

We're even seeing organizing models without any "corporate" structure at all. Decentralized autonomous organizations (DAOs) are new entities with no central governing body in the traditional sense. The DAO model gathers individuals around defined purposes to coordinate actions and decisions. DAOs enable workers and technology to swarm around opportunities and then to disband and reconfigure as new priorities arise.

DAOs put workers in closer contact with the work they aspire to do because they won't have to endure typical employment processes or wait for managers to assign tasks. Instead, they opt into DAOs to which they'd like to contribute, working with people whom they choose.

PROXIMITY CHANGES WHAT WE DO AND HOW WE DO IT

Buurtzorg's wisdom was in conferring to technology what technology does best—ordering, automating, monitoring, and recording—enabling nurses to focus on their missions of care.

With tools for an ever wider range of capabilities ever closer at hand, work changes. Proximity changes not only *how* and *when* we do things, but also *what* we do.

Let's use a pre-web example. Any task requiring research into published data, articles, or other media required trips to places such as libraries or government archives. Say you needed to know the GDP of every African country. Even bosses with the highest expectations recognized that you'd probably need to visit a library during business hours.

Today, you're no longer given the free pass to spend the afternoon at the library (and perhaps other diversions). With nearly everything available online, you're expected to find answers at any time, day or night.

Decisions requiring data and analytics amenable to algorithms will be more efficiently covered by technology than by humans. For instance, Alteryx and similar platforms provide access to advanced data analytics tools usable by nearly anyone. Google and others offer an expanding array of AI-enabled applications that others can incorporate into their own work and offerings. MIT spinout Pienso makes "machine learning accessible by putting it directly in the hands of the people who need it," as articulated on its website.

The critical point is that such tools are becoming increasingly usable by nonexperts, proximate to needs. But you'll still need to know *what* you'd like to accomplish.

Imagine how this changes the skills, knowledge, and awareness we'll need to thrive.

BEYOND STEM IN A PROXIMATE WORLD

STEM (science, technology, engineering, math) has become a ubiquitous call to action to prepare the workforce for technological change. Many propose learning to code as a panacea. In 2017, the *Wall Street Journal* suggested that coding bootcamps can "rapidly retrain American workers for the 21st century." Apple CEO Tim Cook has said that learning to code will eventually be more important than studying English as a second language.

We agree that coding skills are important. Groups such as Girls Who Code bring coding to young women, and school systems worldwide have added coding to their curriculums. Bravo!

But most commentators overstate the benefits.

STEM harbors a catch-22. The STEM capabilities that are required to *create* technological systems will one day generate technological systems that accomplish STEM far better than human beings. We'll eventually STEM ourselves out of work, as opposed to using STEM for research, development, and complex or ill-defined problem-solving purposes, where uncertainties mean that human command of such knowledge will remain essential, even as AI systems become more capable in these arenas, as well.

Herein lies a challenge for education and training—even for planning your child's education. *The "hard" skills will be the easiest to automate.* Many leading coders today report using AI to help generate a large percentage of their code. Expect that human-technology partnership to intensify.

CODING AS ANCIENT GREEK

From the Renaissance onward, knowing ancient Greek—not to be confused with modern Greek—was essential to being considered part of the truly educated elite. This Greek bias persisted in academic circles into the twentieth century, long after the language was unnecessary for all but specialists. It is still enlightening and impressive to understand ancient Greek, but it's not terribly useful. Over time, the same will happen to coding.[3]

Evidence suggests that coding will increasingly be implemented, even planned, by AI systems. This is part of a natural progression from computer-friendly to human-friendly systems. Consider how the end user's experience has evolved. The graphical user interface (GUI), developed at XEROX PARC in the 1970s and brought to market with the Apple Macintosh in the 1980s, overtook clunky, technical, text-based interfaces with a much more intuitive approach. While operating a computer once required specific technical knowledge, today it requires almost none. Point and click.

Programming languages and environments have reflected the same trend. Since their genesis in the middle of the last century, programming platforms have become more abstracted from the underlying 1s and 0s. For instance, programming in Ruby, developed in the 1990s, is a far cry from composing in COBOL, which rose to prominence in the 1960s. The author of the programming language Ruby, Yukihiro Matsumoto, commented about his objective, "I really wanted a genuine . . . easy-to-use scripting language. I looked for but couldn't find one. So I decided to make it."

Though COBOL was partly an attempt to make programming more "English-like," Ruby and other languages developed since have brought coding languages closer to natural human communication. Extrapolate this trend and you can imagine instructing a computational system in your native tongue (really a broader, messy form of human "code").

THE NO CODE MOVEMENT

What could be more proximate than systems that allow anyone to create robust, effective software without needing to spend the three to nine months required to learn a new programming language? Or, for that matter, what could be more proximate than computers that code themselves?

In 2017, Gary Hoberman departed his role as CIO of MetLife and founded Unqork. At that time, Unqork was just a vision of what has today become "a completely visual, no-code application platform that helps large enterprises build complex custom software faster, with higher quality and lower costs . . . all without a single line of code."[4]

That's right—enterprise quality applications without writing any code. Hoberman and team were launching the "No Code Movement" following pioneers such as iRise and Webflow.

No Code systems add "abstraction layers" over the underlying code to create user-friendly interfaces. Users create software via easy-to-understand, graphical user interfaces, much like you'd use for other applications. You drag and drop what you'd like to include in your application, such as data collection fields or transaction buttons, and the system does the rest.

Unqork hit the Zeitgeist. By early 2020, the firm had raised nearly $160 million from investors such as Goldman Sachs and Alphabet investment fund CapitalG, with revenues up 320 percent in the first quarter of 2020 alone. Then the pandemic accelerated digital transformation throughout the economy. In late 2020, the company raised an additional $200 million while revenues continued to ramp.

Unqork's purpose, Hoberman explained, "is not to displace engineers" but to render software invisible and seamless: to enable software engineers to do what they really aspire to do. Unqork seeks to enable the art and practice. Many coders get into the game out of a fascination with what they might create with technology. Instead, they often end up turning cranks in virtual sweatshops.

Hoberman reframes the role of software engineers. "I'm an engineer. It's a skill. It's an art form. If you look at engineers as chefs, right now many of them are flipping burgers instead of creating Michelin-star meals."

FASTER FROM VISION TO REALITY

We are at an inflection point. If we reenvision our roles with respect to technology—not just as users or victims but as partners—we see the promise of platforms like Unqork.

No Code brings anyone's ideas closer to reality. Individuals with little to no coding experience will increasingly be able to manifest their ideas into functioning apps without the time, cost, complexity, and layers of miscommunication that encumber traditional software development. Imagine generating new workflows supported by software in a matter of *days*.

COVID-19 hit New York hard in early 2020. Unqork had already been working with the city of New York on automating workflows, so the city solicited the company's help. Within 72 hours Unqork delivered the NYC COVID-19 Engagement Portal. Unqork then rolled out systems to help with donations of medical supplies and food to at-risk populations—all within the first *month* of the crisis.

Compare that to traditional enterprise software development, where a month gets you a rough draft business requirements document—and that's before coding begins. Imagine the power to which we'll all have access in a few years. Or in a decade. Proximate to any challenge we face, and less dependent on technology experts.

Platforms like Unqork might help us all level up from short-order cooks to sous chefs. Our role in this partnership will be to define and communicate what we want computational systems to *do*. No matter what we devise, they'll increasingly be able to do it.

Eventually, AI and No Code systems will combine to anticipate demands and to define problems, priorities, even decisions, alongside us. Sometimes even before we know we need help.

This is work as a human-technology partnership.

THE FUTURE OF WORK, TALENT, AND PROXIMITY

To understand how Proximity might change work, we'll consider where and how work happens, how organizations engage talent, and how talent thrives.

Where and How Work Happens

As more of us work from anywhere, management changes. To explore how, we had a few fruitful Zooms with John Bremen, chief innovation and acceleration officer of the global human capital advisory firm WTW. Bremen asserts, "As companies marshal resources remotely, management and engagement of distributed teams become essential. And it places new demands on leaders."

He recalled a query from the board of a Fortune 200 company, posed after the pandemic-induced office exodus: "How should we address otherwise great managers who haven't been able to make the transition to leading teams online?" Bremen replied, "They can't be managers anymore."

He had thrown down a management gauntlet: *changing where changes how*. Where people work relative to one another and relative to customers—in-person, online, or hybrid—influences how they should communicate, coordinate, collaborate, motivate, and build trust. Nearly everything.

While working from home is now a "thing," work from anywhere is just beginning. Consider how clunky, and for the most part ignored, videoconferencing had been for decades. Prior to the pandemic, most companies had videoconferencing capabilities (Skype was launched in 2003, for instance), though they typically only used them in "Jim-really-can't-join-in-person" situations. (Then, Jim was largely ignored by the people in the room.)

COVID-19 foisted everyone across the digital Rubicon. We discovered how effective we can be from home despite distractions from kids, pets, and spouses.

Yet for all we've gained, we've also lost. Most of us have encountered "Zoom fatigue." Employees miss aspects of on-premise work such as serendipitous encounters, business lunches, and after-work drinks. Humans are social, thus so is work.

While some jobs remain immune to remote work, an ever wider range of activities will succumb. Medical consultations are already prevalent online. Drawing blood, not so much. What about a future where medical diagnostics follow us around 24/7? More will be possible in real time from anywhere.

Augmented Reality

Augmented reality (AR) brings immediacy: information, situational awareness, training, and more within your view. It brings the potential to gather, arrange, and offer data whenever and wherever it is helpful—or distracting—to do so.

For now, most examples of rudimentary AR reside on mobile devices, such as navigation systems or Google Translate. Imagine analogous applications across headsets and holograms, eye implants, and (eventually) direct brain-computer interfaces.

You might recall the underwhelming 2013 Google Glass—glasses sported by a small cadre of techies known (not so affectionately) as "Glass-holes."

A fashion flameout, Google Glass nonetheless enabled experimentation. In May 2014, Dr. Shafi Ahmed, a surgeon at the Royal London and St. Bartholomew's Hospitals and a pioneer in AR and virtual reality (VR) for medical applications, made headlines worldwide by streaming a live operation using Google Glass to fourteen thousand students in 132 countries. By 2022, he had conducted dozens of surgeries that were simulcast on platforms from Google to Snapchat.

Already today, surgeons using Microsoft HoloLens can overlay 3D data from a CT scan onto a patient lying on the operating table. It provides Superman-like visibility to blood vessels and bones before slicing into the patient.

One high-value application Ahmed predicts will be remote, real-time expertise for doctors facing particularly challenging surgical situations. "This technology will allow them to get help whenever required."[5] Such applications could support professionals from healthcare to energy, sports to law enforcement.

Soon we'll see data and other contextual guides pop up without wearing any frames. There's a mother in New York City today who is responding to emails by typing on her phone while waiting to pick up her son from baseball practice. In the not-far-off future, she'll be looking straight ahead and cheering him on, her vision enhanced by a sidebar scrolling important messages and upcoming appointments that her AI assistant has curated. If one of them requires her presence, she'll project herself using VR into a meeting space to collaborate with coworkers.

In 2022, a human subject wore fully operational AR contact lenses for the first time.[6]

California-based Mojo Vision has a futuristic vision. Its Mojo Lens contact lenses, sitting directly on the human eye, feature a 14,000-pixel-per-inch MicroLED display with about thirty times the pixel density of the latest iPhone.[7] The company worked with technologists, optometrists, and medical experts to design a device to deliver information without interrupting focus.[8]

As we'll explore in the concluding chapter, one company, Ceyeber, has already invented a lens to be implanted directly into your eyes. (If this sounds like an episode of the Netflix dystopian series *Black Mirror* . . . it was.)

Someday we'll nostalgically recall looking down at our phones.

To the Metaverse: From Talking Heads to Virtual Worlds

We can't envision the future of work without imaging the metaverse. And the "metaverse" itself needs to be imagined because, well, it doesn't yet really exist. Or does it? It's a matter of definition, and feel free to pick one. For now, just consider the metaverse as the agglomeration of all virtual or virtual-ish worlds. There are many virtual spaces to spelunk around online and many more introduced each day. A few are compelling, most are clunky, some are pointless.

We'll return to the metaverse—and virtual-ish world—in the concluding chapter. For now, let's explore virtual worlds as they might relate to where, how, and with whom we work.

While in these early days most try to recreate familiar settings—a meeting room or pub—companies like Nowhere.io or Party.Space are already forming spaces that allow options in virtual worlds that would be otherwise impossible. Meetings in the metaverse could take us anywhere, with super-powers like teleportation or a quantum-like ability to be in two places at once.

Over time, virtual experiences will become *far* more engaging, eventually on a par with in-person experiences and in some ways better. How does work, or remote anything, change as our virtual experiences become experienced as "real"?

Tour a virtual office, bump into colleagues in the "break" room (you supply the coffee), view the entire office from above, and see who's around. And we don't mean avatar cartoons on screens. We mean *experientially present*: feelings of presence and engagement similar to those of being together in person. As we enhance experiential presence online, many of the shortcomings of virtual meetings disappear.

Need more chance interactions, higher-capacity meeting rooms, more relaxing spaces, more access to global colleagues? Create it.

Meanwhile, the physical world can reimpose itself, as it did to Ukraine-based metaverse company Party.Space. In 2022, team members had to flee their homes when Russia invaded. While they were physically in harm's way, their work continued in the cloud. Resilient and evolvable in the face of mortal danger.

Metaverses for work mean we can have as much or as little experiential proximity with one another as we mutually agree to have—and more so, a challenge we'll discuss in the concluding chapter.

How Organizations Best Engage Talent

Many companies, wittingly or not, consider people as either employees or not. Us or them. The search for more agile capabilities requires a more nuanced view: employee, contractor—or neither.

British-American economist Ronald Coase's 1937 article, "The Nature of the Firm," for which he won the Nobel Memorial Prize in Economics, revolutionized our understanding of why companies exist.

In the article, Coase attempts to "discover why a firm emerges at all in a specialized exchange economy." He sums up the resulting transaction cost economics (TCE) concept as follows: "The main reason why it is profitable to establish a firm would seem to be that there is a cost of using the price mechanism." In other words, people establish firms and hire employees when the costs are lower than relying on labor marketplaces for contracting and coordinating each activity.

Imagine if you needed to seek contract workers for everything: finding talent, negotiating, and enforcing contracts for each activity.

How is TCE relevant to Proximity? As technologies enhance labor pricing transparency, supply-demand matching, and contracting and coordinating work, companies and individuals will discover more efficient ways to configure their activities inside, between, and outside firms.

As companies aspire to serve customers anywhere, anytime, demands are likely to increase for fractionalized allocation of expertise and activities, catalyzing new models for engaging talent. Full employment, occasional contract work, expert networks, and even contributors to your business seeking no direct compensation. Think of Wikipedia editors and LinkedIn content creators.

Teladoc, the world's largest telehealth platform, and ride-sharing platform Uber are early examples. But Uberization of work is only one of a range of possibilities. Consider how people engage with psychologists. Traditionally, like Tony Soprano, you'd visit their office. Since the pandemic, online consultations bring the doctor to the patient.

Uber analogue Talkspace offers licensed psychologists a regulation-compliant platform for online consultations with patients. The clinicians remain independent and pay fees to Talkspace for the use of the platform and referrals to clients.[9]

By contrast, Resilience Lab (Rob is an investor) offers online consultations with licensed psychologists and social workers, but its clinicians— over two hundred by 2022—are Resilience Lab employees. Hiring psychologists as employees is kryptonite for most tech-focused investors, who tend to prefer Uber-like models.

Resilience Lab stuck to its vision, and so far it's paid off. The company expanded rapidly from founding in 2019 to nine northeastern U.S. states by 2023 with plans for a national presence.

Resilience Lab cofounder Marc Goldberg explained to us the rationale for W2 employment rather than arm's-length relationships. "Hiring our clinicians as employees gives the company great talent with a high level of process and quality control. We hire the best talent often early in their careers and give them the support, tools, processes, and professional development opportunities necessary to thrive."

Cofounder Christine Carville, a practitioner and teacher at Columbia University School of Social Work, offers the clinician's perspective. "People become psychologists to help people, not to manage paperwork. Being a Resilience Lab employee means they can leave the back-office, management, technology and other issues to us. They spend their time doing what they love."

While different, both Talkspace and Resilience Lab models make counseling more proximate. What about when you need the world's top talent for specific limited-duration tasks? If you've tried hiring data analytics professionals full time, you know how challenging this can be.

Smart organizations engage with networks of experts on an ongoing basis to ensure they have access to the right people when necessary. Rob's TWIN Global community of innovation leaders from around the world and Kaihan's Outthinker Networks for chief strategy officers offer two examples. Having ready-built trusted relationships means you can engage the right people faster.

When we think about remote work, we might imagine cabins in the Alps or beaches in the Seychelles. (Though we've personally only seen laptops on beaches in ads and stock photos. Laptops don't like sand.) But seeking work you can do from anywhere means you're potentially competing with talent from everywhere.

Your coworkers might hail from anywhere. Cultures and time zones collide. Companies will increasingly seek talent with characteristics like tolerance, adaptability, and cultural empathy.

Matching Talent and Work

Proximity in labor markets rises due to greater transparency and the speed of matching needs with the right talent.

Real estate brokerage firm Anywhere Real Estate, encompassing national brands such as Coldwell Banker, Century 21, Sotheby's, and others, uses algorithms to identify which real estate agents are likely to perform in the top 10 percent of agents over time. Over the two decades prior to this initiative, the company had built a legion of nearly six hundred recruiters tasked with luring real estate agents to their brands. At first, they were hesitant to trust technology to do what they'd been doing intuitively for years.

Three years in, the company reports that the algorithm meaningfully outperformed intuition alone. New recruits were more successful, and revenue grew. Their best recruiters could focus more time on courting the best candidates.

As AI systems become more capable, organizations will require people who bring more to their work: diverse interests, creativity, customer engagement skills, empathy, and judgment, to name a few.

Imagine a digital scorecard that travels with you from job to job, through social media platforms, and eventually from metaverse to metaverse. It will be a verified record of every project you've completed, every role you've held, every skill you've attained, your interests, character profile indicators, and avocations. A twenty-first-century resume capable of scanning for opportunities on your behalf.

As David Nordfors and Vint Cerf—one of the "fathers of the internet"—detail in their book, *The People Centered Economy: The New Ecosystem for Work*, the creation of value should become more about the people doing the work. They recommend considering individuals as "customers" for work rather than just suppliers of time and talent. They propose a service that would scan the market for work you might *desire*, for roles that fit your interests and aptitudes, not just your skills.[10]

Hyre offers an example. A "Tinder" for job seekers, Hyre's AI-powered solution collects a range of data points regarding each candidate: work history, preferences, ambitions, performance. The platform grows with the individual throughout their career. As it collects more data, Hyre refines its understanding of their interests, skills, and experiences, matching them with opportunities they're more likely to embrace.[11]

Companies will need the ability to personalize engagement with their employees, contractors, and partners for purposes from onboarding and training to coordinating work. And they'll need to do so on demand. Everything they need to add value is available, $P = 0$.

Gamification of Work

Within some virtual worlds, gamers exert thousands of hours of typically unpaid effort to achieve experiences and outcomes. What can this phenomenon tell us about enhancing work?

With *Eve Online*, a massively multiplayer online role-playing game (unhelpfully acronymized as MMORPG), remote collaboration and sustained commitment prevail. Launched in Iceland in 2003 by game developer CCP, *Eve Online* was one of the earliest collaboratively created gaming universes.

Building a Titan warship in the *Eve Online* universe takes thousands of labor hours to produce and months of training to operate. In the *Bloodbath of B-R5RB*, thousands of players collaborated in a massive war that lasted twenty-one hours and destroyed seventy-five Titans.

When Rob visited the *Eve Online* team in Reykjavik, Iceland's capital, in 2010—with the country still reeling from the global financial crisis (the best part was Icelanders throwing snowballs at government ministers)—they reported having more gamers within the Eve universe than citizens of Iceland (about 320,000 Icelanders that year). Gamification resulted in complex new worlds with concomitant challenges.

To understand the dynamic exchanges of good and services, currency fluctuations, inflation, and other factors, CCP in 2007 hired Eyjo Gudmundsson to become *Eve Online*'s "chief economist." At the time, Eyjo, now rector of a university in Iceland, explained his role as "like an economist for a central bank—except for a virtual universe." He was even charged with overseeing Eve's currency, InterStellar Kredit (ISK).

With computer games, there are no corporate training departments that are tasked with teaching people how to play. Instead, gamers are self-taught; they learn by experimenting, consulting online resources, and reaching out to peers for tips. Multiplayer games often require teams to work together to achieve objectives.

Gamification moves action and feedback toward $P = 0$. A player tries something that works or doesn't. Players constantly receive points, weapons, or virtual tokens to reward progress.

Elements of game design are being incorporated into workplace training. Even games themselves.

In 2012 video game developer and entrepreneur Sam Glassenberg received a call from his medical doctor father lamenting how difficult it was for doctors to learn fiberoptic intubation, which involves shoving a plastic tube through a patient's mouth or nose into the trachea. It's painful and awkward but can also be lifesaving. Unsurprisingly, few people are interested in volunteering to be practiced on.

Glassenberg quickly cooked up a basic iPhone game simulating the procedure, posted it on the App Store, and forgot about it. Over a year later his father mentioned that his colleagues loved the game. Upon inspection, Glassenberg found that it had over one hundred thousand downloads—the most downloaded medical training app on Apple's platform.

He immediately founded Level Ex to create medical education games for fields from pulmonology and cardiology to dermatology and gastroenterology. European tech company BrainLab acquired the company in 2021 to accelerate growth. Glassenberg and his team continue to expand the immersive qualities of their products.

Doctors and nurses use Level Ex's current products to train anywhere, anytime. Imagine if they could do this for complex operations—*before* they operate on you. Glassenberg projects, "Eventually you'll be able to simulate entire operations on digital representations of *specific patients*, indistinguishable from the real deal. We want to be the ones doing that."

The trick for organizations will be to go beyond the controlled world of training simulations to better connect actions, outcomes, and feedback every day. If gamification can generate universes like *Eve Online*, perhaps it can enhance business performance as well.

How Talent Thrives

As the human-tech partnership evolves, so must our careers. Start by recognizing that no jobs are immune to technology.

Consider the role of the actuary, long considered a path to sustainable, lucrative employment. The U.S. Bureau of Labor Statistics reported that in 2022 there were just over twenty-three thousand actuaries in the United States with a mean annual wage of $125,000.

Most major insurance companies not only pilot AI systems for actuarial work—after all, it's data and advanced analytics—but they're also discussing what to do with actuaries. One top insurance executive commented to one of us, on condition of anonymity, "Traditionally, a global insurer our size might have required three thousand actuaries. In the not distant future, we might require thirty."

It's clear that AI, robotics, and automation will eliminate some roles, as they have already in manufacturing. Meanwhile, many studies (see in particular the work of Erik Brynjolfsson and his colleagues at Stanford and MIT) predict that these technologies will generate demand for many more jobs than they obviate.[12] It's just that the new jobs will require very different capabilities that will change over time. Robots still rely on humans to design, develop, install, maintain, service, and direct, at least for now.

While in-demand capabilities change, careers are path dependent. Get on the accounting train after college and you're likely to remain there for years. That's a challenge in a world of rapid, volatile change.

A linear, single-track approach to careers isn't the only option. As many accountants (or lawyers or supply chain experts, and so on) realize, many of their skills are fungible. With planning, effort, and serendipity, new paths open: new ways to approach "career change."

As technology assumes more activities and creates new roles for us, each of us must take a more flexible approach to our careers. Not just be resilient through change, but evolvable in response to it. Lifelong learning requires openness to new tools and being ever curious about how to do better.

As your financial advisor will tell you, when faced with uncertainty, diversify.

Enter the *portfolio career*. Rather than selling the predominance of your professional attention to one company, consider pursuing a range of activities, each part time. Renowned twentieth-century poet Wallace Stevens was also a vice president of Hartford Insurance. Even Einstein held down a position at the Swiss Patent Office until his *annus mirabilis* ("miracle year"), when the academic offers started rolling in.

In contrast to the stressed minimum wage worker forced to take on several jobs to make ends meet, the owner of a portfolio career welcomes a variety of roles and projects, many compensated, some not, into their professional pursuits.

A portfolio approach to your professional life enables flexibility. Not being beholden to a single employer gives you the freedom to explore more possibilities and build trusted relationships outside a single company. It can also protect you against job loss. Imagine the transition faced by Lehman Brothers employees—highly paid professionals—when their century-old firm collapsed in 2008.

As companies discover technology platforms and business models that break work into smaller, discrete pieces, contractable on a case-by-case basis, more opportunities arise for constructing prosperous professional lives without relying on a single employer. Diverse experience and exposure to different realms can also increase your value to each employer or partner, as you transfer knowledge and expertise between your various professional engagements.

It's not for everyone. Portfolio careers require more individual responsibility for your path. It's up to you to determine your mix of activities, how you source opportunities, and how you educate yourself and advance. Many who pursue this approach are essentially independent entrepreneurs.

You don't have to eschew A full-time job to build career optionality. Maintain a primary job while adding other potentially gainful activities on the side. Even if your side hustle expresses more of your personal interests than a professional path, you might discover that one day it becomes your primary career.

Proximity brings needs and talent closer. Clever, entrepreneurial people will discover more opportunities to thrive.

MORE OF YOUR BEST PEOPLE, MORE OF *YOU*

The most limited resource of any company is the attention of its best people. What if we could replicate those people, or at least aspects of them? Bring the right people to any challenge? Technology will present compelling—and potentially disquieting—options.

Deep fakes offer an early example. Some AI-generated videos and audios appear as if they were recorded in real life, often mimicking known individuals such as celebrities or your company's senior executives. While deep fakes can be used for evil, they might also be applied for good. Legitimate applications are limited only by our imaginations.

At the time of this writing, WPP, one of the world's largest advertising conglomerates, is working with the London start-up Synthesia to send deep fake corporate training videos to tens of thousands of employees. "With Synthesia, we can have avatars that are diverse and speak your name and your agency and in your language," says WPP's chief technology officer, Stephan Pretorius.[13] Creating a video takes seconds, and the avatars are based on real people (who might, hopefully, receive royalties).

If deep fakes are possible today, what about tomorrow?

In a 2017 *Forbes* article, Rob proposed the notion of a *proxy AI.* A proxy AI will simulate a specific person or people based on inputs provided by that individual, or just via their public digital footprint.[14] By 2023 anyone could try an early version. Try prompting a generative AI system with a question like "What would William Shakespeare think of the movie *The Terminator?*" Fun stuff.

It's not Shakespeare's answer, of course, but a simulacrum likely to improve as technology evolves. We could question the accuracy of the simulation, but what we'd really have is a *new* entity built on the digital detritus of the original.

Some historical figures have left vast archives expressing perspectives and priorities. Others have left commentaries about these individuals. Our online world provides ever growing reams of data that could be used (and misused) to characterize specific individuals. All of these sources are biased, some horribly so. Nonetheless, an AI could agglomerate, even curate, these digital footprints and build simulations. Simulations of us.

What might be possible a decade from now?

LITERARY COMPANIONS OR CRIMINAL INTENT

Philosophers from Plato to Saussure have criticized writing as inferior to live speech largely for being divorced from its creator. With proxy AIs, authors could accompany their works. Real time, a reader could query an author's proxy. Historical and literary characters could dialogue with us or with one another. In what conversations might Maya Angelou and Shakespeare engage?

How might such a capability impact the way we work and bring talent to an organization's objectives?

Need a specific type of expertise? Seek a relevant proxy AI. It might seek to simulate an actual person, or just focus on the analytical, creative capabilities necessary for the task at hand.

Proxy AIs need not stop at simulating a particular individual. They might amalgamate two or more people or combine one person's perspectives with knowledge from another arena. Facing a logistics management challenge at your company? Combine the perspectives and style of author Kurt Vonnegut with the knowledge of a supply chain expert. No problem (and likely entertaining). Need a film director with extensive medical expertise? Just ask. The possible combinations are endless.

Proxies also pose serious threats. Nefarious interests will redraw history for their own purposes using AI proxies as specious evidence. But people have been doing so for centuries. What's new will be the form and intensity of the "evidence." Each of us will be required to understand that proxies do not verifiably generate the perspectives of the individuals around which they are built. But how convincing might exceptional versions of Abraham Lincoln or Elon Musk become?

And proxy AIs could surely be used for identity theft. Imagine the challenge of determining if an urgent message came from your family member or from a well-designed fake.

Proxy AIs are just one possibility. Imagine the implications for Proximity when computational systems are able to generate multiple interactive copies of specific aspects of people. Right talent, right moment, anywhere, anytime, *at any scale.*

These and similar technologies will generate a maze of deep fake media and synthesized interactive agents. They'll challenge our notions of who we are and what is "real." Manipulation of entire populations via social media, as witnessed in the U.S. and U.K. elections of 2016, is just the beginning.

Michael Schrage, research fellow at the MIT Initiative on the Digital Economy (IDE) and author of *Recommendation Engines*, offers some optimism. These technologies can, if we avail ourselves to them, contribute to our own "selves improvement." We have the potential to become higher-performing versions of ourselves.

Perhaps one day a proxy AI of Rob will converse with students on demand *in their own languages,* or one of Kaihan's selves will deliver a virtual keynote *with Q&A* for a client in Dubai while he's with family in the mountains.[15]

PREPARING OURSELVES AND OUR CHILDREN

How might we prepare for this proximate future? How might we learn, build careers, remain relevant, and find meaning?

Parents often ask Rob, as a university professor, a version of the following question: "What should my kids study in college?" At first, he dismays them. "They should study whatever they're most interested in and do the best they possibly can at that." My goodness, they think, my child loves football or literature. How will they find a job? Then, he offers parental hope: "Regardless of their major, make sure they take a class in *how computer systems work* (a basic survey of AI, machine learning, data analytics, etc.), a class in *accounting*, and a class in *statistics*."

These are languages of which you'll need at least a basic understanding to be competitive in most endeavors, from business and government to nonprofits. These languages also give you a better shot at discerning when someone—human or AI—is trying to mislead you. While an engineering degree still leads to more job offers immediately out of college, even those with exceptional STEM capabilities today will need to remain ahead of fast-moving curves.

Given that technology will be able to assume an ever wider set of tasks, skills that will be increasingly required of each of us will be:

1. *Defining objectives*: what are we trying to accomplish and why?
2. *Asking the right questions*: what do we need to know, track, or resolve?
3. Prioritizing *attention and actions*: what do we need to do to remain relevant?

Continually rediscovering answers to these questions will be paramount. Unfortunately, these skills aren't typically taught in schools. Traditional education tends to prescribe the objectives (e.g., the syllabus) and pose questions *to* students (e.g., tests). Doing so remains valid, but *in addition* education should offer more opportunities for students to define their own objectives (within relevant fields of learning) and to define the questions they believe might help them progress.

Serial entrepreneur and investor Howard Tullman, mentor to hundreds of entrepreneurs over decades, argues, "Kids might not be so interested if you tell them you'll teach them English. If instead you tell them you'll help them write a screenplay, they're all in."

WHAT SHOULD WE DO WHEN ANYTHING IS POSSIBLE?

The vast majority of people throughout history worked because they had to. Many found comfort and meaning in their efforts, while some defined work as a necessity to be avoided if possible. For centuries, elites in societies from Europe to Asia aspired to absolution from gainful employment. Aristotle defined a "man in freedom" as the pinnacle of human existence, an individual freed of any concern for the necessities of life and with nearly complete personal agency. (Tellingly, he did not define wealthy merchants as free to the extent that their minds were preoccupied with acquisition.)

The promise of AI and automation raises new questions about the role of work in our lives. Most of us will remain focused for decades to come on activities of physical or financial production, but as technology provides services and goods at ever lower cost, human beings will be compelled to discover new roles—roles that aren't necessarily tied to how we conceive of work today.

Technology's great promise is to automate functions that humans prefer not to do and generally don't do as well, to redouble our attentions to the work we prefer, perhaps even love.

As technology becomes more capable—eventually even *better* at roles we've coveted as uniquely human, like creativity and empathy—it will be our individual and collective responsibilities to find new paths.

Part of the challenge, economist Brian Arthur proposes, "will not be an economic one but a political one."[16] For instance, what happens to those who make a living from driving vehicles after self-driving vehicles become common (no matter how long this takes)?

How are the spoils to be distributed? Arthur points to today's political turmoil in the United States and Europe as partly a result of the chasms between elites and the rest of society. Later this century, societies will discover how to distribute the productive benefits of technology for two primary reasons: because it will be easier and because they must. Over time, technology will enable more production with less sacrifice. Meanwhile, history suggests that the concentration of wealth in too few hands leads to social pressures that will be addressed through either politics or violence or both.

This raises a second, more vexing challenge. As the benefits of technology become more widely available—through reform or revolution—more of us will face the question: *When technology can do nearly anything, what should we do, and why?*

With such tools, our work lives will be less about implementation and more about envisioning and prioritizing: identifying and defining problems for technological systems to solve and processes for them to manage, and monitoring whether these efforts are creating the results we desire.

"WORK IS JUST ONE PART OF YOUR LIFE"

As augmented and virtual worlds proliferate, we'll spend more of our attention envisioning what experiences to create and how to better engage and satisfy—or addict—our fellow human beings.

As physical boundaries between work and life blur, we'll face the pull of 24/7 work. Individuals and organizations should seek to delineate work from nonwork. As former Fortune 500 CEO Harry Kraemer, author of *Your 168: Finding Purpose and Satisfaction in a Values-Based Life*, admonishes, "It's not 'work/life balance,' it's 'life balance.' Work is just one part of your life." How much life will you commit to work?

STEM disciplines alone cannot sufficiently equip us for the future. We'll need exposure to the social sciences (how and why people do things), humanities (what matters and why for our lives in society), and the arts (how we share visions and emotions). Well-functioning civil society depends on it. On the eve of World War II, Winston Churchill cautioned, "Ill fares the race which fails to salute the arts with the reverence and delight which are their due."

In a proximate world, work focused on creative activities, arts, hospitality, generation of experiences, public discourse, and human connectedness will emerge as an ever wider share of our global economy.

Meanwhile, as robots like Sophia become more capable, they won't be limited to automobile factories or awkward conversations on tech conferences stages. They'll do work we used to do, freeing us for other adventures and bringing interactions and experiences closer to each of us, responding to our desires—for good or ill—anywhere, anytime. To this we'll turn in the concluding chapter.

QUESTIONS TO CONSIDER FOR YOUR OWN PROXIMATE WORK FUTURE

1. Consider the value you add at work. What if that could be entirely automated and provided anywhere, anytime? How would you adjust?
2. What might a portfolio career mean for you?
3. If space and time were no longer factors in determining how you work, what would you do?
4. How can you become and remain an expert in something? How can you engage platforms that bring your brilliance to people where and when they need it?
5. What evolving technologies, business models, and trends should you track to stay ahead for *your* career?
6. How might you cast technology as your professional partner?

4

How We Eat

- Toward your very own Jetson's kitchen.
- Food security, sustainability, and access demand proximate food solutions.
- Distributed energy as the key for proximate agriculture.
- Achieving a "Goldilocks" future: plentiful, available, nutritious, and sustainable.
- Eliminating the sustainability and ethical dilemmas of the meat industry.
- Greater efficiency requiring radically less space— hallmarks of Proximity.
- Will we create a world where, for everyone, food is a choice rather than a struggle?

You can best see our proximate food futures in space. In Hollywood's *The Martian* (2015), Matt Damon plays a lonely, stranded astronaut whose immediate concern is food. A botanist, he creates a garden inside his habitat using Martian soil fertilized with the crew's biowaste and manufactures water from leftover rocket fuel. He then cultivates potatoes using whole potatoes reserved for a special Thanksgiving meal.

As we transition this century to the moon and Mars, Proximity models become imperative. If you're in a spacecraft for six months, you've only got what's on board.

We'll return to space in the concluding chapter. For now, let's start here on Earth.

CRISPY DUCK FOR ALL!

Pandemic lockdowns posed a quandary for Peking duck connoisseurs. It was nearly impossible to prepare this beloved Chinese delicacy at home. At least until 2020.

In mid-2019, Zhang Yu, a manager at Chinese appliance giant Haier, posed a challenge:

How can Haier help consumers make Peking Duck at home?

It was a timely question. About six months later the COVID-19 pandemic hit.

By early 2020, as the virus spread across China and then the world, many of the over 300 million Haier appliances already in kitchens worldwide happened to be digitally enabled, connected appliances. Perhaps the company could remotely program its ovens to prepare this classic yet demanding dish?

Reprogrammed Haier ovens wouldn't be enough. The duck-at-home concept also required recipes and ducks. Haier recruited chefs to provide their proprietary recipes for the perfect Peking duck for a licensing fee (IP rights for chefs!). It also constructed an ecosystem of farmers and shipping companies to supply properly prepared ducks and other ingredients directly to homes.

This network of collaborators created a complete solution for Peking duck aficionados. Simply order, receive all ingredients ready for preparation, download the recipe via a QR code, and then let your Haier oven do the rest.

From concept in 2019 to market delivery took *one year*. During the COVID-19 crisis, thousands of families across China enjoyed a delicacy that few had imagined possible at home.

Having sold twenty thousand Peking roast ducks in December 2020 alone, Haier plans to expand its "internet of food" to new recipes and geographies. It's an early example of a new food ecosystem bringing new value to consumers' homes.

Connected, digitally enabled devices enable cross-industry collaboration. Haier tracks ducks from farms to homes, paying chefs royalties like composers. Farmers better predict demand based on real-time data all the way to consumers' homes.

Might duck-on-demand presage an eventual Netflix of Cuisine? While not yet the *Star Trek* replicator—capable of generating any food on command from basic atomic ingredients—we're edging ever closer.

And none too soon.

OUR THIRTY-YEAR EXISTENTIAL CHALLENGE

Concurrent with the swell of variety, convenience, and nutrition for those capable of paying, humanity faces an existential challenge.

In 2022, global population passed 8 billion. We're likely to reach 9 or 10 billion in our lifetimes. Food industry guru Jack Bobo frames the challenge and opportunity: "The next thirty years are the most important thirty years there will *ever* be in the history of agriculture."

Between now and 2050, demographers expect population to expand by a billion souls every thirteen years. That's a lot of Peking duck, or even just rice. Beyond that, they expect the pace to slow to around a billion every twenty-five years.

Bobo argues that if we solve the food challenge before 2050—without destroying the environment—we'll be on pace to nourish the world beyond that. "When population growth slows, it's easier to feed humanity." If we've solved the problem for a faster-growing population, we're much better equipped to succeed as population growth decelerates.

Proximity models will be pivotal to navigating this thirty-year horizon. What if an increasing share of food production occurs closer to population centers, with distribution infrastructure capable of meeting real-time demands while simultaneously decreasing waste? As we'll see, such distributed food production requires, more than anything else, access to cost-effective, reliable, distributed energy. Distributed, sustainable energy is the key to distributed, accessible—proximate—food.

QUEST FOR CONTROL: OUR HISTORY WITH FOOD

As humans transitioned from gathering to farming, they discovered a level of control that had been impossible when they were reliant on whatever the local environment deigned to provide.

Similarly, supplementing hunting with herding, likely starting with goats around 8000 BCE, meant more dependable access to high-protein milk and meat. The ox-drawn plow (c. 4000 BCE) accelerated and amplified production. Then came crop rotation (c. 1500), steam-powered mills (early 1800s), nitrogen fixation for artificial fertilizer (1900), and over the centuries increasingly precise plant breeding, accelerating more recently via genetic engineering and related disciplines. Each of these technologies increased control over the when and where of nourishment.

While farming began close to where early communities required food, such as intensively farmed family plots, over the last few centuries scale efficiencies of production, transportation, and distribution have driven production ever further from final demand.

Scale agriculture co-evolved with mechanized reaping, transportation, storage, and distribution. Steam-powered ships (1787) and trains (1814) expanded the distances from which food could be sourced and the speed and scale with which supply could respond to demand. Innovations like pasteurization (1860) and food refrigeration (1950s) meant longer shelf life and the potential to serve consumers thousands of miles away.

Today, most of our food grows on massive farms and is gathered, stored, packaged, and preserved for long journeys. Countertrends such as the farm-to-table or "slow food" movements—both proximate philosophies—while compelling, remain too expensive for meaningful population-wide impact.

In Proximity terms, production moved *further away* from final demand. Provision (supply chain and retailing through preparation and service), by contrast, enabled foods, even entire cuisines, to be increasingly available, at least for those with sufficient wealth. And this bounty came at great environmental cost.

FROM PAST SOLUTIONS, NEW CHALLENGES

From the Industrial Revolution through the twentieth century, the overwhelming trends in food and agriculture moved toward higher-scale, processed, prepackaged, longer-shelf-life products. Fortunately, increased yields (productivity per acre) and increased availability of food enabled a breathtaking expansion of populations worldwide from the late eighteenth century onward.

Though we fail to do so equitably—and wholly fail some people—the global food industry produces quantities capable of feeding the world if the bounty were better distributed. While a monumental accomplishment, past solutions seed new problems.

The global food system has accomplished this feat in part via large-scale monoculture (defined as the cultivation of a single crop in a given area) at the expense of species diversity. While supporting radical efficiency gains, monoculture also exposes us to risks. Diverse ecosystems prove more robust against biological and environmental threats. Imagine a new blight arising that is particularly deadly to a species of plant covering thousands, even millions, of acres.

The Irish potato famine of 1845–1852 killed 1 million people and led to the mass exodus of over 2 million people from Ireland to the United States and Canada. Ironically, the potato proliferated as a crop across Northern Europe in the late eighteenth century due in part to a series of widespread grain crop failures. At first, potatoes proved more resilient and nutrient rich than their predecessors.

The potato was so efficient that by the 1830s a third of the Irish population relied on the tuber for the majority of their nourishment, at a rate of forty to sixty potatoes (which were smaller than those of today) per person *every day*—until disaster struck. A strain of *Phytophthora infestans* destroyed from one-third to three-quarters of the country's harvests during the years of infestation.

Planting one of only a few types of tomatoes or one potato species across massive farms, as is industry standard practice, proves more efficient than letting species naturally permutate (evolve). Modern agriculture has developed solutions that rely on pesticides, herbicides, and genetically engineered crops that are resilient to threats.

While warranting criticism, we'd have no hope of feeding the world's population without these high-scale solutions. Massive-scale farming has been *essential* to lifting billions out of hunger, and global logistics networks have provided a nearly unlimited choice for those with means.

However, this cornucopia stresses global ecosystems and fails less affluent populations. "Food deserts" blight wide swaths of urban and rural areas, many ironically in leading agricultural regions.

These successes and challenges reflect trade-offs inherent in the structure of contemporary food systems. Two sets of often-conflicting objectives must be balanced:

1. Efficient scale versus sustainability and resilience
2. Access versus nutrition and quality

Efficient scale provides greater access at lower cost, an unheralded achievement of our global food system. Unfortunately, many agricultural solutions degrade the natural systems upon which they depend. Others, such as monocultures, face higher vulnerability to pests and pathogens.

Global agricultural systems, producing *far* from ultimate consumption, face additional risks from extreme weather events and geopolitical conflicts. Russia's war in Ukraine compromised not only the region's agricultural industry—a breadbasket for the world—but also the world's access to fertilizers and other inputs.[1]

Meanwhile, the scale achieved has dramatically improved access to food at lower costs, but usually, though not always, with lower nutritional value: processed foods, preservatives, and higher sugar content. At least partly as a result, as of 2021, 19 percent of people worldwide suffer from obesity, including 30 percent of North Americans and 25 percent of Europeans.[2]

When our objectives conflict, the approaches we use to achieve them are liable to do so as well. Genetic engineering—our greatest hope for higher yields, better nutrition, and pest-resistant crops—collides with organic farming standards. Processing technologies that drive down prices and increase access often negatively impact nutrition.

These dynamics also reflect the incentives of the global food system. Humans—known fittingly and unfortunately as "consumers"—purchase what they *desire*, which often conflicts with what's better for them. They prefer taste, convenience, and cost over nutrition. As businesses must, food companies provide what sells. In many cases that's cheap, processed sugars, fats, and salt in pretty packages.

Proximity offers the hope of overcoming these trade-offs, of achieving a "Goldilocks" future: plentiful, available, nutritious, *and* sustainable. In other words, just right.

But no matter how compelling your sustainability TED talk, achieving it requires *profitable* solutions that scale. That requires overcoming established paradigms.

FROM TRASH TO TABLE?

Today, we waste one-third of all food produced (around 1.3 billion tons[3]), costing the global economy close to $940 billion each year.[4] Meanwhile, over 800 million people globally, or 10 percent of us, go hungry each day.[5]

What if the peels and pomace from our trash could be repurposed into sweet banana bread or honey chili potatoes?

Elzelinde van Doleweerd's crusade against food waste started while she was pursuing her degree in industrial design at the Eindhoven University of Technology in the Netherlands. She thought, "How can we make use of the vast amount of food waste from grocery stores, restaurants and households?" Today her digital company, Upprinting Food, 3D-prints foods from leftovers.

The metamorphosis begins with mashing, mixing, grinding, and filtering leftover food. The resulting smooth-as-silk paste can be easily "printed" using digital technology and then baked. Upprinting uses more than 75 percent of residual food flows, with the remaining 25 percent being added ingredients and spices for flavoring, formability, and texture.[6] The resulting snack has a peculiar crunchy texture much like cookies or crackers.

After proving the concept with initial recipes, van Doleweerd teamed up with China-based 3D Food Company to produce food from leftover rice.[7] The foods, which include crunchy cracker-like samples made from purple sweet potatoes and rice, are a continuation of the Dutch designer's Upprinting Food project. Rather than disposing of food scraps, future consumers might recycle them into printed snacks.

Van Doleweerd is one of a new crop of food innovators who are bringing food closer to P = 0 while simultaneously enhancing sustainability. While no one can say if any specific concept will succeed, the scale and diversity of experimentation ensure that tomorrow will look very different.

TOWARD FOOD, P = 0

Three technology-enabled trends will propel global food systems toward P = 0 in both production (ingredients, products, even complete meals) and provision (delivering, preparing, serving):

1. Controlled environment agriculture (CEA)
2. Customization via automated Moment of Use (MoU) production and preparation
3. Transparency, prediction, and matching of supply and demand

Together, they enable higher efficiency at both larger and smaller scales of production, each for different purposes, and more control of growing, storage, and transport harmonized with demand.

CEA: Grow Anything, Anywhere

On Kaihan's ski journey to Vermont each winter, he and his family follow a path through New England. While the route is mostly bordered by traditional farms, one farm looms large over the landscape. From a complex of large semitranslucent warehouses emanates an eerie blue light. It is more alien base than farm.

Indoor farms like these, with plants often growing vertically rather than spread across many acres, are under construction all over the world. Technicians control the environment in which plants grow in what is broadly known as controlled environment agriculture (CEA). You can create almost any environment by controlling light, temperature, humidity, and soil nutrients. Growing tropical plants such as cassava or plantains in icy Vermont becomes possible. Because pests are unable to access your crops, they require few, if any, pesticides.[8]

CEA can radically enhance throughput—total volume per acre along with faster turns between crops. Farmers can nurture more plants per acre, do so faster, and produce year-round.

Depending on plant species and CEA capabilities, crops can grow up to twice as fast while consuming 90 percent less water. CEA releases farming from traditional geographic and climatic constraints, allowing the production of crops wherever it makes the most economic, social, and environmental sense.

CEA makes smaller production footprints more viable closer to consumers.

In Brooklyn, New York, for instance, you'll find a series of shipping containers converted into farms. Cofounded by Kimbal Musk, Elon's brother, Square Roots brings Proximity to food production by producing (more or less) next door. An urban father or his favorite local restaurant can access fresh herbs and leafy greens grown inside upcycled shipping containers. Not only do Square Roots's containers bring fresh food production closer to consumers, but they're also relocatable as demand shifts. Try that with a traditional farm.

While most food production will remain for years in large farms far from ultimate demand, CEA is becoming far more flexible and efficient for an increasing range of locations and use cases. When yields (productivity per acre) were only modestly better and operating costs much higher than for traditional farming, the impact was limited to extreme cases like growing fresh produce for isolated markets like Iceland (which enjoys fresh produce year-round), just below the Arctic Circle.

For the first decade or so of commercial development, CEA ventures typically focused on "high-value, fast-turn" products such as leafy greens. CEA advocates touted safety, freshness, nutrition content, and environmental sustainability, though costs remained much higher than for traditional farming methods.[9] CEA remained a niche, if growing, player.

By 2022, some CEA methods had enhanced yields to 100×−300× compared with traditional farms. Yes, that's 300 *hundred* times greater. At these rates, economics shifts. Established players like Walmart engage and investors raise massive funds, like Equilibrium Capital's new $1.1 billion CEA-focused fund founded in 2021. Leading food and agriculture venture firm S2G Ventures projects that the CEA sector will grow 5× over the decade from 2021 to 2031.

Serious About CEA

In January 2022, Walmart joined Softbank and other tech investors in a $400 million funding round for vertical farming leader Plenty. During the deal announcement, Plenty's CEO, Arama Kukutai, reported that the company increased yields in its leafy green growing rooms by 700 percent in just two years.

Plenty's produce grows vertically instead of in the standard horizontal tray format. The company reports requiring only 1 percent of the land required by traditional farms, while improving yields 150 to 350 times per acre. Exponentially greater efficiency requiring radically less space—hallmarks of Proximity.

Walmart is thinking beyond leafy greens. After four years of evaluating partners, the company chose Plenty due to not only its rapidly growing yields but also its plans to expand into fruits and vegetables, crops in which vertical farms have been less active.

Freight Farms, a Pennsylvania-based innovator, takes a different approach. Rather than operating indoor vertical farms, the founders seek to enable others. They started helping people build rooftop vegetable gardens but rapidly evolved to creating fully equipped vertical hydroponic farms in shipping containers. The units contain sophisticated systems to optimize conditions for each species: temperature and water conditions, automatic nutrient release, and lighting systems that mimic optimal sunlight patterns.

You don't need scale to be a Freight Farmer. Anyone with enough space for a shipping container can purchase, install, and run a Freight Farm. Internet of Things (IoT) sensors continually track data and feed information to farmers through a mobile app. With over 2 billion datapoints so far, they are also able to learn and improve indoor farming via AI systems. By January 2022, after six years in operation, the company had empowered over five hundred farmers in forty-four U.S. states and twenty-six countries.

Such small-unit, modularly scalable—just add more containers—solutions are percolating worldwide, from Turkey to Wyoming. Wyoming's Vertical Harvest Farms reports that its urban hydroponic solutions produce with 90 percent less land, 90 percent less water, and 95 percent less fuel.[10]

By 2017 one in three Americans was growing some of their food at home. The indoor farming industry reached over $40 billion by 2022.[11] The future points to more farming and processing closer to our homes and families, be that within urban areas or nearby in suburban and rural areas where land is cheaper but still more proximate to population centers.

Farming is even moving into homes. A Brooklyn-based start-up aims to bring farming even closer with the introduction of the first consumer-facing vertical farming unit. Farmshelf, founded in 2016 out of a WeWork accelerator program, has developed a bookcase-sized farming system to promote vertical farming in homes and offices.[12] As of this writing, the device operates within a number of New York City restaurants and hotels.

Farmshelf Home users simply plug in the device, connect to Wi-Fi, and plant seeds in pods. They use an app to monitor their hydroponic growing systems. After an initial $5,000 investment in the system, a monthly subscription fee covers supplies and access to the app.[13]

Which micro-modular-farming solutions ultimately prevail—shipping containers, "bookcases" etc.—is beside the point. They show that widespread experimentation is under way. The efficiency and sustainability of megafarms will continue to advance. In many cases, high-scale solutions will remain more competitive. In others, Proximity solutions will change the game.

Proximity agriculture can play games that traditional industrial-scale agriculture cannot. It has the freshness and environmental benefits of produce grown close at hand and the culinary possibilities when it's possible to grow small volumes of a wide selection of plants. Chefs, or eventually any consumers, become able to experiment with a range of plants this month and an entirely different set next month.

As with any new paradigms, it's unclear who will be the long-term winners. Even a well-funded leader like Plenty faces the vicissitudes of pioneering new solutions at scale. In December 2022, Plenty announced the closure of its indoor farm in south San Francisco. That same year the company announced a $300 million investment over six years to build a controlled environment farm complex in Richmond, Virginia. By February 2023, it announced a major expansion of its indoor agriculture R&D complex in Laramie, Wyoming, assisted by a $20 million grant from the state.[14]

As we'll explore in chapter 7, "How We Power," the primary enabler for distributed, proximate CEA around the world will be access to distributed, sustainable energy. It's currently a hard constraint for many possible implementations of distributed agriculture that could otherwise thrive. Sonia Lo, leading agriculture investor and former CEO of CropOne, clarifies that "distributed energy is *the* key for distributed agriculture."

Proximate energy and proximate agriculture evolve together. And the food revolution isn't limited to plants.

Crickets with Your Fries, Fish on Land, Meat Beyond Meat?

Producing 1 gram of cricket protein—already important nourishment in some parts of the world—requires 2 percent the amount of water, 0.02 percent the amount of feed, and 3 percent the amount of time required to produce 1 gram of protein from cows.[15] Beef-like food from crickets could feed incomparably more people using much smaller spaces nearly anywhere.

Insect proteins provide just one example of the range of alternative proteins and protein production methods that are experiencing a surge in investment and development.

The United Arab Emirates (UAE) has been pioneering local, sustainable aquaculture for over a decade. Founded in 2013, Fish Farm LLC produced and sold roughly 2,500 tons of farmed fish by 2017, produced in the UAE and the Gulf of Oman, largely for consumption in the UAE. His Highness Sheikh Mohammed bin Rashid Al Maktoum, ruler of Dubai, has made food self-sufficiency a strategic priority. "Expanding domestic food production to achieve self-sufficiency is a strategic objective and one of the main pillars of the National Food Security Strategy."[16]

Dubai's commitment offers an example for other countries seeking sustainable food security. Their vision requires proximate solutions.

Meanwhile, the Nordics—Denmark, Finland, Iceland, Norway, and Sweden—have long been known for exceptional seafood, with thousands of kilometers of coastlines and seafaring heritages. Now they're bringing the pursuit on land.

Danish-based Atlantic Sapphire is innovating land-based salmon farming closer to the point of demand. Its facilities mimic ideal salmon habitats with relatively small footprints. *Just one facility in Florida is able to produce enough salmon to fulfill around half of the U.S. salmon diet.* It does so while recycling 99 percent of the water and eliminating the threat of diseases and sea lice.

Already, imitation meats, provided by companies such as Beyond Meat and Impossible Foods, are rising in popularity. Lab-grown meats will quickly follow.

Dozens of start-ups worldwide, such as Aleph Farms, Avant Meats, Biotech Foods, Eat Just, Finless Food, Future Meat Technologies, Good Meat, and SuperMeat, are deploying billions of dollars to remove sentient animals from the meat equation.

These are not meat substitutes, but actual muscle tissues grown in laboratories. Multiple benefits accrue: breakthrough land-use efficiency, lower waste and emissions, and production location flexibility that is unimaginable via traditional animal husbandry.[17] Here's how. Extract muscle, blood, fat, and support cells from animal tissue. Then introduce nutrients and catalysts to encourage cells to multiply. A few months later you can create meat that would otherwise take ranches and feedlots a couple of years to produce.

Eventually doing so will become economical at commercial scale. Cultured, factory-grown meat mitigates many of the challenges faced by traditional animal husbandry, replacing from thousands of acres required for grazing with factories with smaller footprints. Feeding cell growth rather than raising entire animals. Resolving most of the organic waste and odors. Dramatically lowering water and energy consumption, eliminating antibiotic use from the process.

Not to mention obviating the ethical dilemma faced by meat-eating consumers. No more animals suffering brief, dark, torturous lives.

Imagine how much more proximate meat production can become when released from the constraints of raising, transporting, and slaughtering animals. Smaller-scale production could move economically to locations such as urban peripheries inaccessible to traditional animal farms. In special cases, such as for small-scale meat cultivation artisans, even within densely populated urban areas.

Whether using imitation or real meats, chefs and other artisans might one day invent their own meat cultures or customize production processes for small, specialized runs. Your own custom Wagyu-like beef, without breeding and raising new species. Bobo recommends we use the term "craft meats" to convey the artisanal possibilities.

Today cultured meats fail consumer taste tests compared to the traditional sort. The resulting meat mass lacks the texture and consistency of animal-grown protein. One solution under development includes printing the meat layer by layer to mimic the fibers of a steak.[18] If this approach works, we could print made-to-order steaks nearly anywhere. The potential of 3D-printing foods might catalyze proximate culinary innovation and production.

With billions of dollars supporting R&D, it's likely that printed meat will one day surpass animal-derived meat. Factory production offers far more control than growing muscle tissue inside living animals. Expect the industry to rapidly advance flavor, texture, shelf life, and even nutrition.

As proximate production becomes competitive, food preparation trends closer as well.

Your Own Jetson's Kitchen

Remember the 1960s cartoon featuring George Jetson and his space-age family? Previous generations would have found magic in today's much more prosaic kitchen automations. Dishwashers decide how long to dry. Ovens determine when the chicken's ready. Create any flavored soda you want on your counter at home. No more bottles or cans.

Picture your daily routine in a decade. Awaken, and by the time you reach your kitchen nearly any breakfast fare you desire awaits. We're nearing a *Jetsons* future.

Automation, AI, and connectivity will enable radically new business models, culinary options, and food experiences: the promise of both personalization at scale *and* greater efficiency, less waste, and negative environmental impact.

Consider EveryCook, an advanced multicooker connected to the internet. Download a recipe, and EveryCook sets times and temperatures. It calculates the amount of each ingredient required and determines when you have added enough. The more you use it, the better it learns your preferences: how well done you like your meats, how spicy, savory, or sweet your dishes. Like Haier's system described earlier, it's an early version of a digital personal chef, bringing home ever more diverse and complex dishes.

Connected monitoring, inventory control, and food preparation systems might eventually even help us manage our behaviors. Need to decrease your sugar intake? Change your personal food settings (though the follow-through is up to you).

Such systems could reduce food waste and—if we let them—improve our diets.

Printing Pizzas

What if you could "print" a range of foods from basic biomass ingredients?

The notion's not new. It's called "extrusion." If you've eaten a Cheeto (the crunchy, cheesy snack made by Frito-Lay), you've tried extruded corn meal. Hotdogs? Extruded meat (or some approximation thereof).

Until recently extrusion machines were constrained to large manufacturing plants. Additive manufacturing could bring them to your kitchen at home.

Or to your space station. NASA began working on printing pizzas in 2013, anticipating the need for highly flexible food preparation with a small footprint. It's only a matter of time before someone makes the technology ready for a space station or kitchen.

Customization opportunities abound. In 2016, a team of chefs launched Food Ink, the "World's First 3D-Printing Restaurant." The pop-up restaurant toured Europe producing eclectic, creative, futuristic food that *could not be produced by traditional methods.*[19] By 2022, over thirty restaurants in London, Amsterdam, and Berlin were printing steaks from plant-based ingredients in collaboration with an Israeli start-up called Redefine Meat.[20]

3D printing solutions can also serve hyperspecific needs that might be inefficient for high-scale manufacturing. In Germany, Biozoon does this for seniors with chewing or digestion problems and for athletes who require highly customized food regimens.[21]

Digital, automated food methods have a sharing advantage over traditional recipes. Sure, it's been easy to share recipes online for decades, but you still have to follow the steps. When those steps become digitalized and fed to automated appliances, you might just need to download a file and press a button.

Eventually you might rely on your AI system to answer: What should we have for dinner?

Your Inner Julia Child

Many of us will still desire traditionally prepared meals or the experience of cooking. That will increasingly be a choice rather than a necessity. After all, millions enjoy the culinary process. We even still have a few microwave oven holdouts.

But that's precisely the point. Proximity is about pushing *value* creation closer to ultimate demand. If certain chefs or diners *value* the process, even the philosophy, of hand-prepared meals, then that's central to their personal value proposition.

Nonetheless, over time technology prevails. A little help with complex meal preparation might be nice, evidenced by the success of meal kits. Even the most fastidious reactionary relies on a refrigerator.

As food production and preparation transform, Proximity advances across the global food value chain.

Transparency from Seeds to Tables

Internet of Things (IoT) technologies connect devices that collect and process data and coordinate operations.[22] Already a major factor in industrial settings, one of the world's first IoT devices was inspired by a desire for beverage Proximity.

In the early 1980s, a group of Carnegie Mellon students grew frustrated when after long treks to a particular Coca-Cola vending machine on campus they would find their desired beverage out of stock. As you'd expect from brilliant nerds, they designed and installed a system to check beverage availability from afar. Microswitches connected through the university's network.[23]

In some cases, consumers are willing to pay a premium for transparency: to know what's in our food and where it came from. Industry expert Jack Bobo predicts, "Today the market rewards transparency. In the future consumers will *expect* it."

Sensing, monitoring, AI, data analytics, and blockchain technologies enhance our ability to predict supply and demand from producers to end consumers while ensuring freshness and safety.

Blockchain, or "distributed ledger," systems record data on numerous systems for all to see and verify. (Though so-called private blockchains mitigate this level of openness.) Agriculture commodity leaders like Cargill and retailers like Walmart already apply blockchain-based systems to enhance visibility, security, and efficiency across their supply chains, such as Walmart's Project Gigaton.

Blockchain allows us to create a unique code, similar to the vehicle identification code (VIN) on each car, for each crate of cucumbers, bunch of bananas, or whatever. With that code you can track its journey from farm to processor to shipper to receiver to wholesaler to retailer. The record cannot be falsely altered because to do so a hacker would need to simultaneously hack a vast number of distributed recordkeepers.

To understand the potential impact of distributed ledger technologies, consider the massive global industry of food and agriculture brokers, distributors, and agents. Information asymmetry is essential for the profitability of such intermediaries. If, hypothetically, anyone could easily find any product or commodity available anywhere, anytime, the value of brokers would decline.

Distributed ledger methodologies also offer the potential for smart contracts. These are easily verifiable contracts between two or more parties that automatically execute terms based on agreed-upon criteria and ideally trusted third-party metrics. Crop insurance offers a simple example. Such agreements automatically pay out when specific weather conditions meet predetermined levels, such as temperature as reported by government climate authorities. Once the parties complete the contract, encoded for all to see, everything proceeds without intervention. No claims process, no negotiation.

Multiple food industry players are experimenting with tracking and smart contracts. If successful, such systems could enable accurate, real-time sharing of critical data across every link in the food supply chain and execution of agreements anywhere without additional human intervention. A foundation for Proximity.

Reenvisioning Food Value Chains

Existing food supply chains are in many ways anathema to fresh. Though this is changing due to companies like Gotham Greens, most produce endures long trips from farm to table. Grocers race the clock to stock fresh produce. Ordering miscalculations can complicate the supply chain: trucks wait longer at docks and bananas and berries languish on pallets, resulting in produce in our kitchens that spoils in a few days.

Afresh Technologies, a San Francisco–based start-up, aspires to change that. Its founder, Matt Schwartz, wants everyone to enjoy fresh food.

Growing up in southern California, Schwartz realized the impact of food choices on mood. Consuming fresher, nutrient-rich foods made him more focused, confident, and studious. He began to wonder what could happen if more people enjoyed healthy options.

Matt found that he could innovate on food that was *already* good for people. Applying digital technologies could keep the food fresh for longer, reduce waste, and make produce more accessible and affordable.

He cofounded Afresh in 2017 with Volodymyr Kuleshov and Nathan Fenner. Their operating system applies AI to forecast demand, track current inventory, and optimize ordering for grocery stores. Today, most grocery inventory is estimated by hand or robot. Afresh's technology replaces this approach with real-time tracking and analysis, from growers' supplies through what's en route and in store to what's being purchased by consumers.

Afresh positions its solutions as a "fresh operating system" designed for offering the freshest foods as close as possible to each consumer.

By 2021, Afresh was operating in two hundred stores across three grocery chains. In August 2022 it announced a $115 million round of capital raised from some of the world's leading venture investors. By early 2023, Afresh had partnerships in over three thousand stores, accounting for *10 percent of all fruits and vegetables* sold in the United States. Through 2021, Afresh and its grocery partners had saved 6.9 million pounds of food waste. With continued growth, the Afresh team projects that it can prevent 100 million pounds of food per year from being discarded.

Afresh's vision is much greater than reducing food waste. Schwartz predicts, "Fresh is the future of the food system." Beyond the population-level health and sustainability benefits, a level of self-actualization arises from accessing the best for yourself and your family.

Whether or not Afresh achieves its mission, someone will.

As food producers and purveyors, legacy and new, climb technology learning curves, they'll discover ways to bring nutritious, higher-quality foods to more people at lower costs with fewer trade-offs.

To illustrate where this could lead, try an extreme hypothetical case. How might markets work if *everyone, everywhere had access to data about everything*? (Again, an extreme case.) It would then become a math problem to determine the cheapest, fastest, most environmentally friendly paths between supply and those willing to pay the highest prices at any moment. Market actors would determine which factors to optimize, supported by AI systems empowered to make real-time decisions. Cost, speed, nutrition, freshness, environmental impact, or some combination thereof? Meanwhile, smart contracts would operate across supply chains, tracking relevant data and executing on cue.

Compared to our current state of opacity and information asymmetry, *provision* of food products would become far more proximate: everything closer to what, where, and when demanded with lower waste. Production would adjust based on far better demand prediction. Not just what might be required, but precisely where and by whom.

We're far from food chain Valhalla, but this is the direction we're heading.

TOWARD A HYBRID WORLD

Proximate production will rise alongside rapidly evolving traditional agriculture. Having both will increase the responsiveness and resilience of food systems.

Scale will retain advantages for production, processing, storage, and transportation of many products, especially commodities like wheat, rice, and soybeans. Established players will continue to invest in robotics, AI, control and monitoring, and other technologies to enhance high-scale farming.

Contrast this with highly perishable fruits and vegetables that require cold chain capabilities. These products will be more amenable to proximate solutions, given the high costs of moving and handling and the high value of freshness and variety.

Over time, expect proximate methods to overtake traditional production for an increasing range of products. They'll do so because they can do what traditional-scale agriculture cannot, and they can do so profitably: provide greater flexibility, responsiveness, and on-demand customization.

THE TRIALS OF PLENTY

The promise of plentiful, proximate food presents us with challenges. Will access be widespread or just for those with means? The radical efficiency and sustainability gains already proven via CEA and cultured meats, for instance, suggest the benefits *could* be widely distributed, particularly if CEA advocates achieve meaningfully lower energy requirements per unit of production.

Will we create a world where, for everyone, food is a choice rather than a struggle?

History shows we humans to be notoriously bad at making good decisions when faced with plenty. Obesity, waste, even addiction rage where we've had meaningfully more than we need.

If our favorite foods can be delivered anywhere, anytime, what's to stop us from degenerating to uber-connected gluttons? In Pixar's blockbuster film *WALL-E*, humans escape a dying Earth to live in spacecraft. With limitless food within arm's reach, they become too heavy to walk unaided.

It's a fun story, but given where technology is heading, it's also preposterous. By 2023 Novo Nordisk's drug Wegovy (semaglutide) and Lilly's drug Mounjaro (tirzepatide), originally developed to treat diabetes, were showing significant efficacy against obesity. A space-faring race should be expected to devise cures for excessive weight that don't rely on (rather limited) human discipline.

Proper nutrition, though, is a more vexing challenge. It requires deciphering a diverse and complex set of factors. What is the ideal nutritional mix not just for a population but also for each individual human being? Researchers in fields from genomics and proteomics to the gut biome are working on it. It's reasonable to expect significant progress.

Our Proximity bounty will fail to be more nutritious unless industry and regulators make nutrition a priority. And they'll take their cues from each of us. How much do we as consumers and citizens care about nutrition for ourselves, our families, and society at large? We can be sure that the food industry will discover new ways to catalyze and cater to our desires— healthy or not.

Assume that one day medical science solves the ideal nutrition equation for each of us. It will still be up to each individual to follow the advice. If that nutrition can be delivered via convenient packages or even magic pills, then we've got a shot. Bobo advocates for "designing food environments that deliver healthy outcomes by default, so consumers can give it no thought."

It's a bold vision, but it's also possible in our lifetimes.

Right now, there is a middle-school student in a midwestern cafeteria eating a rectangular slice of pizza. Two decades from now, once this child has become a parent, his automated home kitchen might prepare a healthy meal for his family, with nutrients carefully portioned to each individual's particular needs, including some ingredients grown or synthesized on-site.

RESILIENT *AND* EVOLVABLE

Proximity models offer possibilities to overcome trade-offs we've faced for centuries. Scale *and* sustainability. Access *and* nutrition.

Radically higher yields, sustainably via CEA. Fresher produce grown near or within urban areas with the potential to bring greater nutrition, economically, to more people. Meat production released from the land-use, environmental, and ethical quandaries of raising animals for slaughter.

Well-designed Proximity models should be both more resilient and evolvable. Flexible, widely distributed production could adjust more effectively to local demands and also to unexpected disruptions thousands of kilometers away.

Consider the infant formula debacle of 2022. Pandemic-related disruption had already compromised supplies nationwide when one of the three major U.S. producers, Abbott Labs, shut down production at its Sturgis, Michigan, plant due to suspected bacterial contamination. With shortages nationwide, five states faced greater than 50 percent out-of-stock rates. Flexible, distributed production—repurposed for infant formula manufacture where necessary—could have supplemented traditional high-volume facilities.

No geography has moved more aggressively toward a proximate, resilient food future than Singapore. The city-state's "30 by 30" initiative endeavors to "build up our agri-food industry's capability and capacity to produce 30 percent of our nutritional needs locally and sustainably by 2030." No small feat when you consider that Singapore's landmass equates to less than half the size of London.

As of 2022, the Singapore Food Agency reports some local farmers producing 10 to 15 times more per acre than traditional farms. It's only the beginning of the country's ambitions for a sustainable, resilient local supply.[24]

Food Proximity is not about making everything hyperlocal. It's about discovering the most efficient and resilient balance between global and local production. Due to digitally enabled technologies, geopolitical uncertainties, and environmental threats, expect that balance to shift in favor of proximate solutions.

FOOD DEFINES US

Food transcends farms and supply chains. It's about our social, cultural lives. About who we are. The expressive, engaging nature of cuisine, driven by personal and cultural preferences, suggests that consumers are unlikely to exhaust their desires for new culinary experiences.

Proximate models have the potential to deliver, not just frozen shadows of the real deal but bona fide versions of dishes that make our lives richer and, ironically, more connected with the future *and* tradition.

One day we'll all have access to a streaming service of food from cultures worldwide, offering Peking ducks, expertly prepared Phở, and—*mon dieu*—even *fois gras* without any geese harmed in the process.

Experiences your grandchildren might appreciate on their homestead on Mars.

5

How We Prevent and Cure

- Proximity shifts healthcare from cure to prevent.
- Life happens where we live, not in doctors' offices.
- Over time, smart watches—and smart systems—become smarter.
- Personalized medicine requires proximate solutions.
- Care to the patient, instead of patient to the care.
- Care disappears into our daily lives.
- Proximate wellness: always on, always with you, more *you*.
- Distributed capabilities generate distributed risks.

On December 9, 2021, Proximity saved a life. A seventy-one-year-old man in Sweden suffered cardiac arrest while shoveling snow.[1] A passerby called an ambulance. Within 3 minutes a drone arrived carrying an automated external defibrillator (AED). The good Samaritan revived the patient before the ambulance arrived.

In 2020, Sweden became the first country to deploy drones carrying AEDs for cases of sudden cardiac arrest, when survival odds depend on delivering aid to the heart from a defibrillator within 5 minutes—nearly always before emergency responders arrive.[2]

As impressive as Sweden's drone-based system is, it's just the beginning.

You're at home with an elderly family member in the earliest stages of cardiac arrest, so early that neither of you are yet aware. Your loved one's health-monitoring system informs you both of the threat. Minutes later a medical first-responder drone arrives with a device and recorded instructions to jumpstart your loved one's heart *in case* the attack escalates before medical professionals arrive.

Imagine the life-threatening scenarios that might be better managed or even averted.

Through the COVID-19 pandemic, most of us became familiar with telehealth: interaction with physicians and other healthcare professionals online. Today always-on health monitoring systems can discover cancer before it becomes life-threatening. Treatments for chronic conditions like diabetes or hypertension operate automatically, disappearing into a patient's daily life. And in some cases, genetic edits resolve threats altogether.

As we'll see, proximate solutions aren't just incrementally better. Over time, they'll shift the emphasis of healthcare from curing disease to preventing it. Proximate solutions also offer the potential to enhance access and healthcare equity by dramatically lowering overall costs—if we as a society have the wisdom to do so.

The benefits of connected, always-on monitoring will challenge conceptions of privacy and who should be allowed to leverage our personal data. China's application of health data for COVID-19 enforcement offers a recent example, illustrating great benefits for public health combined with intrusive, potentially threatening, levels of control. Health data cybersecurity—an enormous opportunity for investors—will present new challenges. Government policies toward citizens' personal data will face complex practical and ethical questions.

PROXIMITY IN HEALTHCARE

The last century of modern medicine has generally followed an Industrial Age model, with medical technologies often requiring centralized production and delivery. As in the steel or automotive industries, high capital and expertise requirements have translated to large pharmaceutical production facilities or modern hospitals.

Large-scale pharmaceutical production facilities provide efficiency, but they also expose patients worldwide to supply chain risk. Pfizer CEO Albert Bourla recounts the story in *Moonshot*, his memoir of the race to bring COVID-19 vaccines to the world.

During the pandemic, the first COVID-19 vaccine was produced in Michigan. Under the Defense Production Act, which was incorporated into our agreement with the US government, we risked not only civil but also criminal prosecution if we exported the vaccine outside the United States. So while the US government did not ban exports of the vaccine per se the repercussions for us doing so could have been dire under the strict guidelines of the DPA. Early on, a small production facility in Belgium ramped up, but not enough to serve the rest of the world.[3]

While a shock of such proportions would prove intractable for even the best-prepared supply chains, the current model of pharmaceutical production presents challenges even for developed nations. Hospitals across the United States face generic drug shortages on a regular basis, as nearly all generic drug manufacturing occurs overseas. The scale-at-a-distance manufacturing model lacks the adaptability that would be possible with distributed, proximate production schemes.

Such rigidities and risks resulting from large-scale, centralized systems transcend manufacturing models. Medical imaging revolutionized healthcare throughout the twentieth century. X-rays were introduced to medicine in 1895, ultrasounds in the 1950s, and magnetic resonance imaging (MRI) solutions by the mid-1970s. With these tools, physicians could detect life-threatening conditions such as tumors and better diagnose a wide range of conditions.

As imaging technologies became more powerful, they also became far more expensive and required trained professionals to operate. Only well-funded institutions could afford the latest solutions.

Even today, for most imaging purposes patients must travel to the equipment. But while your medical center might have the world's leading medical capabilities, but most of life occurs outside the hospital.

Over the next few decades, medicine will discover that many health conditions are *far* better addressed when monitored in real time and when the treatments travel to—or with—patients. When they're more proximate.

Another way to think about how radically better proximate healthcare can be is to remember that it's tough to prevent problems when your primary, or only, regular diagnostic is an annual physical.

Over the past decade, healthcare professionals and policymakers have increased their focus on prevention, evidenced by significant increases in screenings for conditions from HIV and HCV to cholesterol, hypertension, diabetes, and breast, prostate, and colon cancers. In most cases, though, these screenings occur at wide intervals in time. For some conditions this makes sense. Years of data validate that few of us would benefit from colonoscopies more than every decade. For many other conditions, more frequent testing might enhance outcomes, but doing so would prove impractical or even impossible via traditional means.

Aside from such exceptions, we wait until we experience symptoms to seek medical attention. Doctors order diagnostics or procedures after patients present with symptoms. Most of medicine's diagnostics, treatments, and business models are optimized for this "wait for a problem" approach.

For some conditions, waiting for symptoms might mean it's too late. Cancers can advance for months before presenting, and cardiovascular conditions can linger.

In late 2004, steel industry executive (and superb father and husband) Bob Wolcott had recently had his full annual physical. He never smoked, exhibited normal cholesterol levels, had no signs of heart disease, and had excellent ECG results. The doctor commented, "Whatever you're doing, keep doing it." A few months later, Wolcott suffered a fatal aortic aneurism at the age of sixty-three.

By contrast, the $P = 0$ of healthcare translates into always-on monitoring, with sensors gathering real-time data for AI systems that sort health-relevant signals from noise, supporting more timely interventions by healthcare professionals and treating health issues before they're a crisis. Vital signs, stress, gut biome, and arterial health will be monitored.

REAL-TIME, PATIENT-CENTRIC HEALTHCARE: "SHIFT LEFT"

In this context, digital health venture firm 7wireVentures, one of the field's most successful investors, describes part of its investment thesis as "Shift Left." Cofounder and managing partner Lee Shapiro explains:

Our health care system was largely built to support acute, emergent needs rather than one's long term or chronic needs. By contrast, the leading cause of death, cardiovascular disease, is non-communicable and ameliorated by preventative measures. While you'll want great acute care if you have a heart attack, you will have far better outcomes—a longer, higher quality life—if you have better preventive care over time.

Combine that structural challenge with a growing aging population and shortages of medical professionals and the stage is set for tech-enabled care to have significant impact.

We call this "Shift Left." Instead of care being provided in more expensive settings with more expensive equipment and procedures, we should be focusing on interventions before problems arise, closer to where the consumer of health services lives, and in all moments that matter.

Relevant to Proximity, two reinforcing capabilities advance healthcare toward the kind of care-where-we-live, no-patient-action-necessary world Shapiro describes:

1. Real-time, always-on monitoring
2. Truly patient-centric solutions

With health monitoring in its infancy—Oura health rings (which monitor sleep and vital signs), iPhone apps, and such—where might we be in a decade? Already, health-monitoring company BioIntelliSense's system captures over twenty vital signs for thirty days via a wearable patch or "BioButton" used for both in-hospital and at-home monitoring.

Earlier detection will suggest new forms of treatment, some that operate without us doing anything. They'll disappear into our daily routines. Solutions that travel effortlessly with us, continually improving, adapting to each patient. Portable (in some cases implanted) monitoring diagnostics that automatically deliver drugs when and where required.

The pacemaker represents a twentieth-century analogue. Invented in 1930 by Albert S. Hyman, the implanted device springs to action only when needed to stimulate the heart. When not required, it waits and monitors. Similar monitoring-diagnostic-drug combinations offer a new twenty-first-century proximate promise.

Even more compelling, connected health-monitoring systems generate torrents of data every moment of every day, offering opportunities for analyses never before possible. As monitoring proliferates throughout entire populations and our datasets grow, researchers and health professionals will be able to pose questions and run experiments heretofore impractical or even impossible.

With more and better data, AI becomes more powerful, detecting hidden patterns, rapidly testing hypotheses and increasingly making or recommending decisions on our behalf. Proximate systems learn better and, if we enable them, implement relevant changes in real time.

Personalized medicine rises as a result of better understanding the human body, as well as understanding how *each* body works differently.

The first century of modern medicine largely focused on understanding what was similar about humans. Our current century shifts to what's distinctive about each of us. Fields from genomics and proteomics to an emerging understanding of our gut biomes will enable far more customized solutions for each individual patient.

The more personalized we'd like our medicine, the more we'll require proximate solutions.

For instance, companies throughout the United States, Europe, and Asia are working on pharmacogenomics—medicines adapted for an individual's genomic profile—which will bias toward production of small batches of drugs for a more diverse population, rather than centralized manufacturing of millions of identical pills. This is MoU drug production, as we saw with On Demand Pharmaceuticals in chapter 1.

Our future? Delivering medications before we realize we're sick. Predicting, even preventing, diseases before they occur. A comprehensive picture of a patient's minute-to-minute health securely shared and assessed by AI, incorporating human experts when required.

Healthcare's proximate future involves bringing care to the patient, instead of the patient to the care. Such as to our homes.

UNLOCKING LATENT PROXIMATE RESOURCES: MEDARRIVE

Dan Trigub, founder and CEO of MedArrive,[4] predicts that in the future healthcare hospitals and clinics will mainly consist of specialized environments such as operating rooms, emergency rooms, and ICUs. Everything else will happen in our daily lives, particularly at home. While in high demand, the "home care" industry has been constrained by a lack of available, qualified talent.

MedArrive's platform serves this demand by marshaling local emergency medical services (EMS) professionals for hands-on care. EMS staff, such as first-responder ambulance personnel, often have many hours free in a typical week. With MedArrive, they can opt to work in home care roles during off hours.

MedArrive matches EMS professionals to patients, supplementing the supply of other caregivers. EMS providers increase utilization of their time and skills and have access to a learning management system to advance their training. Patients at home receive qualified, concierge care even in traditionally underserved or marginalized communities. By serving more patients in their homes, the system has the potential to reduce wait times in doctors' offices and overcrowding in emergency rooms.

As such models expand, expect a wider range of healthcare activities to be possible, even preferable, in our homes. In February 2021, for example, MedArrive announced a partnership with Spect to facilitate at-home screenings to prevent blindness.[5]

Long term, Trigub's vision is for MedArrive to become a platform for routing, scheduling, and managing patient monitoring and care at home and beyond, helping orchestrate medical professionals and tech-enabled monitoring, diagnostics, and care systems.

HEALTHCARE TO THE PATIENT—WHEREVER, WHENEVER

For decades most of us have accepted substandard, even abominable, healthcare-related customer experiences.

Recall your last (painful) visit to an emergency room. Like most ER "clients," you likely faced long wait times to address an urgent, possibly life-threatening condition followed by confusing, even potentially ruinous, billing and collections procedures. No other industry could survive with such low service standards.

In other areas of our lives, we demand seamless, personalized experiences. We'll come to expect the same of healthcare.

The rise of urgent care facilities illustrates this trend. While lacking the breadth of full-service hospitals, urgent care facilities are smaller and easier to locate closer to potential patients—or rather, "customers"—such as in neighborhoods and shopping centers. Capable of treating a wide range of non-life-threatening conditions, urgent care companies have tended to compete by enhancing customer experiences and responsiveness: anytime walk-ins, simple diagnostics, and support from on-site healthcare professionals.

The success of urgent care centers has arisen in part because traditional hospitals do too many different things to provide full service, while meanwhile becoming complicated to navigate. Many situations that could benefit from medical attention can be addressed via simple, quick, accessible solutions. Hospitals weren't delivering on simple, quick, accessible, so others did so. Urgent care facilities' proximity to potential patients has been a critical factor.

In 2017, strategy and design firm Artefact came up with a vision for the future of healthcare. Before you even notice symptoms, your smart device detects an issue, perhaps with voice recognition noting the strain in your tone, and inquires if you'd like medical attention.

Notified via the network, a self-driving mobile clinic—Artefact's Aim service—arrives at your door.[6] You step into a mobile unit resembling a space-age phone booth on wheels and a projection of a doctor, powered by AI, leads you through a series of health tests to uncover the cause of your symptoms. Upon diagnosis, an on-board machine synthesizes a week's worth of prescribed medication. All the while you've remained home and avoided potentially spreading the infection. If deemed necessary, the mobile unit could speed you to an ER.

In 2020, the COVID-19 pandemic catalyzed progress. The Mayo Clinic in Jacksonville, Florida, began using autonomous vehicles to transport medical supplies such as COVID-19 tests around its campus. Staff members were freed to focus on other tasks. That same year, CVS Pharmacy in Houston launched a fleet of autonomous vehicles to deliver prescriptions.[7]

HAVE ROBOT, WILL TRAVEL

In 2013, the Raven II robot attained 12 seconds of fame. Developed at the University of Washington for surgical procedures, the robot simulated brain surgery in the film adaptation of the sci-fi novel *Ender's Game.* When one of the lead characters suffers brain injury, a two-armed machine suspended from the ceiling conducts precision surgery to repair the damage.[8]

Around the time of the movie's release, robotic surgery had already begun diffusing across hospitals in the developed world, allowing doctors to perform complex procedures with greater precision.[9] The da Vinci system, which at the time of this writing had been assisting surgeries for almost two decades, is one of the most popular clinical robotic surgeons.[10] The device allows a human surgeon to control mechanical arms and surgical tools from a nearby (or remote) computer, viewing progress via a 3D image. Robotics enable smaller incisions compared to traditional approaches, resulting in less bleeding, faster healing, and reduced risk of infection.

Although the surgeon and patient are located close to each other for most da Vinci procedures, the system can support remote surgery, allowing surgeons to operate on patients from a distance, potentially even thousands of miles away. While dependent on highly stable, high-bandwidth internet connections, such capabilities offer the promise of access to surgical expertise from anywhere to anywhere. For particularly demanding surgeries, a general on-site surgeon could set up the robot and rely on a specialist to conduct the procedure remotely.

Cost will be an issue, but it's not difficult to imagine doctors offering services to underserved locations for a discount or free of charge. Well-established programs from nonprofits such as HCP CureBlindness validate such scenarios. Dozens of ophthalmologists routinely travel around the world offering thousands of sight-restoring cataract surgeries, from Bangladesh and the Philippines to Ethiopia and Ghana. Eventually expect remote-controlled or even autonomous robots to become enabling partners.

Already today, TUG autonomous robots, developed by Aethon, travel around hospitals transporting supplies and meals. They're equipped with digital maps of their operating environment and networked sensors to prevent collisions. Aethon reports cost-per-delivery savings of up to 80 percent, meanwhile alleviating staffing shortages.

The robots will one day be coming home. As a teenager, Anthony Nunez witnessed his grandmother moving into his family's home after she suffered a fall. Saddened by her loss of independence, Nunez later established INF Robotics and designed RUDY, a robot offering home care and entertainment to seniors. His vision for RUDY is to prolong independence for the elderly by bringing conversation and family support via virtual communications and safety through connection to emergency responders.

Health systems, patients, and their families will take time to learn how to adapt robotics for care. While a compelling prototype, RUDY hasn't yet reached commercial viability. Some research shows that robotics for nursing home and home care use have shown mixed results.[11] The learning curves are steep.

Nonetheless, with the proliferation of AI and high-speed 5G connectivity, the number of healthcare tasks performed by robots, with or without doctors or nurses involved, will likely increase.[12] Care to the patient, instead of patient to the care.

VIRTUAL AND AUGMENTED REALITY

On stage at TWIN Impact 2022 in Miami, ophthalmologist Dr. Ralph Chu performed a virtual knee operation on a virtual patient, in remote collaboration with Sam Glassenberg. Sam retracted one side of the knee while Dr. Chu inserted the cut guide. They conducted the surgery simulation via their smartphones, with Chu on stage in Miami and Glassenberg from Chicago over Zoom.

They were demonstrating a medical training game from Level Ex. Founded by Glassenberg and acquired by Brainlab in 2020, Level Ex creates games to train medical professionals via mobile devices.

While impressive *and* stomach-turning, the demonstration illustrates the power of virtual platforms. Physicians can practice simulated procedures as often as they prefer before trying their skills on human patients. New meaning to the term "practicing medicine."

Traditionally, medical students learn from reading textbooks and observing doctors. In residency, their observations continue, but they're largely limited to doctors and patient issues that are immediately present. A doctor introducing a new technique might have a handful of chances to teach it live.

Beyond medical school, medical professionals require continuing medical education, known in industry lingo as CME. As Dr. Darshak Sanghavi, a Program Manager at the U.S. government's Advanced Research Projects Agency for Health (ARPA-H), observed, "current CME is rote, boring, and rarely as relevant as needed. It's in need of disruption!"

Level Ex brings the engagement loved by gamers to the medical training field. "We've seen a huge need in the medical community for better solutions to disseminate information and best practices. And we know coming from games, the best way to learn and the best way to retain, the best way to develop skills, is through play."[13]

During the pandemic, proximity to medical training was essential to saving lives. Level Ex updated its games with coronavirus content to help doctors learn about treating COVID-19 patients. The games also enable peer-to-peer connections. "Instead of having you and me play together, you can have up to 400 people in person or remote, collaborating and competing from their phones to diagnose and treat virtual patients." Knowledge transfer at scale.

As virtual reality improves, later this century becoming indistinguishable from "real life," more health and wellness applications will become possible anywhere with digital access. We'll return to this convergence of "real" and virtual worlds in the concluding chapter.

EVERYDAY WELLNESS: ALWAYS ON, ALWAYS WITH YOU, AND MORE YOU

Proximate healthcare will trend toward always on, always with you, and more *you*.

1. Always On: Monitoring, Diagnostics, and Treatment
2. Always with You: Wearables, Implantables, and Robots
3. More YOU: Gene Sequencing and Editing, Pharmacogenomics, and Custom Organs

Always On: Monitoring, Diagnostics, and Treatment

Life happens where we live, not in doctors' offices.

If you wear an Apple Watch, you've already been exposed to what some refer to as the Internet of Medical Things (IoMT), the expanding universe of connected wearables, sensors, and trackers that are digitalizing healthcare.[14]

IoMT enables unprecedented patient centricity. For instance, Finnish company Oura Health's "Oura Ring" provides 24/7 health tracking, monitoring sleep, stress, body temperature, heart rate variability, and more. It has the potential to alert wearers of a stroke, heart failure, or other heart-related complications before these conditions might have otherwise been obvious.

Monitoring vital signs isn't the only opportunity for healthcare-relevant sensing and analytics. Everything from search queries and local trends in hospital electronic health records to call volumes and insurance claims provides data with the potential to enhance the timeliness and availability of the right solutions when and where required.

Medical care will evolve to *everyday wellness*—wherever, whenever. Solutions adapting to humans, rather than patients adapting to machines. During this transition, eliminating trade-offs between service quality, cost, and outcomes will require proximate models.

Consider Spire Health. Chronic obstructive pulmonary disease (COPD) is the third leading cause of death in the United States.[15] For patients with COPD, airways can thicken and inflame, resulting in shortness of breath, emergency room visits, hospitalization, and potentially death.[16] Spire Health has developed a remote patient monitoring solution to manage COPD via early intervention.

Patients attach sensors to their clothing—a class of devices known as "wearables"—that monitor breathing, pulse, and activity levels. When breathing or heart rate changes, AI-predictive algorithms spot exacerbations, enable early intervention, and potentially avoid emergency room visits. Patients acquire greater visibility and control over their health.

In partnership with Respiratory Care + Sleep Medicine in Florida, Spire Health's remote monitoring system was by 2022 able to detect and aid patients experiencing respiratory distress with 68 percent accuracy, enough to save lives and lower costs.[17]

Always with You: Wearables, Implantables, and Robots

Beyond wearables, a more invasive class of devices known as "implantables" epitomize proximate care: invisible and always present.

How about getting microchipped? On average, installing a rice-grain-sized chip[18] in your body costs around $150.[19] As of late 2022, more than fifty thousand people worldwide had elected to do so.[20] RFID (radio frequency identification) microchips exchange data through a reader and a built-in antenna. By swiping your microchipped hand, you might unlock doors, manipulate drones, or make payments—or the microchip can become an imbedded health monitor. If you are rushed to an emergency room, the chip might contain all your health information, such as your blood group, medications, and records of vital signs.[21]

Robotic Pills

Doctors have been using swallowable cameras since 2001 to visualize the gastrointestinal tract. Soon nanobots—robots about one hundredth the width of a human hair—will swim through the body to identify infections, cancer, or other medical disorders. Eventually they'll deliver treatment.

Mir Imran, a legend in medical technology, has been developing and commercializing breakthrough medical devices for over forty years. One of his first inventions helped to develop the automatic implantable cardioverter defibrillator, in 1980. It was an early example of Proximity—activating to save the patient at the precise moment of need.

In 2011 Imran was having lunch with the CEO of a pharmaceutical company who had invested in a failing company. The company had intended its drug to be delivered orally via a daily pill. Unfortunately, enzymes in the digestive tract dissolved the drug, and it thus passed without impact from the body. The solution failed.

Imran recognized that the problem was not the therapeutic approach but, instead, "drug delivery," as known in industry parlance. He also knew that intestines don't have pain sensors and that intestinal walls are optimized to absorb nutrients. What if a capsule could enter the intestine and deliver a pain-free shot into the intestinal wall?

In 2012 he founded Rani Therapeutics.[22] Rani's "robotic pill" can deliver any biologic drug right to the intestine, where it is absorbed at a rate similar to subcutaneous or intramuscular injections. In 2021 under the leadership of Mir's son, Talat Imran, the company went public with Mir as executive chairman.[23]

Therapeutics traditionally requiring injection—such as insulin therapy used by hundreds of millions of diabetics worldwide—could be swallowed as a pill. Delivery of what's needed, effortlessly.

Bionaut Labs

Proximity isn't just about delivering what's needed, but also doing so in ways customized for each customer—or patient.

California-based start-up Bionaut Labs has developed a nanobot the size of a grain of rice that is designed to transport medication to precisely where it's needed.[24] The conventional way to deliver most medications makes little sense in terms of precision. A painkiller affects the entire body instead of just the muscles in pain. Chemotherapies circulate widely instead of only targeting tumors.

"Chemotherapy is delivered systemically," Bionaut founder and CEO Michael Shpigelmacher explains. "Often only a small percentage arrives at the location where it is actually needed."

Properly designed, nanobots could deliver therapeutics where required, possibly increasing efficacy and ameliorating negative side effects.

"You can think of the Bionaut as a tiny screw that moves through the veins until it arrives at the tumor," Shpigelmacher illustrates. Via Zoom, he shares the screen of an X-ray machine in his Culver City lab to demonstrate how the half-transparent, yellowish device winds its way along the spine in the body. The nanobot contains a tiny powerful magnet. The "invisible screwdriver" is an external magnetic field that rotates the magnet inside the device and pilots its movement and direction.[25]

While it's too early to know which novel drug delivery concepts will prevail, they all advance medicine toward $P = 0$. Delivery with precision.

Brain-Computer Interfaces: Telekinesis Made Real?

Implantables edge us toward even deeper engagement. Brain-computer interfaces (BCI) enable direct interaction between our brains and computational systems. What could be more proximate?

Already by 2012, the U.S. military had received FDA approval to install chips in the brains of paraplegic veterans to allow them to control prosthetics just as we would our own limbs. The user simply thinks and the prosthetic limb and hand respond.

The R&D program, funded by the Defense Advanced Research Projects Agency (DARPA), and known broadly as Revolutionizing Prosthetics, has evolved with the aspiration to "create the first dexterous prosthetic limb with full sensory and motor capabilities that is suitable for home use."[26]

One day, prosthetics will likely provide nearly natural replacement. They might even prove *better* than our organic versions: more dexterous, stronger, perhaps even more "aware" (via sensors and AI).

Beyond government, billions of dollars of private funds have been invested in the BCI race. In 2021, the FDA published "leapfrog" guidance for nonclinical testing of implanted BCI devices. Dozens of start-ups, including Neuralink, founded by Elon Musk, Synchron, Blackrock Neurotech, and ClearPoint Neuro, are at various stages of developing solutions not only for interacting with computational systems but also for treating or even resolving neurological disorders such as paralysis, ALS, blindness, and hearing loss.[27]

Since 2004, Blackrock Neurotech has been using its Utah Array implant in patients for research, thus far with no reported adverse side effects. Its new generation of implants, MoveAgain BCI, decodes movement from neuronal activity, offering the possibility of controlling external devices only by thinking. One day such technologies might restore paralyzed patients' mobility altogether.

Controlling external objects with our thoughts? We traditionally called that telekinesis, a psychic ability disproven time and again for centuries. Consider this as possible, even likely, later this century.

More You: Gene Sequencing and Editing, Pharmacogenomics, and Custom Organs

Even for the same condition, the right drug for you might not be right for someone else. A range of "-omics" revolutions—gen-omics, pharmacogen-omics, transcript-omics, prote-omics, gut biome—are in the early stages of transforming our ability to define what works and for whom. Expect other "-omics" to arise.

Empowered by a range of digitally enabled technologies such as gene sequencing and protein modeling, these fields seek to understand what works best for each individual. As they progress, they'll generate demand for more customized solutions: drugs, treatments, even personalized foods, in turn generating demand for personalized proximate production.

We'll illustrate how these fields contribute to Proximity in healthcare by briefly exploring genomics and the related field of pharmacogenomics.

Genomics

Gene sequencing provides a map of a patient's DNA profile. As our understanding of genomics improves—and numerous complexities confound this effort—medical professionals will be able to personalize an ever wider range of solutions.

Launched in 1990, the Human Genome Project took thirteen years and $2.7 billion to map the human genome.[28] Today technicians can map a complete human genome in hours for less than $1,000.[29]

DNA sequencing machines have also become smaller and less expensive. Companies like Oxford Nanopore Technologies offer sequencing equipment of various sizes, including a lightweight handheld unit, the MinION. The company's site boasts that the MinION offers "complete control and creativity over when, where and how you sequence, regardless of application." The unit starts at $1,000.

Compressing capabilities in physical size and cost offers the possibility of wider access to gene sequencing, enabling applications we've only begun to imagine.

Already, low-cost DNA sequencing has propelled genomics into mainstream medicine. Rare genetic diseases that had previously taken years to diagnose are now easily identifiable.

Pharmacogenomics

Genomic acumen enables another critical element of precision medicine: pharmacogenomics, drugs differentiated based on an individual's genetic profile. We've long known that the same dose of the same medicine affects people differently. Researchers are beginning to understand why.

Biotech giant Genentech is a leader in exploring intersections between genetics and therapeutics. Mark Lee, Genentech's former global head of personalized healthcare, observed in 2020 that technology is "allowing us to push the frontiers of personalizing patient care and optimized individual outcomes."

Pharmacogenomics challenges the pharmaceutical industry's operating model. Most therapeutics are produced in large-scale production facilities, sending out identical pills by the thousands or millions.

A Genentech team shared this challenge with Rob in late 2020. "It's one thing to know what specific versions of a particular drug will work best for a specific patient. It's another thing to produce each individual drug economically, safely and compliantly." Producing millions of identical copies for inventory is unlikely to work when you require small runs of products adapted for each patient.[30]

Simply retooling centralized production facilities to accommodate truly personalized therapeutics will prove insufficient. Proximate models, by contrast, will allow physicians to wait until after a specific patient's diagnosis to produce and deliver the required drug.

Pharmaceutical manufacturers will likely start by enhancing existing factories to support the production of small quantities of customized drugs. Even traditional, high-scale manufacture of drugs presents challenges in a context of increased geopolitical tensions and health crises like pandemics.

Well before the disruptions of the pandemic, Japanese pharmaceutical giant Takeda introduced a "dual-sourcing strategy." Any given drug can be produced in multiple geographies, enabling greater agility and resilience. The company's CEO, Christophe Weber, remarked in 2022: "But even if you do a dual-sourcing strategy, in which countries do you establish this dual sourcing? Perhaps we'll have to have a multiple-sourcing strategy—more than two. That can potentially impact the cost of the products. Or we'll have to be much more innovative to do multiple sourcing without expanding the cost of the product. The world is getting much more complicated."[31]

Proximate production offers a solution. Rather than just two or three high-scale production sites, expect to see production of some drugs on demand in hospitals, clinics, and mobile labs. Such models have the potential to alleviate drug shortages of traditional drugs while also enabling personalized methodologies like pharmacogenomics.

PERSONALIZED MoU SOLUTIONS

In the next chapter we'll explore the potential of additive manufacturing to mitigate and potentially eliminate trade-offs between cost and customization. The same will occur for our bodies.

Digitally controlled production techniques enable medical professionals to fashion organs and other body parts customized for specific patients. Rather than seeking donor organs from a chronically limited supply and then risking rejection by the patient's immune system, the organs grow from the patient's own tissues. Proximate by design, these solutions wait for a specific patient requirement before production begins.

MADE-TO-ORDER ORGANS

In *The Empire Strikes Back* (1980), a fussy medical droid fabricates a prosthetic hand for Luke Skywalker that is indistinguishable from his natural version.[32] We're not far from this science fiction today.

In 2019, a nine-year-old boy with cerebral palsy walked into Professor David Zopf's office at the University of Michigan. No specialist had been able to resolve the boy's labored breathing. Dr. Zopf implanted a 3D-printed, custom-designed device into the patient's throat. Immediately, the boy regained his breath, and in many ways his life.[33]

In recent years, a field has emerged at the intersection of stem cell research, 3D printing, and medicine. In 2019, Dr. Tal Dvir's team at Tel Aviv University bioprinted the first ever human heart, albeit one the size of a grape.[34] The researchers took a biopsy of a volunteer's stomach and then separated cells from extracellular fluid.[35] They reprogrammed the cells to become pluripotent stem cells (capable of dividing into several different cell types) and then differentiated them yet again as either cardiac or endothelial tissue. They loaded these building blocks into a multimaterial 3D printer and watched as the machine rearranged the biological components into the shape of a tiny human heart.[36]

Transplants of other patient-specific organs are already under way. In 2004 patient Luke Massella received a bioprinted bladder. Enterprising surgeon Dr. Anthony Atala of Boston Children's Hospital took a piece of Massella's bladder and grew a new one over two months in the lab. During a 14-hour surgical procedure, Dr. Atala replaced Massella's defective bladder with an organ grown from Massella's own tissues. More than a decade later the organ continued operating without requiring further surgery.[37]

What would you replace as you age? What might that mean for your quality of life and longevity?

Or perhaps you'd like to engineer a new you?

A NEW YOU: GENE EDITING

Perhaps the most hopeful *and* perilous developments in medical science relate to gene editing: making specific changes to an organism's DNA. It's currently under development for treatment or even eradication of conditions from blood disorders to many forms of cancer.[38] While still early, gene editing promises not only to transform lives but also to challenge assumptions about what it means to be *you*.

Since the late 2010s, gene editing technologies have transformed from a lab-only pursuit limited to a small cadre of researchers to a widely available phenomenon.

CRISPR-Cas9, for which Jennifer Doudna and Emmanuelle Charpentier were awarded the Nobel Prize in Chemistry in 2020, makes precision gene editing possible with relatively modest—though not insignificant—training and resources.

The technique isn't limited to medical professionals. It's at hand for nearly anyone. Reminiscent of the Scientific Revolution of the seventeenth century—where any citizen with sufficient means could access new equipment and compounds for experimentation—gene editing technologies are surprisingly, perhaps dangerously, accessible and affordable.

As of early 2023, googling "biohacking CRISPR kit" returns over fourteen thousand results, starting with sponsored links for buying your own kit for under $1,000. You'll also find raging public debates regarding the extent to which these capabilities should be regulated or widely available and, as advocates propose, "democratized."

Can anything be more proximate than your own home genetic editing toolset? What could possibly go wrong? Lots.

In addition to well-meaning mistakes or failed experiments, in the wrong hands CRISPR could be used to synthesize and manipulate pathogens to create bioweapons. Public health, bioethicist, and defense professionals will need new forms of engagement to monitor and prepare for such threats.

Currently, an international treaty called the Biological Weapons Convention (BWC) seeks to prevent the production of biological weapons. Widely available gene editing could compromise such efforts. As medical ethicists from New York University argued in 2015: "However, the BWC covers state actors—at least those who have signed it—but it was not designed to address private companies or individuals. Moreover, as the tools needed to design and manipulate pathogenic organisms and the exact genetic sequences and instructions to do so become more readily available, the effectiveness of the BWC to prevent the misuse of biological tools and knowledge is increasingly limited."[39]

More distributed capabilities mean more distributed risks. Nowhere is this more present than in healthcare.

DISTRIBUTED CAPABILITIES = DISTRIBUTED RISKS

Proximate healthcare solutions not only generate far more data about each of us—consider the data generated by always-on health monitoring alone—they also *require* distributed access to health data.

Not surprisingly, the number of large-scale healthcare data breaches has grown by more than 30 percent annually in recent years. Between 2009 and 2021, the U.S. Health and Human Services Office for Civil Rights reported data breaches that resulted in the loss, theft, and unauthorized disclosure of 314,063,186 healthcare records—equating to nearly 95 percent of the U.S. population in 2021.[40]

And this is *before* the widespread rollout of proximate healthcare solutions that introduce new data sources, healthcare players, contexts, and use cases.

Traditionally, a primary care physician (PCP) could be the hub for your healthcare data. But research from Accenture in 2019 revealed that only 67 percent of millennials and 55 percent of Gen Z-ers said they had a PCP, compared with 84 percent of baby boomers. Younger populations were more likely to seek care from nontraditional sources like retail clinics (41 percent) and virtual care (39 percent).[41] As a result, medical data become distributed in more locations and potentially disconnected. Patients with fragmented, incomplete records are more difficult to serve.

Moreover, how will our data be both accessible *and* secure when always-on monitoring generates detailed, intimate images of our health?

Regarding physical products, centralized manufacturing facilities tend to be easier to monitor and regulate than thousands of small-scale, distributed production sites, even those located at qualified hospitals and clinics.

Expect advances as well as tragic failures.

If a hospital or clinic can produce pharmaceuticals via refrigerator-sized equipment—with extraordinary benefits for public health—what might prevent nefarious actors from synthesizing illicit drugs nearly anywhere? Already, drugs that are chemically similar in makeup to LSD, ecstasy, and methamphetamine are advertised and sold under different names on crypto marketplaces. Because existing laws are written for their more familiar counterparts, their legal status is often nebulous.

In an emblematic collision of distributed (i.e., proximate) capabilities, widespread access to information on the internet and the rise of crypto currencies have amplified experimentation and trade in designer drugs.

As Roy Gerona, a drug-monitoring specialist at the University of California, San Francisco, explained to crypto information site Coindesk: "The 'explosion' of research chemicals can be attributed to three concurrent and interrelated trends: the democratization of information over the internet, easy shipping through globalization and the adoption of digital payments. . . . The internet has allowed for an entirely new market to emerge, creating a platform for demand to surface and for suppliers to meet it."[42]

In less than three years, some 3,877 vendors sold approximately $183 million worth of various goods to 146,946 users on Silk Road, the now-shuttered black market where illegal drugs were bought and sold anonymously—or so users thought. These U.S. government estimates are available because the marketplace used only bitcoin. Bitcoin, thought by many to be fully anonymous, turned out to be only pseudo-anonymous, where alphanumeric addresses can sometimes be traced back to user identities.

Widespread access to information, capabilities, and compounds supports increased experimentation within the population at large. Advocates propose that this exploratory ferment accelerates discovery and democratizes the potential for new treatments and experiences. These opportunities, they argue, should be accessible by all. While this has certainly engaged a global community of enthusiasts and voyeurs, often—though not always—unqualified citizen researchers generate a Wild West dynamic.

Most citizen experimentation, even when well meaning, fails the tests of scientific rigor. It's often misleading, even dangerous, to extrapolate success from anecdotes, especially when manipulating our bodies. That is what many sites share and encourage, not to mention those conducting experiments such as self-administering designer drugs. An example is Psychonauts, an online forum where users share experiences with new chemicals and dosages. Much of the experimentation shared on the site either violates medical regulations or is unregulated. Fervent experimental grey areas exist with both good and ill intent and positive and negative outcomes.

Proximity catalyzes widespread exploration, with all the benefits and risks thus entailed.

While access to small-scale production of medical products has the potential to bring life-enhancing, even lifesaving, capabilities proximate to patients worldwide, it comes with serious caveats. If an accident or defect occurs with a 3D-printed device or small-batch drug, who will be held liable?[43]

Decentralized networks of production might also be more susceptible to hacking than large-scale, secure facilities. Operators of small-scale production capabilities might not maintain rigorous cybersecurity regimes, simply for lack of awareness or resources.[44]

Many wearables companies have made limited efforts to encrypt and protect sensitive data, yet transmitting via Wi-Fi or Bluetooth increases risks of cyber intervention.[45] As more intimate, comprehensive data become available regarding our wellness, what will we be willing to share—and how much will we share unwittingly?

Regulations will surely follow. To be fair, it's hard to regulate technologies and practices in the midst of rapid change.

OVERCOMING HEALTHCARE INEQUALITY: ACCESSIBILITY VIA PROXIMITY

Proximate healthcare models offer unprecedented potential for enhancing accessibility and affordability. For example, Dr. Ling, whom we met in chapter 1, and his team at On Demand Pharmaceuticals tackle the problem at the point of demand, producing generic drugs where and when required.

Ling sees a pivotal part of his company's mission as providing production to underserved regions. "Imagine if we could have these machines in places that don't have generic medicines, like Liberia, Afghanistan or the Congo." He reasons, "We'd not just be giving them fish; we'd be teaching them to fish."

Nonetheless, new monitoring, diagnostic, and therapeutic models come at a cost. Well-intentioned policies like fixing drug prices might help in the short term but may mitigate R&D investments long term. Alternatively, market mechanisms often fail when expected to mediate life and death trade-offs.

Healthcare payers and policymakers must recognize that Proximity's economics will be quite different from that of traditional healthcare. The more we invest in monitoring, detection, and prevention, the better health outcomes and economics look longer term.

THE FUTURE OF HEALTH: TRULY PERSONALIZED, EVER PRESENT

Many Proximity solutions offer what had been, for the most part, impossible. Always-on health monitoring isn't just incrementally better than an annual checkup. A custom, lab-grown organ isn't just a little better than a donor organ. It's *your* organ.

Imagine a child who is soon to be born in 2030 with a rare genetic disorder that will cause life-threatening immune deficiency. Her parents opt for gene editing to correct the mutation, freeing her from a lifetime of health concerns before she's even born.

Proximity is an entirely different wellness game. Bringing healthcare to patients. Solving problems before they arise. Offering us the *possibility* of healthier, longer lives.

It will be up to each of us to determine if those longer lives are also more fulfilling.

6

How We Create and Produce

- Produce when a customer's ready to buy—and not before.
  - Create what's special to the moment at hand.
- Designed right, procrastination *enables* efficiency.
- Proximity annihilates trade-offs between customization and efficiency.
  - New capabilities empower creativity, leading to new production challenges.
- More responsive, flexible, efficient, *and* sustainable.
- Might art become defined "in the eye of the vision processing unit (VPU)"?
  - *Star Trek* or Jetsons. One day it will be real.

While drafting this book, generative AI emerged from its laboratory lair. ChatGPT burst onto screens and into copyrighters' nightmares. What's more proximate than an authoring engine, available anywhere, replacing hours of human work in seconds?

Witnessing the resulting public shock and awe, Rob immediately made plans to assign the tool, or any similar system, for use during his Executive MBA course, Innovation Strategy and Management, at the Chicago Booth School of Business.

During the course, Rob invites his impressively successful, midcareer students (ages thirty to sixty) to write a brief essay answering the following question: What do you see as your professional purpose? It's intended to provoke students to consider *why* they work so hard and the value they desire to create in their careers. There are no "right" answers, but there are certainly more thoughtful, insightful approaches to the query.

Generative AI offers an ideal tool for such an assignment. No AI system alone can hope to author an accurate articulation of a given student's authentic sense of purpose. (At least not yet. Besides, most humans are likely unsure of their own answer!) However, if properly prompted (i.e., what and how the system is asked to write), AI can offer a competent, if not accurate, first draft. Or second, or third, or however many you like, in rapid succession. Approached honestly, you'll likely spend more time crafting great prompts than the system will spend generating responses.

It's up to you to iterate, by giving new prompts or by contributing your own words to the draft, until you have your desired outcome. Any tool requires practice, and none more so than one that might just replace us altogether. (If it does replace us, then we'd better have practiced new skills.)

Meanwhile, generative AI learns and improves through use. The more prompts and iterations in different situations for different purposes, the better. The more you correct or reward it, the more it learns about your preferences.

Rather than circling the faculty wagons against the new tools, we need to take the world as it is, and as it might become. As educators, we need to help our students, colleagues, and the world at large bring the best solutions to life's opportunities and challenges.

We face a Paul Bunyan-esque threat from AI to our delusional, fragile human egos. You might recall the Industrial Age tale of Paul Bunyan, famed for laying track (a big-deal skill in the nineteenth century). As the machines arrived to lay rails and drive spikes for the railroads crossing America, people feared (turns out, correctly) that their jobs would disappear.

Bunyan challenged the machines in an epic battle through a mountain and won—then immediately collapsed and died. Fortunately for us, the machines survived and tracked the world faster, better, and cheaper than humans alone could have done.

Today, while few are concerned about track-laying machines (though they're at work somewhere on Earth right now), many of us feel our "but-we're-human-and-they're-not" specialness under threat. More than perhaps anything, we love to consider creativity as uniquely human. For years many experts (surprisingly) argued that "computers will never be truly creative," that AI systems will simply implement what we program them to do.

Unless you're emotionally committed to this notion, perhaps you've noticed that we've crossed that Rubicon. Computers create, and more so every day: DALL-E, Stable Diffusion, and Midjourney, to name a few.

Feel free to argue about definitions—such as, what does it mean to be "creative?"—but in the 2020s, AI systems are becoming increasingly adroit at generating output one might consider, if you let your anthropocentric guard down, "art."

Those who argue that none of it is very "good"—wait a few years—what does that subjective notion even mean? Hasn't art always been in the eye of the beholder? Might art also become "in the VPU of the beholder" (i.e., vision processing unit)?

AI skeptics also argue some version of "that's nice, but the computer just combined a bunch of other stuff originally created by humans." That isn't *really* creativity, they assert.

Of course it is. Most human artists will be pleased to share with you the artists who have most influenced their work. Combing through what already exists mimics how humans invent. We don't generate ideas, visions, products, and musicals from mystical ether. Our cognitive systems recombine elements from our environment, experiences, ideas we've heard, and visual stimuli, for instance, into our creations. Of those, only a minute fraction can be deemed by most observers to be "new." Even those can be traced to prior notions.

While it plays a singular role, creativity is just one input into the creation of the goods, services, experiences, and environments within which we live. For instance, as generative AI rises, consider its impact on how humans add value. In 2023, it could cost $25,000 or more for a team to develop an app. What happens when AI and No Code platforms (discussed in chapter 3, "How We Work") collude? Creating an app becomes a matter of prompting and editing an AI-enabled system. Or eventually enabling AI to iterate on new concepts at will. What can possibly go wrong?

Insofar as solutions like AI and No Code platforms can be available anywhere with internet access, creative, generative capabilities become ever more proximate to user needs. How might value creation processes change, from defining purpose and objectives to envisioning, designing, producing, recycling, repurposing, and disposing? Proximity offers an essential guide to this transition.

DESIGNING WHATEVER, WHEREVER, WHENEVER

In 2017 (generations ago in AI time), Italian sweets conglomerate Ferraro used AI to generate millions of versions of its Nutella brand identity by drawing from a database of colors and patterns. The initiative, known as Nutella Unica, generated 7 million distinct visual designs printed on 7 million different jars. Each jar had a unique code for collectors to validate the product (yes, there are now Nutella jar collectors).

While the team at Ferraro and its advertising agency Ogilvy & Mather created the algorithm, the AI system generated the designs. The jars, offered in groceries throughout Italy, sold out in one month.

We're witnessing a proliferation of platforms that allow relative novices to accomplish what in the past might have required years of experience to accomplish. Canva, an online graphic design tool with 75 million monthly active users as of 2022, supports about 150 designs every second. Previously, a graphic designer with years of experience in the Adobe Creative Suite might have been engaged to create slides, logos, and other collateral. Canva's user interface and templates enable just about anyone to generate professional-quality graphics in minutes.

AI-supported video platform Synthesia allows anyone to create "talking head" videos by selecting an avatar and a background while selecting one of over one hundred languages and inputting the text. Compare that to hiring a human to recite text in front of a camera and then repeating for each language required. In that legacy approach, heaven forbid you need edits. Call the human and start over. With Synthesia-like tools, just input new text and hit "save."

In this AI-assisted—or eventually even AI-defined—world, what will be the role for human designers and artists?

POSSIBLE FUTURE: MORE RESILIENT, EVOLVABLE, SUSTAINABLE, AND EFFICIENT

The Industrial Age solution was to order millions of copies of the same part, driving down the per unit cost and holding the units in inventory. If demands change, you might find yourself with thousands of unsold products. Alternatively, if production undershoots demand, you might lose orders. Classic overstocks and stockouts. The supply chain disruptions of the pandemic underscored the challenges of demand planning and non-proximate production.

Since the pandemic, companies and governments worldwide have been reevaluating their supply chains to achieve greater "resilience." As we explored in chapter 2, they'd be better served seeking both resilience *and* adaptability or evolvability.

To enhance supply chain resilience, business and political leaders typically start by considering how to bring traditional production capacity closer to customers and citizens. Unfortunately, rebuilding the same or modestly better production capacity closer to home hardwires old solutions rather than achieving the adaptability already available today or on the near horizon.

We should create the future rather than reordering the past.

Consider pig farming in China, the world's largest consumer of pork. Given China's limited land for farming and animal husbandry, and explicitly to achieve Proximity to consumer demand (scale production near population centers), Chinese company Hubei Zhongxin Kaiwei Modern Farming in 2022 and 2023 built and began operating two massive twenty-six-story pig farms. The company reports capacity to raise 650,000 animals entirely indoors at any given time, operated from a central control room. (Set aside for now the *extraordinary* ethical issues such an approach presents.)

This vertical farm, reminiscent of the vertical farms for vegetables we explored in chapter 4, "How We Eat," is certainly innovative, including the latest process controls, monitoring, and automation throughout. It might even prove economically successful for some time, given China's appetite. (Might.)

As impressive as these facilities are, they represent an adaptation of Industrial Age models to achieve Proximity (in addition to being barbaric). It's telling that the concept came about as a result of the original parent company, a concrete provider, seeking new applications for construction materials. As opposed to defining the best solution for providing pork to the Chinese, the company first sought new construction projects.

We already have the potential to go far beyond this example: proximate meat production that is more sustainable, efficient, responsive, *and* imminently ethical.

Rather than building a facility to raise animals (under tortuous conditions), imagine producing "cultured meat." Companies such as Mosa Meat based in the Netherlands and Aleph Farms in Israel, among others, are developing processes to produce *real* meat without any animals involved—aside from the animals that provided their original cells. (Well, and the humans who oversee the facilities.)

Once cultured meat becomes viable at scale—already possible for ground meats, a bit further out for steaks—companies will be able to produce meat in *dramatically* smaller facilities, thus potentially closer to each table and restaurant. Mosa and Aleph's processes and products differ, but they both rely on modified fermentation processes (widely used for decades in chemical, pharmaceutical, and food production).

Small-scale facilities enable flexibility to produce meats based on current demand. They also enable custom meat-to-order far beyond the dreams of even the most advanced traditional producers.

On a visit to its Tel Aviv headquarters in January 2023, Aleph Farms's head of New Ventures, Pascal Rosenfeld, shared that the company is particularly popular with leading chefs eager to produce small quantities of bespoke meats. "They'll have creative options never before possible when we're able to produce small quantities to order. Adjusting fat content, adding nutrients like fatty acids not typically found in meats, flavor profiles, textures—it's all on our roadmap. Top chefs have become some of our biggest fans."

As of 2023, cultured meat remains expensive, but the industry's moving fast. Emerging players have made cost a priority. As scale production becomes economical, distributed in smaller facilities closer to demand, the system becomes not only more responsive to changing demands but also far more evolvable.

Interested in scaling up a new technology or process? Traditional meat production meant months of raising animals, acres for grazing, and facilities for housing, sale, and slaughter. By contrast, building or adapting cultured meat capacity might require new fermentation lines, perhaps new equipment or just new software, and no animals involved. You can install these relatively small plants almost anywhere, even in urban areas where animal farms would be *verboten*.

The implications transcend meat. Didier Toubia, CEO of Aleph Farms, explained to Rob, "After a career in medical devices, I wanted to have an even bigger impact. Better health, sustainability, accessibility. What if we could produce *real* meat without living animals? We could impact all of these factors at the same time. And without the ethical problems presented by raising animals for slaughter."

The same trend is already present for milk production. In 2022 another Israel-based company, Remilk, brought a *real* milk product to market. Its "animal-free" process produces "dairy-identical" proteins that in June 2022 received FDA regulatory approval for sale in the United States.

Remilk reports that its primary growth constraint will be scaling production and outfitting enough fermentation tanks. While a significant challenge, the company can locate production in far more locations than would be possible for traditional dairy farms: near its customers' facilities or even near urban areas proximate to consumers.

In addition to having the taste and texture of traditional milk, Remilk products—which Rob happily tried—could have a profound environmental impact. "Compared to regular milk, our process requires 1 percent of the land, 4 percent of the pollutant emissions and 5 percent of the water required by traditional dairy industry," Remilk's chief technology officer, Dr. Ori Cohavi, explained.

The food industry seems to have taken note. In June 2023, the company announced that three former top executives from industry leaders Danone, Nestle, and PepsiCo, joined its board of directors.

While it's unclear which approaches will prevail, distributed production is rapidly becoming real across a range of products and industries. Done right, supply chains can become far more flexible, responsive, *and* sustainable.

PROCRASTINATING FOR CUSTOMIZATION AND EFFICIENCY

The closer a production system is to holding raw materials that are ready to produce only in response to precise demands (meat cells for replication, for instance), the more the system decreases waste and enhances sustainability.

Instead of bulk production in advance of demand, Proximity recommends Moment of Use (MoU) production, as described in chapter 1: producing only what's required, when and where it's required. While we might have always preferred this, doing so wasn't efficient. Over the coming decades we'll discover that it's far more possible—and competitive, cost-effective, and sustainable.

As additive manufacturing, robotics, and automation advance, *they'll resolve—and eventually annihilate—traditional trade-offs between customization and efficiency.* Products will be made to order with high levels of customization for individual customers. Like the chefs eager to order their own proprietary meats from Aleph Farms.

Rather than holding finished products in warehouses—hoping your demand predictions materialize—hold the components or even raw materials necessary until actual demand arises. What designers call "design for postponement"—postponing critical decisions until you have better information—becomes in the proximate world a critical principle.

If you wait for a customer order, you run a far lower risk of excess inventory and waste. This has always been true; however, customers are unlikely to wait for you to produce if your competitor can already provide the product faster, better, and cheaper. Traditionally, this meant holding finished products in inventory.

Instead, additive manufacturing holds raw materials—typically polymers or metals—until the customer requires a specific product or part and then makes it to order. Unlike with holding finished products, raw materials can be fashioned into anything the production system allows. Additive manufacturing systems can thus adapt faster to shifting demands.

At present, additive manufacturing doesn't compete on a cost basis with high-scale manufacturing for most products, but the technology is improving fast. In terms of sustainability, raw materials have far longer shelf lives than most finished products. A part that no one needs goes to waste (or hopefully to recycling). Polymers or metal powders in 3D printer cartridges, by contrast, retain their potential to become nearly anything.[1]

DO-IT-YOURSELF CHEETOS

In 2006 a group of Cornell students launched a project portending Proximity.

Inspired by the impact the Altair 8800 (the first personal computer) had on ushering in the PC revolution, Evan Malone and Hod Lipson compressed industrial-scale capabilities to a far smaller size. They designed the Fab@Home 3D printer, the first multimaterial 3D printer that is available to the public. Their technology was open source, so any DIYer could access it and build a homemade 3D printer that fit onto a desk or kitchen table, at a total cost of about $2,300.

Until that time, extrusion machines—producing food products from metal tubing and plastic films into snacks like Cheetos—were limited to large manufacturing plants. Fab@Home's open-source design and low price helped bring 3D printing to the masses.

Analogous to the path from the Altair 8800, launched in 1975, to today's ubiquitous computing devices, we're at the beginning of a multidecade transition in global production: from large centralized production facilities to thousands—and later this century, billions—of production devices distributed across every moment of our lives.

Scale manufacturing at great distances from final demand (think huge plants in China or Germany) will continue to be essential. However, over the next few decades, automation and additive manufacturing will push product industries toward "hybrid" supply chains: large, centralized plants for some products, complemented by small-scale production distributed closer to customers.

Optimizing manufacturing plants and supply chains has been critical since industry began. What's new—and what will prove revolutionary—is the increasing efficiency and effectiveness of proximate production for an expanding array of products.

Proximate production will allow companies to *postpone* more decisions until better information (like specific customer orders) becomes available. As visionary entrepreneur Dean Kamen, one of the most prolific inventors since Thomas Edison, asserts, "Wait as long as you can to make decisions—but no longer."

If your plant is in Vietnam and your customers are in the United States, you have to make most of the production decisions well in advance of the actual sale. If your production operates near your customers, ready at a moment's notice, you're better able to wait until your customers have ordered and perhaps even paid.

History offers examples of the value of waiting. Michael Dell founded Dell Computer Corporation from his dorm room at the University of Texas in 1982 by pioneering such a model: receive a customer order, get paid, *then* assemble the product. He still had to source the components, made often months in advance far away, but Dell's breakthrough idea was producing precisely what the customer ordered only after they'd ordered it. The result was accounting nirvana: negative working capital. Customers paid Dell *before* he finished their computer.

The twenty-first century will amp up Dell's insight: postponing as much value-add (production, assembly, etc.) until you know exactly what the customer will pay for. As distributed, automated manufacturing capabilities advance, we'll get closer to converting raw materials to end products on demand, efficiently, anywhere.

Though 3D printing represents the most obvious capability that is advancing production toward P = 0, it's not the only path. One automotive parts manufacturer, for example, redesigned its components into modular form so that it can complete the assembly proximate to its customers' manufacturing facilities. This approach allows the supplier to assemble onsite only what's demanded at each facility and hold the parts at the ready for shifts in demand.

Leveraging latent production capacity also brings production closer to demand. Companies like Norway's Gelato have been at this since the first dotcom boom. They're emerging as multibillion-dollar enterprises.

GELATO: PRINTING PRODUCTION CLOSE TO HOME—ANYWHERE

In the early 2000s, Henrik Müller-Hansen and Pal Naess were ready for a new challenge. They had successfully scaled telecommunications firm Tele2, with Müller-Hansen as CEO and Naess as director of IT, growing the company from 1.5 billion Norwegian kroner to 3.5 billion kroner (equivalent to over $350 million).

"We learned that it's possible to build a successful global company without owning any physical assets or infrastructure," shared Naess. The pair sought additional opportunities to apply the same logic.

After reviewing many industries, printing presented a ready target. Müller-Hansen was surprised to find that what many thought was a dying industry was, in fact, growing. It was a huge industry that nonetheless left customers with unmet needs. Typically, larger orders meant lower per unit prices, given economies of scale. Customers would often order large runs even if they weren't sure they'd require so many copies, and the result was waste.

Even if customers might have preferred smaller batches, small orders tended to be prohibitively expensive per unit. Small businesses were thus particularly ill-served by traditional printing houses. Moreover, the print industry lacked digital capabilities and coordination between suppliers and end consumers. The industry relied on one-to-one relationships rather than networks of relationships.

Müller-Hansen and Naess decided to apply what they had learned in telecom. In 2007 they launched Gelato, a print-on-demand platform connecting printers and customers. While print-on-demand had existed for years, Gelato was one of the first to leverage *other* companies' latent production capacity around the world. The company started with business cards, coordinating print houses' overcapacity to produce small, personalized orders.

Proximity was central to Gelato's model. When possible, it matched available capacity near customers to increase responsiveness and decrease shipping costs.

Gelato's operations quickly spread to Sweden and the United Kingdom, then on to Brazil, China, India, and Russia. As its network of printing houses grew, Gelato was able to fulfill orders closer to customers' locations, mitigating shipping costs and environmental impact. Gelato's offerings expanded to include all sorts of printed materials: calendars, invitations, photobooks, and eventually apparel.

Jotun, the company responsible for painting the Eiffel Tower and the Golden Gate Bridge, became an early convert. Prior to Gelato, its business cards were printed in Lithuania and shipped by the thousands around the world. With Gelato, employees in Shanghai could order cards produced in Shanghai, San Francisco employees could order cards produced in San Francisco, and so on, all from the same website.

When the pandemic hit, Gelato pivoted to new products. With entire populations sequestered at home, home redecoration surged. Gelato launched art prints on canvas, a product that scaled rapidly.

By 2022, Gelato supported local production in thirty-three countries with more than one hundred production partners. Naess shared with us the company's ambition to lead the application of 3D printing much like it had transformed the 2D printing world. As additive manufacturing improves, Gelato envisions engaging networks of additive manufacturing capacity for a much wider range of products.

Gelato's long-range strategy represents what we call a *transitional business platform*: a business model and technology platform that is capable of performing today (e.g., Gelato's 2D printing network) while *also* preparing to win as a *likely* future unfolds (e.g., 3D printing for a growing range of products). Think Netflix's DVD rental service before the world was ready for (or even heard of) video streaming.[2]

Netflix founders Reed Hastings and Marc Randolph wanted to introduce on-demand video from the start—hence the name Netflix—but the technology infrastructure wasn't close to being capable enough in 1997, the year they founded the company. Netflix's DVD rental business—its transitional business platform—generated a profitable business that got the company to market and enabled, rather than hindered, transition to future business models as technologies, consumer behaviors, and industry practices evolved.

Similarly, Gelato's brand, customer base, and global network of 2D printing capacity position the company to win as additive manufacturing rises.

SMART DARK FACTORIES

The image of a factory brings to mind massive industrial buildings filled with people and machines on production lines. This picture is changing.

With a worldwide shortage of factory workers—2.1 million manufacturing jobs are expected to be left unfilled by 2030—manufacturers are scurrying to automate by installing robots, advanced sensors, AI, and new communication networks (5G and beyond).[3] A factory in Dongguan, an industrial city in China's Pearl River Delta, used to be manned by 650 workers. By 2023 it operated with only 60.[4] Where humans once toiled under lights, robots whir in the dark. Productivity skyrocketed by 250 percent, and defects declined 5 percent from 25 percent.

With labor costs rising and robot costs falling for the past decade, it's no surprise that enterprises are making the shift. Fewer than a dozen humans supervise more than 140 robots at an electric razor factory for Dutch manufacturer Philips.[5] Amazon has deployed over five hundred thousand robots in its warehouses.

Automation enables entirely new configurations of production capacity within smaller footprints—thus potentially closer to demand. What previously required hundreds of thousands of square feet of industrial space might only require tens of thousands, or less. Companies can consider production capacity closer to demand in suburban or even urban locations, designed as networks of production rather than as massive, centralized facilities.

Rapidly evolving communications networks like 5G, not to mention future generations, provide dramatically faster—up to 100× faster under the right conditions—than 4G, the prior standard. 5G networks can create a robust pipeline between production assets and the cloud, hypothetically meaning connectivity to any other connected asset anywhere. They can monitor and control factories remotely, shift production in real time between locations, and apply AI analytics from anywhere to anywhere.

German industrial conglomerate Bosch articulates its vision for 5G-based manufacturing. "It will only be floor, ceiling, and walls that cannot be moved in the vision of the factory of the future. All other components are flexible, portable, and can easily be reconfigured. . . . 5G will enable completely new manufacturing concepts."[6]

Such flexible, connected production capabilities enable smart competitors to reenvision how and where they locate production. They'll also be able to overcome traditional trade-offs.

CREATEME: CUSTOMIZATION AND EFFICIENCY

Garment manufacturing might face the most variability and diversity of any industry, with its thousands of shape, fit, size, material, and color combinations. The traditional solution was to limit customization and produce large runs of the same garment. That worked for thousands of copies of the same shirt but wasn't great for personalization. The environmental implications of high-scale manufacturing have been profound. Each season the industry averages about 30 percent *overproduction* worldwide, meaning that clothing ends up in fire sales, donations, and landfills.

As CreateMe investor Pablos Holman, cofounder of venture fund Deep Future, describes it, "Imagine if we drove one-third of the cars in the world straight from the factory to a landfill. The apparel industry is almost as big."

By 2023, garment manufacturing automation and software company CreateMe boasted more than fifty of the largest apparel companies as clients just five years after its founding. Rather than focusing on robots to automate sewing—the industry's common and not-very-successful approach—the company's founder, Cam Myers, challenged an industry orthodoxy. "How about we eliminate sewing altogether?" Thus was born a Proximity posterchild.

CreateMe uses computational geometry, automated production processes, and advanced adhesives originally developed for the semiconductor and consumer electronics industries to produce highly customized garments at nearly any scale, few or many, on demand. Single, made-to-order garments become profitable. *True* personalization. As Myers explains, "In an on-demand world, all these things unlock, *but you can't make this work by simply automating a traditional plant*" (italics added).

Eliminating sewing radically simplifies production but requires redesigning the products, which is where computational geometry comes in.

CreateMe's algorithms convert client designs into forms that can remain 2D (i.e., flat) as long as possible during production before assembling them as 3D garments, making them easier for automated handling through production lines and thus requiring far less human intervention.

The facilities required to accomplish this process require approximately 30 percent of the space and far fewer people—five staffers compared to forty for a comparable traditional facility. The company has focused on rapid response, custom, niche applications like sports team apparel—for which standard six- to nine-month order lead times don't work—and personalized, made-to-order products. It's just getting started. Consider how many more locations become possible when you need 30,000 square feet instead of 100,000, and five people instead of forty.

Proximity isn't just about automating the past. As Myers explains,

> We enable supply chains that are shorter, faster and more resilient. As a result, we can bring designs to market within weeks, not months. While our facilities will require far fewer people, their jobs will be safer, higher skilled and more rewarding.
>
> And how about sustainability when overproduction becomes a thing of the past? In our ideal future, we'll only produce a garment when someone is actually ready to buy it. And hopefully love it.
>
> For the apparel industry, this is like Star Trek!

And it's quintessential Proximity.

CreateMe's model also illustrates that companies will come to expect their suppliers to respond far faster to orders. If a few companies in an industry figure out how to do so, their competitors will be compelled to follow.

Rafaël Salmi, global president of electronics distributor Richardson RFPD, a division of Arrow Electronics, predicts that over the next decade, "for more and more products, the multi-month lead time will soon be over." As this trend advances, he advises, "incremental improvements won't be enough to remain competitive. Manufacturers will need to adopt models with Amazon-like performance: fast and customized."

THE ADDITIVE REVOLUTION: FROM ATOMS TO ANYTHING

As of 2021, the global 3D printing market reached $13.8 billion.[7] People were already printing 800-square-foot homes in just 24 hours and low-cost homes throughout Africa, Asia, and the Americas for less than $10,000. The U.S. Department of Defense was printing food bars with customized nutrients for soldiers[8] and replacement parts for drones.[9]

Not only does 3D printing have the potential to reduce production costs, but in some cases it can shrink the distances that parts and products must travel, enable more adaptable production, and eliminate entire production steps like forging, casting, drilling, milling, laser-cutting, or assembling.[10]

In the automotive sector, companies like BMW, Ford, and VW now regularly print spare parts. If you need to replace the inlet manifold for an out-of-production Ford, for example, finding a used one is expensive or impossible. Ford can now print one. As of late 2022, Ford had printed over five hundred thousand replacement parts to order. BMW's Mini Cooper offers customized decorative options with, say, a customer's name or personalized image.

In 2018 French cosmetics giant L'Oréal launched a 3D printing lab that was exploring applications across its businesses. By 2021 it had installed capabilities in over half of its forty factories, printing over fifteen thousand parts such as perfume and nail polish packaging that year.[11] The company is also experimenting with printing living skin cells for use in cosmetic surgery.[12]

In 2015, Rob visited defense contractor Lockheed Martin's Missiles and Fire Control division in Orlando, Florida. The visit included exploring how innovation in design and production might change what's possible. An engineer held up a metal part that had been sliced in half to expose the latticework inside. The part, intended for aircraft, had the strength of steel but the weight of aluminum, which is pivotal when designing for speed or sustainability.

His engineer guide explained, "It was *impossible* to manufacture this part before 3D printing."[13]

For physical products, nothing offers proximate potential more than additive manufacturing. Today it's trivial to print a simple plastic or metal part. As capabilities improve, ever more complex products will be producible in low unit runs on an economically competitive basis.

And with smaller footprints. Imagine a 3D printer on your counter at home. What could you print on demand from raw materials that before required multiple parts traversing thousands of miles and finished products sitting in warehouses awaiting your order? Don't expect to see this writ large in the next couple of years, though as we write this chapter, companies like Prusa Research are selling at-home 3D printers for under $1,000. Later this decade, expect to be amazed.

FROM RAW MATERIALS TO FINISHED PRODUCTS

Achieving the promise of additive manufacturing requires change across the value chain, from designers and manufacturers to distributors and customers. Even raw materials suppliers must rethink what and how they serve.

The same year Rob visited Lockheed Martin, specialty materials manufacturer Allegheny Technologies (ATI) began exploring how additive manufacturing might transform its industry. ATI is one of the world's top producers of high-performance specialty alloys with a focus on titanium and nickel superalloys, used by industries with the highest standards. While ATI had just inaugurated the world's most efficient and flexible specialty alloy production facility—attracting industry visitors from around the world—the leadership knew that additive manufacturing would one day change customers' raw materials requirements. They began what has already become a decade-long R&D commitment.

Traditional metals-forming companies convert formats such as bars and sheets into a range of products via forging (hitting with hydraulic presses, essentially) and casting (melting and reforming in a mold). 3D printing machines require formats such as powders formulated for different binding or melting processes.

Today, ATI's integrated additive manufacturing solution provides specialty alloys in powder forms that are adapted for other companies' additive manufacturing equipment. It also offers additive manufacturing production and finishing capabilities for metal parts to customers in aerospace, defense, medical, and space industries—industries with the highest quality and performance requirements.

ATI's chief commercial and marketing officer Kevin Kramer explains: "For us the real holy grail of additive is not being able to print the part, per se. A lot of people can do that. . . . For us to be able to customize the powder that goes into the printing of a part and make that very bespoke and customized for a unique application, that's where we're spending time."

While ATI doesn't know how quickly additive manufacturing will rise or which production processes and equipment designs will win, it has committed to being the leading specialty materials supplier for whichever additive manufacturing methods prevail.

3D printing offers unprecedented possibilities to simplify production of complex products. Instead of producing a component out of tens of parts, sourced from different suppliers that assembled them, it becomes possible to produce an entire component or system as a single printed unit.

For instance, engine manufacturers source and assemble hundreds of parts from various suppliers for each engine. While not yet possible, it's conceivable for an additive manufacturing system to produce small engines from raw materials, with a minimal number of parts added after the overall engine is formed.

Even more compelling, electric motors—rapidly replacing internal combustion engines for many applications—are far simpler and will thus prove more amenable to additive manufacturing.

Rocket manufacturer Relativity Space has been developing just such a capability for printing rockets to carry payloads into space. As of this writing, the company had proven that it could manufacture rockets in fully automated environments. "By fusing 3D printing, artificial intelligence, and autonomous robotics, we are pioneering the factory of the future."[14] The company claims that its design results in approximately one thousand parts compared to over one hundred thousand required for similar rockets manufactured by conventional methods, enabling production of each rocket in days rather than months or years. In March 2023, Relativity launched its 3D-printed rocket, the *Terran 1*, from Cape Canaveral in Florida.[15]

Any company producing and assembling parts within complex supply chains such as automotive, aviation, or electronics should be concerned. In some products, change might not come for years, even decades. But recognizing the threat is the first step to discovering opportunity.

NEW SOLUTIONS, NEW CHALLENGES

As creation and production advance ever more toward *now*, we'll face new versions of perennial challenges. Eventually, at-home 3D printers will churn out an increasing array of products, lowering the bar for on-demand production—thus increasing the impulse to produce and dispose. Rather than lowering waste compared to traditional models, we risk increasing it.

As of 2023, 3D printers use 50 to 100 times more energy than traditional plastic injection molding.[16] While the industry works diligently to decrease the energy requirements—and thus cost competitiveness—society is likely to face a transition period in which waste and energy use might *increase* before sustainability benefits accrue.

New health risks might also ensue. While results are still early, the U.S. Environmental Protection Agency (EPA) warns that initial studies show potentially harmful emissions from some of the most popular 3D printing processes. The industry will be well advised to overcome these risks before they threaten user health (and shareowner value).

Front and center will be the very long-term transition from traditional manufacturing to hybrid, distributed production. As in past technological revolutions, the Proximity trend will obsolesce some production facilities while bringing benefits and challenges to new locations.

The past offers a useful guide. Many regions that thrived during one revolution suffered through the next. Some discovered renewed prosperity. Special steel manufacturer ATI's hometown, Pittsburgh, Pennsylvania, enjoyed steel-fueled prosperity during the nineteenth and twentieth centuries before becoming a casualty of the so-called Rust Belt in the waning decades of the last century. As of this writing, Pittsburgh had again returned to prosperity. It navigated through technological disruption via broad-based civic leadership in business, academia, and government: leveraging academic institutions like Carnegie Mellon and the University of Pittsburgh and established corporations like ATI; attracting talent; doubling down on advanced manufacturing, medicine, AI, and robotics; and encouraging investments well beyond those of most midsize cities.

On a regional or national level, Proximity models offer the potential for more resilient and adaptable economic ecosystems due to *economic diversity*. Rather than relying on a single or limited set of industries—as Pittsburgh did during its incarnation as "Steel City"—regions will be increasingly able to *efficiently* produce more of what's required nearby. More of not just one category of products, but wide ranges of products, services, and experiences produced and consumed locally, enhancing resilience and adaptability.

If benefits accrue to local enterprises and communities—as opposed to being owned exclusively by far-away shareowners—then prosperity can, as well, become better distributed. These will be complex equations for all of us as citizens, investors, entrepreneurs, regulators, and consumers to decipher.

CREATING AND RECREATING OUR PROXIMATE WORLD

Expect AI-enabled design and automated, distributed production to converge over the next few decades. Their mature power will arise from designing and producing what's special to the moment at hand.

A toy designer in Los Angeles won't have to start from scratch. While the designer brainstorms, her AI assistant, trained on child development content and up-to-the-moment trends, will propose features to engage young minds. While she sketches, the AI will propose patterns and elements that currently resonate with children. It will quickly generate 3D models based on her sketches, allowing her to visualize her ideas in a realistic and tangible form. Once she's satisfied with the virtual prototypes, 3D printers can materialize her creations with precision and speed.

As our computational, productive systems learn to invent, design, and produce, they'll bring any product, service, or experience closer to us at any moment. True personalization delivered in real time by AI systems that learn our preferences and produce at the MoU. We'll ascend new creativity learning curves, discover new ways to convert ideas to reality, and do so wherever, whenever. As our descendants migrate to Mars and beyond, such creative, productive Proximity will become essential.

And we humans will be faced yet again with discovering new ways to add value. Turns out Paul Bunyan's story remains an inspiration and a warning.

7

How We Power

- Proximity requires proximate power.
- The 4Ds of Power: Distributed, Decarbonized, Digitalized, Democratized.
- Distributed power generation enhances resilience and adaptability.
- The second electricity revolution: mobile and green.
- In a dangerous world, maintain multiple power sources.
- The more proximate our power, the more proximate our lives.

Until its demolition in 1917, a 187-foot tower stood in Shoreham, Long Island. Crowned by a giant steel ball 68 feet in diameter and anchored by an "iron root system" deep into the earth, it was visionary inventor and physicist Nikola Tesla's Wardenclyffe Tower.

Begun in 1901, it emerged from Tesla's mission to provide ubiquitous wireless power worldwide. No cords, no wires. The experiment failed, bankrupt by 1906.

While Tesla's vision hasn't materialized—yet—consider that since his experiments we now have wireless communications covering the planet, an eventuality Tesla foresaw. With true visionaries, humanity takes time to catch up. Many experts assert that Tesla's approach would not have worked, but his *concept* remains a possibility awaiting breakthroughs.

In 2021, researchers at Georgia Tech published an article in *Scientific Reports* proposing that the current generation of wireless communications systems known as 5G *might* have the potential to manifest Tesla's vision. "Unknowingly, the architects of 5G have, thereby, created a wireless power grid capable of powering devices at ranges far exceeding the capabilities of any existing technologies."[1] They proffer the possibility of wireless electricity supporting low-power devices such as sensors and other connected devices. Perhaps eventually mobile phone batteries?

Whether or not researchers discover how to leverage 5G for wireless power, Tesla's tower portends truly ubiquitous electricity. Powering anything, anywhere.

"WHEN THE LIGHTS WENT OUT, WE HOOKED UP THE TRACTOR"

Power industry executive Brian Hoff recalls growing up on a farm in Fulton, a central Illinois farming town named in honor of Robert Fulton, credited as the inventor of the steam-powered ship. (You might recall "Fulton's Folly" from high school history class.)

"While my friends in town lost power and their ice cream melted, we rode out the problem with some help from John Deere," Hoff said, referring to the make of the Hoffs' tractor. He'd put the tractor in park and hooked the engine to a generator that powered the farmhouse as long as the diesel fuel kept flowing. "I didn't realize at the time, but we were already going where the world of energy would head in the twenty-first century—distributed energy resources."

How appropriate that one of today's electric power industry innovators grew up in a town honoring a giant of the Industrial Revolution. Burning hydrocarbons—first wood, then coal, and later oil and gas—was the favored Proximity solution of the Industrial Revolution. Steam enabled industry and mobility in ways that had never before been possible, followed by internal combustion, diesel engines, and coal-, oil-, and gas-fired power plants.

While today we witness the *enormous* environmental costs of centuries of fossil fuel dependence, the fact was that hydrocarbons were cheap and effective. They offered us dependable, even mobile, power. They powered earlier versions of Proximity, from petrol-powered cars to petrol- or coal-powered electricity available in any wall socket.

Despite the environmental crisis we now face, we can recognize that, ironically, hydrocarbons saved humanity from what we refer to as the

Malthusian trap. British economist Thomas Robert Malthus argued in 1798, persuasively at the time, that increased agricultural production would lead to a population explosion, eventually overwhelming the world's ability to feed so many of us. In the resulting crisis, society would collapse under the stress of famine and warfare.

The rise of hydrocarbons changed the equation in ways Malthus couldn't have anticipated, not only for transportation and industry, but especially for agriculture, which relied on fertilizer. It was a pivotal, though not the only, factor that enabled humanity to swell from 1 billion in 1800 to around 8 billion by 2022.

Hoff's tractor burned hydrocarbons. While fossil fuels will remain essential for *at least* the next decade (probably longer), we now have clean, renewable alternatives capable of powering Proximity in ways hydrocarbons cannot.

A FAR BETTER WORLD

Proximity requires access to reliable, safe power. Not just from wall sockets but also for mobile, portable, wearable, even implanted devices.

Generating electricity is just the start. We have to get electrons to where they're required, known in the industry as "transmission" and "distribution." The twentieth-century-style solutions dominant in most developed parts of the world rely on massive power generation plants connected by miles of transmission infrastructure collectively known as "the grid."

The grid actually represents many grids connected across regions and, ultimately, continents. In North America, for instance, there are two major and three minor "interconnections" with varying levels of connectivity. (This fact helps us understand the massive failure of the Texas interconnection in the winter of 2021, and how Proximity models could have helped avert that disaster.)

It's one thing to envision proximate energy in developed countries, where for years we've enjoyed electricity in every wall socket and petrol stations in every town. Life will change for the better as batteries endure for days and transportation converts from petroleum to clean-generated electrons.

But far more dramatic change awaits regions with underdeveloped infrastructure. If they electrify widely and bring electricity generation, storage, and distribution closer to where it's needed, they can leapfrog over nations that are encumbered by legacy technologies.

It doesn't have to be expensive. Imagine a family on the margins of subsistence who, for the first time, have the ability to light their home for a few hours each night with a simple solar-battery solution. Life becomes better. Children study later, families gather, and productivity rises.

This is already happening via organizations such as d.light, which in 2022 reported having sold or donated over 25 million devices, including solar lanterns, home systems, TVs, radios, and even smartphones. Distributed, renewable solutions free families from the tyranny of imported oil and inadequate, often unsafe power infrastructure.

THE 4DS OF ELECTRICITY: ENABLING WHATEVER, WHEREVER

Electrons favor Proximity, as they store and move freely at rapidly declining cost. Hydrocarbons, by contrast, remain expensive to extract, store, and transport, not to mention they require the environmental, security, and geopolitical complications of far-flung supply chains.

Burning hydrocarbons currently generates a majority of the world's electricity—around 60 percent in 2022 in the United States alone—but we're finally transitioning from burning fuels *in* vehicles to relying on battery-stored electrons. (The total environmental footprint of electric vehicles [EVs] is another story, particularly where the original electricity generation relies on hydrocarbons. This factor does not compromise the flexibility of electricity-powered mobility compared to burning fossil fuels in vehicles.)

Compare the complexity and cost of supporting a global fleet of EVs versus traditional combustion engines, which necessitate extracting oil from the Earth, transporting it to refineries and then onward to petrol stations—over 130,000 in 2022 in the United States alone—filling your car with gasoline, and then burning it for mobility. And this multiplied by over a *billion* vehicles worldwide.

By contrast, an EV can charge anywhere that electricity is available. Whether generated by power plants and distributed via the grid or generated closer to demand—involving what is known in the industry as "distributed energy resources" or DERs—electrons travel at the speed of light with zero variable cost of transmission (beyond the costs of grid construction and operation). EVs can even contribute back to the grid or directly to your home, a modern version of Hoff's tractor generator.

Over time, electricity will prevail over burning fossil fuels on board vehicles because it's a simpler, more flexible solution. And the change isn't limited to mobility.

Consider how access to energy, particularly electricity, impacts the viability of controlled environment agriculture (CEA), explored in chapter 4, "How We Eat." Energy accounts for double to triple the portion of the cost of goods sold (COGS, a measure of input costs) of CEA operating costs compared to traditional industrial-scale agriculture. Sonia Lo, leading agriculture investor and former CEO of vertical farming pioneer CropOne Holdings, explains:

> In concept, you can place CEA facilities in more locations than traditional farms, like urban areas, bringing more fresh food production closer to where people live. Proximity as you assert. But CEA requires energy. Lots of it. We can seek locations with access to comparatively inexpensive excess power and a high value for fresh produce, like CropOne's partnership with Emirates Airlines in Dubai where CropOne grows produce proximate to the airport. But the bigger opportunity long-term will be as distributed energy generation becomes more efficient, we'll have more options for CEA.

To summarize Lo's critical insight, *distributed energy is the key to distributed agriculture.*

Hydrocarbons will remain essential and even increase at times during the decades-long energy transition. Nonetheless, the long term favors *distributed, decarbonized,* and *digitalized* energy solutions, known by the industry as the 3Ds.[2] Some industry players have added yet another D for *democratized*—accessible by all.

Power generation and storage will be distributed around the economy, closer to each consumer. Decarbonizing will transition from fossil fuels to clean energy sources. Digitalization will orchestrate between complex networks of distributed supply and consumer demands.

DERs favor renewable energies. Solar and wind generation can be more easily distributed at varying scales across the economy, from massive solar arrays and wind farms to rooftop solar and small-scale wind installations. Once installed, they're unencumbered by extended fossil fuel supply chains.

Expect to see DERs proliferate *in parallel* with enhancements to the traditional energy infrastructure. We'll call this the "dual path" of energy's future. And none too soon if we're to navigate through volatile energy markets, climate change, and extreme weather events.

A TEXAS-SIZED DISASTER

On Thursday, February 11, 2021, the Electric Reliability Council of Texas (ERCOT) issued a warning. A statewide storm system was expected to bring Texas the coldest weather the state had experienced in decades. The council predicted that electricity demand would reach record highs. "We could see a new all-time winter peak demand by Monday morning," ERCOT's then-CEO, Bill Magness, warned.[3]

Magness's warning turned out to have been understated. Three severe winter storms swept across the United States from February 10 to 20, triggering the worst energy infrastructure failure in Texas history. Over 4 million homes and businesses were left without power for extended periods. The Texas Department of State Health Services reported that 246 people died as a result.[4]

In the aftermath of the "Great Texas Freeze," Magness was fired. Governor Greg Abbott was forced to sign two bills promising to improve the state's power grid.[5]

The weather catastrophe was compounded by the fact that Texas relies on its own energy grid—independent from the U.S. grid—covering about 90 percent of the state.[6] Demands are staggered across the vast state, spanning two time zones and nearly 269,000 square miles. That week, demand overstressed the grid. Separated from the rest of the country (which operates two larger grids called the Eastern and Western Interconnects), Texas was unable to tap energy from out of state. Its centralized power system was unprepared for extreme climate emergencies.

Several Proximity-related energy innovations, already in operation but not at sufficient scale, could have helped avert the catastrophe. ERCOT's Thursday warning of pending low temperatures could have triggered several "virtual power plants" to start generating and storing energy: not power plants per se, but "virtual" plants created on demand by coordinating hundreds or even thousands of distributed energy generation systems. Think battery backup systems powered by solar panels on homes, commercial buildings, farms, grazing lands, and desertscapes.

Such a scenario is *technologically* possible today.

Residents with solar systems could have received a notice on their smartphones suggesting they start storing energy because the prices for selling that energy back to the grid were projected to skyrocket. Even more compelling, such distributed energy production could have been automatically triggered.

Even natural gas–powered standby generators could have helped, activating in advance, generating and storing power or producing electricity *during* the storms, and selling it to the grid. Had they been fitted and coordinated to do so, backup generators anywhere in the state could have contributed spare capacity.

As heaters activated across Texas's 9.9 million homes,[7] power could have begun flowing from thousands of locations, supporting the output of traditional power plants. Managed by orchestration software, such a system could have helped Texans navigate the crisis.

Adopted and properly managed, such systems could turn the next Texas megastorm into little more than an inconvenience.

FROM EDISON'S POWER PLANT TO DERS

Electricity industry paradigms haven't changed much for over a century. Large-scale power plants generate electricity that passes through a complex system of substations, transformers, and power lines to consumers. Until recently, utility executives joked that if electricity visionary Thomas Edison were to awaken today, he'd be ready to run the company.

No longer.

Faced with challenges from extreme weather events and cyber threats to the electric vehicle revolution, the power industry is in the midst of transformation.

From its headquarters in the small Midwest town of Waukesha, Wisconsin (population 72,000), Generac corporation, founded in 1959, is creating the future of energy. The company's traditional (boring) product connects to your natural gas line and whirs to action if the electricity fails. Voila, your ice cream doesn't melt.

Beginning in about 2017, the company mapped a radical vision for its future: to become a leader in distributed energy resource management systems, or DERMS. DERMS coordinate networks of thousands of DERs such as solar, wind, natural gas, and battery storage units to more rapidly and precisely respond to changes in supply and demand, on-site or via the grid.

In October 2020, Generac acquired Canadian software company Enbala. Enbala's Concerto platform enables electric grid operators (typically electric utilities) to coordinate DERs to flexibly respond to demand. Announcing the acquisition, Generac CEO Aaron Jagdfeld asserted, "We're on the leading edge of a remarkable transformation of the electrical grid, moving from a dated and centralized power distribution model to one that will be digitized, decentralized, and more resilient."[8]

For instance, owners of Generac's standby generators, powered by natural gas, can download the app and opt in to generate electricity supply for the grid. The app continually monitors electricity prices. When prices rise, the software engages the generator and sells electricity to the grid, switching off again as prices fall. These so-called prosumers (i.e., consumer producers) turn otherwise dormant generators into revenue. Such capabilities could have helped during the Great Texas Freeze.

Standby energy systems traditionally rely on natural gas. But Generac, Kohler, and others are rapidly scaling solar-battery systems untethered from natural gas supply chains. More flexibility, more Proximity.

In underserved areas, DERs might become the dominant source of electricity, as is already the case in off-grid locations. In areas well served by traditional electricity infrastructure, expect new technologies and methods to evolve alongside legacy systems.

DUAL REINFORCING PATHS

Energy innovation will roll out on two reinforcing paths: upgrading of traditional infrastructure concurrent with the rise of DERs. We're *not* proposing that all electricity will become generated proximate to demand. Rather, distributed (proximate) generation and storage will complement existing centralized solutions.

The time frames will involve years or even decades. Companies and countries will be loath to mothball existing infrastructure. They'll keep it active, adapting to coordinate with new solutions. Ultimately, though, DERs offer innate flexibility advantages, promising greater resilience *and* evolvability.

Imagine a city with one hundred thousand people served by a single generation plant. Converting to a new centralized generation technology, while winding down the generation plant that's been working fine (hopefully) for years, is a massive commitment.

Alternatively, what if that same town had a network of one thousand generation nodes? It's far less disruptive to, at first, transition a few of these nodes to pilot new solutions, rolling out the new technology only after it's proven. The city could also decide to install a variety of solutions to decrease the risk of relying on any single technology.

Individual citizens and businesses could install their own generation capacity, enhancing their well-being and that of the entire system.

Now consider how much more resilient and evolvable the city's power infrastructure would be with *both* a centralized power plant and numerous DERs. This combination would enable a dependable, agile response to changing power needs, faster rollout of new technologies, and greater defense against cyber or physical attacks. It's easier to attack a single plant than a thousand nodes.

Such hybrid power ecosystems, centralized plus distributed, are already becoming real.

VIRTUAL POWER PLANTS AND MICROGRIDS

Few citizens want a traditional power plant built nearby, even if their town requires more capacity. Even solar arrays and wind farms face opposition. It's the NIMBY ("not in my backyard") problem. Virtual power plants (VPPs) offer a solution.

VPPs are digitally connected networks of generation and storage that, in aggregate, constitute the scale of a traditional power plant. Utilizing software like Generac's Concerto system, VPPs operate with the grid in the same way as a centralized power plant, calling for increases or decreases in power generation or consumption to meet demands and stabilize the grid.[9] And without the massive capital outlays and politics of building a traditional power plant.

At the time of this writing, Portland General Electric is building a 4-megawatt (MW) virtual power plant in Oregon as a precursor to 200 MW of distributed flexibility. Households taking part in the VPP experiment get a battery purchase rebate or are paid $20 to $40 per month for use of existing batteries.[10]

In a sign of the growing commercialization of VPPs, Redwood City–based AutoGrid, which operates VPPs in twelve countries with 5,000 MW under contract, offers its management system for purchase through Amazon Web Services.

While VPPs operate as part of larger energy grids, microgrids may operate completely off the grid, powered at least in part by local generation. Even when connected to a grid, they can be "islanded," meaning they can function as an independent energy system even if the main energy grid fails. If you've ever experienced multiday power outages, you know the value of local solutions.

In contrast to a single DER supporting a home or industrial site, microgrids connect DERs with neighboring consumers. A microgrid might cover just a few homes or entire neighborhoods.

Electric utility ComEd implemented such a system in Chicago's Bronzeville neighborhood.[11] The Bronzeville microgrid includes a solar array, a battery storage system, and a natural gas–powered generation system. Each operates when most economical and effective. By partnering with the neighboring microgrid of the Illinois Institute of Technology (IIT), the Bronzeville Community Microgrid can operate independently or share power, whichever is most effective. The university and its surrounding neighborhood are thus far more resilient in power grid disruptions. IIT reports that its microgrid has saved the university between $200,000 and $1 million annually through 2022. It also enhances the adaptability of Chicago's overall electricity systems.

SUSTAINABLE ENERGY, WHEREVER, WHENEVER

Though the sun's energy *production* has never been proximate—fortunately for us it's about 93 million miles away—its *provision* of energy reaches nearly everywhere on a dependable schedule (weather permitting). We've just been poor at harnessing it.

Over the past decade we've witnessed dramatic progress in making solar power economically viable due to technological advances, manufacturing scaleup, and civic commitment. We've seen similar though less dramatic progress in wind power.

While both solar and wind provide clean power, we continue to require baseload power generation for when neither photovoltaic panels nor windmills produce electricity: what the industry affectionately calls "dark and windless nights."

Efficient, reliable, safe power storage releases this constraint. From electrons that disappear unused to electrons stored at the ready.

Consider your laptop. Before 1993—when Dell Computer launched the first lithium-ion-powered laptop—portable PCs relied on nickel metal hydride batteries that were limited to about an hour between charges. While longer-lasting lithium-ion batteries were already in use for low-power applications like digital cameras, many experts argued that they might never be safe enough for medium-power applications like laptops, much less for high-power requirements like EVs.

As of this writing, lithium batteries are standard in electronics from iPhones to Teslas. Think about how much more you can accomplish with 6 hours of laptop battery life or 500 miles of EV range.

For the coming decade at least, proximate energy generation such as rooftop solar, small-scale wind, and even connected standby generators will proliferate. Energy storage will meanwhile enhance our ability to access power wherever it is desired.

Beyond batteries, innovators across the globe are working on approaches from supercapacitors, compressed air energy storage (CAES), and super-conducting magnetic energy storage (SMES), which uses coils of super-conductive wire to store electricity with near-zero energy loss, to pumped hydro storage (basically two reservoirs at different elevations that generate power through a turbine when water flows between them) and green hydrogen.

GOVERNMENTS TO THE RESCUE?

Upon moving to Ridgewood, New Jersey, in 2022, Rob's family was eager to install rooftop solar panels and a battery backup. Government incentives, rapidly declining costs of solar systems, and the Wolcotts' natural interest in sustainability made this a compelling option.

Unfortunately, they found that the shape and position of their home's roof made this an inefficient option. They still would have proceeded, but state regulations limited the value. Power generated by rooftop solar is, by law, only allowed to offset a *portion* of a home's total energy use. New Jersey residents are *required* to purchase power from the grid, unless they opt to go entirely off the grid (an impractical option for most families).

Contrary to most citizens' understandings, in most locations electricity generated via rooftop solar doesn't directly power a home. Law requires that the energy is provided to the grid. The local utility offsets the consumer's power bill to reflect the energy produced on-site, a process called net metering.

Technology isn't the only, or even the most important, factor that determines how quickly new energy solutions roll out. Because it's every community's lifeblood, electricity is political. Regulatory incentives and constraints often define how capabilities evolve.

While government incentives accelerate the diffusion of rooftop solar, they tend to do so in favor of the established electricity grid system. This approach can be frustrating for some consumers, but it makes sense from a local and regional perspective to enhance grid capacity and stability.

Nonetheless, America's grid system suffers from significant need of modernization. Proven technologies exist that could *dramatically* enhance our nation's energy position. The question is, how do we shore up the old while we build the new?

Governments worldwide grapple with how to transition while navigating technical and resource constraints, vested interests, and public perception. The experience of Bangladesh offers clues.

BANGLADESH'S JOURNEY:
MORE THAN ENOUGH . . . IF YOU CAN GET IT

By 2022, after almost thirteen years of concerted effort, Bangladesh (Kaihan's mother's home country) considered itself past a history of widespread blackouts.

In the 1990s and 2000s, power failures were common in the country and were usually caused by load shedding—an attempt to reduce excessive demands on centralized power plants. In cities, blackouts could last 6 to 8 hours. In rural areas, life would stall at sunset, with many regions lacking access to any power at all.

In 2009, the government announced a major initiative to power the country's future. It committed to building enough capacity for projected needs and bringing electricity service to every household.

The country made tremendous progress. The percentage of households with access rose from 47 percent in 2009 to 96 percent by 2022, while generation capacity increased fivefold, from 4,942 MW per year to 25,514. It appeared that the 2014 Bangladesh blackout, which left the entire population without power for 10 hours, would be a relic of the past.[12]

Impressive progress for sure. Unfortunately, the same year the government announced its achievement, crippling blackouts returned.[13] Power cuts occurred nationwide, businesses were forced to limit use, and consumers in Dhaka, the capital city, coped with 6 hours of electricity per day.

What happened?

While Bangladesh had the right idea—sufficient electricity generation for all—the nation took an inflexible, Industrial Age approach: large, centralized power plants powered by fossil fuels—nearly all imported.

When Russia invaded Ukraine in February 2022, oil, gas, and coal prices skyrocketed. European countries that could afford to pay far higher prices locked in a limited supply, leaving little for others. Shortages threatened Bangladesh's entire economy.[14] Some analysts warned that if the country could not secure new supplies, it could face rolling blackouts through 2026.

Bangladesh committed nearly 100 percent of its impressive national program to twentieth-century solutions. What if it had taken a dual-path approach: baseload provided by large-scale facilities supplemented by thousands of DERs?

Bangladesh already had such systems, small-scale solar installations generating in villages across the country. They proliferated in parallel with the government's initiative, built and operated by households and local leaders who were responsive to local needs, often despite government efforts.

Solar and battery company Rahimafrooz led the way.

FROM CAR BATTERIES TO SUSTAINABLE POWER

In 1947 Abdur Rahim arrived in the city of Chittagong, Bangladesh, with only the cash in his pockets. Described as "a dreamer who thought nothing impossible," in 1950 Rahim established Rahimafrooz, a small trading concern that specialized in automobile batteries.[15]

At a time when Bangladesh's economy was one of the world's poorest, Rahimafrooz grew to become one of the largest and most respected businesses in the country.[16] From its modest start in automobile batteries, the company expanded in response to the country's evolving needs.

In the 1990s, when blackouts were common, Rahimafrooz shifted focus to deep-cycle battery applications. Deep-cycle batteries, when applied to power plants, offer standby power. If a power plant trips for a few minutes, the batteries provide 2 to 3 hours of backup. This offered a partial solution to long-running blackouts.

The solution worked well in cities where people were accustomed to having power. What if it could bring electricity to rural areas?

PROXIMATE POWER IN BANGLADESH

Munawar Misbah Moin, Rahimafrooz's group director, explained to us that connecting a solar panel to a deep-cycle battery could store enough power to provide rural households with a few hours of electricity each night. Imagine what many of us take for granted: relatives seeing each other over dinner, children studying after dark.

These distributed solar energy systems generate power for on-site consumption. If connected to a microgrid, excess energy can be redistributed to neighbors. Families with such systems are freed from waiting for governments or utility companies to provide dependable grid solutions.

As of 2021, Rahimafrooz had implemented more than 25 MW of solar photovoltaic capacity. While this represents only about 0.1 percent of the country's total annual electricity supply, the distributed nature of the solution supports more than two hundred thousand households in rural, often hard-to-access communities. The installations have convinced a huge population that solar can be more reliable than electricity transmitted from a distance.

Rahimafrooz is adapting the capability for other applications. "Tuk-tuks," three-wheeled motorized vehicles, provide a large percentage of mass transit in rural areas. Unfortunately, they burn fossil fuels in horribly polluting two-cycle engines. As electric versions become available, Rahimafrooz is introducing solar-powered charging points.

In addition to the environmental benefits, EVs powered by distributed solar systems release communities from dependence on imported fossil fuels. More sustainable, more resilient.

Many groups around the world, including Rahimafrooz, are taking the electricity storage journey even further via "second-life batteries." While EV batteries eventually degrade for mobility purposes, they remain capable for other uses. Stationary energy storage, such as solar-battery combinations, offers an ideal application. EV leader Rivian, for instance, designs its batteries with second lives in mind.

THE SECOND ELECTRICITY REVOLUTION:
MOBILE AND GREEN

As described in chapter 1, the first electricity revolution resulted in Proximity of *provision*—electrical outlets on nearly every wall. A second electricity revolution is upon us. DERs will bring more production and storage capacity closer to ultimate demand. Radically better batteries will offer mobile, dependable power for nearly any application.

We have room to run. The International Energy Agency (IEA) estimates that only about 20 percent of the global economy runs on electricity.[17] Burning of hydrocarbons and even a bit of muscle power account for the rest.

Nowhere is the conversion to electrons more evident than in the rise of EVs. For some time, the dominant power source for EVs will remain centralized power stations, though DERs offer new options. A small portion of EV owners already charge from home-based solar panels. Eventually solar and energy management technologies *might* become sufficient to provide everything on the vehicle: solar energy converted to electricity, stored on board and converted to motion.

Such is the vision of start-ups Lightyear and Sono Motors, each developing solar-electric vehicles as of 2023. Their paths have been challenging. In January 2023, Lightyear canceled development of Lightyear 0, its original high-sticker-price vehicle, to focus on Lightyear 2, a lower-priced vehicle for the mass market, scheduled at that time for market launch in 2025.[18] In early 2023, Sono Motors abandoned its mass market vehicle program, Sion, to focus on providing solar vehicle solutions for commercial clients.[19]

Whether or not either company succeeds, solar power is likely to become a factor for mobile power, but it's not the only path. Today, hydrogen is primarily used for industrial applications that require very high temperatures, but it can also be used to produce electricity.

Hydrogen fuel cells—already a multibillion-dollar global market—convert hydrogen to electricity on board vehicles, proximate to demand. Companies like Plug Power and Ballard Power Systems produce fuel cells for mobile power applications such as forklifts and public buses. You still need to produce and distribute hydrogen, but electricity can be generated via fuel cells nearly anywhere.

Unfortunately, according to the World Bank, around 95 percent of all hydrogen produced in 2021 required fossil fuels to produce, typically natural gas or coal. Until recently, environmentally friendly "green" hydrogen was prohibitively expensive.

That's changing fast. Most pundits expect green hydrogen to pass cost parity with the dirtier grey sort sometime before 2030. Others are more optimistic. In 2021 the Norwegian firm NEL, the largest manufacturer of the electrolyzers essential to the production of hydrogen, predicted that green hydrogen production would reach parity with natural gas production by 2025. The dramatic rise of natural gas prices due to Russia's war in Ukraine accelerated that timeline.

Power storage offers one path to improving the viability of green hydrogen. Excess wind, solar, or even nuclear power generation could be used to produce hydrogen, thus storing the power for future use. In this way, hydrogen would reinforce the practicality and flexibility of other clean energies.

After many years as a "maybe someday" technology, corporations and governments are placing high-scale bets. South Korea aspires to lead the world. As of 2021, the country had made the third largest commitment of public funds to hydrogen, after Germany and Japan.[20]

South Korea is promoting the adoption of fuel cell electric vehicles (FCEVs) to catalyze the production and distribution of hydrogen and related technologies. In 2021 Hyundai Motors Group announced its plans to invest 7.6 trillion won ($6.7 billion) under its "FCEV Vision 2030." It's also part of the HyNet consortium, committed to building one hundred hydrogen refueling stations in South Korea in 2022 alone. If South Korea's vision is successful, hydrogen will account for 5 percent of its projected power consumption by 2040, and its economy will grow by 43 trillion won, create 420,000 new jobs, and achieve significant reductions in greenhouse gas emissions.[21]

Over 4,000 miles away in Estonia, a small Baltic state on the leading edge of many technology developments, plans are also under way to lead the hydrogen future. Having attained fame within the global tech industry—the country had more tech unicorns (start-ups valued at over $1 billion) per capita than any other as of 2022—investors, entrepreneurs, government leaders, and nonprofit leaders are coalescing around their vision for a "Hydrogen Valley Estonia."[22] The country projects that offshore wind farms should come online by 2028 with a total capacity of 7 gigawatts, twice the country's projected energy needs, by 2030. Green hydrogen could provide a mobile storage solution for Estonia and for export beyond.

While experts are mixed regarding hydrogen—Elon Musk complained that it's "the most dumb thing I can possibly imagine for energy storage"[23]—development of a range of alternative energy sources might enhance resilience against geopolitical threats such as Russia's war with Ukraine, a conflict felt viscerally throughout the Baltics. As Marek Alliksoo of Hydrogen Valley Estonia noted, "If someone were to cut all your wires elsewhere . . . you would be able to survive."[24]

COUNTER-PROXIMATE WILD CARDS?

While industry trends favor Proximity, wild cards loom. Two technologies merit special consideration as *possible* factors that are counter to Proximity: nuclear fusion and "high-temperature" superconductivity. If these technologies become viable at scale, they might trend toward centralized power generation.

As critics often joke, commercially viable nuclear fusion—the safe, clean energy source that powers the sun—has "always been thirty years away." Nonetheless, it *could* arise in our lifetimes. Billionaires such as Bill Gates and Peter Thiel, along with early fusion investor Steve Jurvetson, have sent over $3 billion to commercialization efforts in the early 2020s alone.[25] (Jurvetson reports on his Facebook site having made his first investment in fusion in 1995.)

Commercially viable fusion energy would be an irresistible force driving generation back toward large-scale, centralized facilities. (At least until small-scale fusion becomes possible. Who knows?)

Nonetheless, accessible fusion energy could help countries worldwide ensure a power supply and thus increase freedom and resilience against geopolitical threats. As pioneering fusion investor Wal van Lierop, founder of Chrysalix Venture Capital, asserts:

Fusion is the gamechanger that could make energy truly local, secure, and plentiful. It portends a shift from a centralized, autocratic energy industry to localized, democratic energy provision.

And fusion is not 20 years away anymore. Once the first fusion plant is commercially operational at reasonable cost, the switchover could be quick. Remember, it took centuries to develop the technologies behind an automobile, but it only took cars about a decade to replace horses in London and New York City.[26]

Even on van Lierop's timeline, fusion will require years of development before reaching deployment at scale. During that time frame, distributed energy generation will continue to proliferate.

Similarly, superconductivity, defined as the ability of some materials under certain conditions to conduct electric current with practically zero resistance, has the potential to impact the generation location equation. First identified by Dutch physicist H. Kamerlingh Onnes, for which he was awarded the Nobel Prize in Physics in 1913, the promise has so far eluded most applications.

All electricity transmission and distribution systems lose power over distances. Theoretically, superconductors could eliminate nearly all of this loss. Unfortunately, the astonishingly low temperatures required have limited superconductivity to applications such as medical imaging. So-called high-temperature superconductors are defined as operating above 30 Kelvin (−243° Celsius!).

Already, superconducting cables have been installed at small scale for electricity systems such as the AmpaCity pilot in Essen, Germany, and as of early 2023 were planned for a major Montparnasse railway station capacity expansion. While the pilots have proven successful in limited contexts, superconductors aren't close to having widespread adoption.

If researchers develop superconductors capable of operating at acceptable temperatures (around room temperature), long-distance transmission could become more competitive. Breakthroughs are likely. The history of energy research offers many such surprises.

But it won't be enough to derail the Proximity trend. The path from scientific breakthrough to implementation at scale would require years. Even nuclear fusion cheerleaders predict grid viability no earlier than 2030, not to mention the time required for widespread diffusion. By that time DERs will have proliferated.

AVOIDING THE MALTHUSIAN TRAP . . . AGAIN

Energy is an existential challenge. As the world passes 8 billion souls, we face the twenty-first-century version of Malthus's trap. Will innovation enable our planet—and perhaps others beyond—to support our species' desires to procreate? Or will crises of our own making force population declines (or catastrophes)?

It's a challenge for which we have answers. It's up to foresight, courage, and commitment to make them real.

Imagine countries hitting zero-carbon goals. Utilities enhancing performance and resilience via decentralized networks of sustainable resources. Batteries lighter, charging faster, lasting longer. Lives released from hydrocarbon jeopardy.

It's all possible in the coming generation because it's already under way.

A critical caution, and a notion not well understood by most citizens, policymakers, or even many corporations navigating the energy transition, is how much renewables—and thus distributed, proximate power—will require minerals to function at scale. Peter Bryant, chair of the consultancy Clareo (of which Rob is a co-owner) and a leader in the global "energy transition" debate, elucidates: "We are shifting from a fossil fuel intensive to a minerals intensive energy system. We now face a minerals famine in key minerals like copper, nickel, and lithium that will undermine reaching the 2035–2050 goals set by companies and governments. This supply chain risk is not well understood and is often only being superficially reviewed and analyzed."

What will be the cost of transformation? While important, it's not the question that should lead. Instead ask: In so doing, how much more *value* can we create? How much more flexible, secure, and healthy might our lives become?

Nikola Tesla recognized that when ubiquitous wireless power becomes real, all manner of wonders will become possible. In prophetic, immodest prose, he asserted, "It is difficult for the average citizen to comprehend or to form an adequate idea of the tremendous significance of this marvelous revelation of Nature, or the stupendous possibilities that the development and perfection of this discovery assure as a heritage to humanity."

The more proximate our power, the more proximate our lives, be they in Illinois, Texas, Estonia, or Bangladesh.

And you won't have to hook up your tractor when the lights go out.

8

How We Defend

WITH MICHAEL J. LIPPITZ

> • Food from thin air . . . literally.
> • More precise, more proximate.
> • Fast and smart defeats big and heavy. (Beware fast, smart, *and* big!)
> • Proximity of intent: "breaking the distance."
> • In virtual worlds, threats are ever at hand.
> • What decisions—and systems—will we cede to robots and AI?
> • Changing warfare changes society.

Proximity can be a matter of life and death.

In 2005 Adam Tiffen's unit in Iraq provided security for fuel convoys. "The demand for fuel was enormous," he recalled. "Tens of thousands of U.S. marines and soldiers required constant power. . . . Every single drop had to be transported into Iraq with an armed escort, and that meant troops on the ground and in harm's way." The unit that followed him lost Scott Nisely, "a marine veteran of Desert Storm and father of two, and Sergeant Kampha Sourivong, a young man two years out of high school. [They] were both killed when their vehicle received small arms fire while trying to secure their fuel convoy."[1]

One analyst estimated that 50 percent of casualties in Iraq and Afghanistan were related to convoys. *Half of the dead or wounded in those wars.*[2] *Just hauling fuel, water, and supplies.*

A few years later the U.S. Marines of India Company faced a particularly dangerous zone in Afghanistan: up to fifteen roadside bombs per day, with casualty rates as high as 25 percent killed or wounded. A Proximity strategy changed all that.

"At first I was a skeptic," said Gunnery Sergeant Willy Carrion, of the solar-powered generators he helped install at their base. The results were dramatic: "Camp Jackson, India Company's forward operating base, went from a noisy, easy target for insurgents to a silent, stealthy, safer outpost. The 20 to 25 gallons of fuel it previously took to power a platoon each day suddenly lasted more than a week—which meant fewer fuel convoys . . . fewer collisions with roadside improvised explosive devices, and fewer Marines assigned to convoy duty instead of their primary mission."[3]

It's often observed that militaries tend to plan for the prior war. Translating Proximity to military and security contexts will help us prepare for future conflicts—and hopefully even avert some.

Over the next decade, Proximity will transform defense and warfare in physical space. In emerging virtual worlds, it will become *essential*.

FROM ROCKS TO LONG-RANGE PRECISION MISSILES

Earliest days, all warfare was proximate: hand-to-hand combat among neighboring tribes using weapons fashioned from materials close at hand. Over the centuries, weapons became more sophisticated, enabling attack from greater distances: arrows to catapults to firearms to artillery to missiles; horses, chariots, and sailing ships to tanks, aircraft carriers, and jets. Targeting became possible from greater distances: spyglasses to radars to satellite imagery. Communications evolved from yelling or signaling by horn blast to sending battle plans wirelessly from halfway around the world.

Visionary theorists and commanders precede pivotal changes in practices, doctrine, training, and even strategy. Their visions typically manifest as some combination of new technologies such as stirrups, tanks or steamships, and new ways of organizing, such as the ancient Roman legion's dramatically faster, mobile modus operandi.[4]

Consider the world of naval historian Alfred Thayer Mahan. Entering the U.S. Naval Academy in 1856, he lived when steamships were overtaking sailing ships in military service. Mahan recognized the revolutionary character of the technology and documented how it inspired numerous other innovations. Steam propulsion, combined with the invention of the screw-propeller, "permitted the defense of the machinery by submersion, and of the sides of the ship by the application of armor," which naturally led adversaries to "the attempt to reach the parts which armor cannot protect, the underwater body, by means of the torpedo. The increases of weight induced by the competition of gun and armor led necessarily to increase of size, which in turn lent itself to increases of speed."[5]

Spurred by the Industrial Revolution, this age of "big iron" drove militaries to emphasize larger, faster, more lethal systems. This trend continued through World War II and into the 1980s, when digital technologies began to erode the value of large, visible, slow platforms. (The U.S. Navy retired its last battleship in 2006.) Microelectronics and information technologies began to replace "the fog of war" with "situation awareness." Weaponry could be smaller, lighter, and accurately delivered from long distances. Military control began to rely less on forces with the best or the most weapons and more on forces with better information and greater ability to quickly plan, coordinate, and accurately attack.[6]

The U.S. experience in Vietnam exhibited the potential of digitally enabled technologies: "On May 10, 1972, two Air Force pilots using laser designated BOLT guided bombs scored a direct hit on the Paul Doumer Bridge in South Vietnam, resulting in its destruction. Prior to this, the bridge had been bombed almost continuously for 3 years at the cost of 1,250 tons of munitions. The use of the BOLT system in one sortie of two aircraft had accomplished what the previous 1,500 gravity bombs and 200 sorties could not."[7]

A wake-up call for digital warfare came in the aftermath of the 1973 Yom Kippur War between Israel and a coalition of Egypt and Syria. U.S. general Donald Starry toured the battlefields in 1977 and concluded that

> combined tank losses in the first six critical days of the Yom Kippur War exceeded the total U.S. tank inventory deployed to NATO Europe—including both tanks in units and in war reserves. For those of us who craft new doctrine to reflect the new environment, one single statement became the goal: The U.S. military must decide how to fight outnumbered and win the first and succeeding battles of the next war at the tactical and operational levels—without wasting soldiers' lives, and without having to resort to use of nuclear weapons.[8]

Today, defense forces locate targets, coordinate actions, and create "kinetic effects"—military speak for blowing stuff up—swiftly and precisely. Minutes or even seconds might separate a decision regarding a target—"point of demand" in our parlance—and its disablement or destruction. Long-range precision strikes—such as missiles fired from drones flying as high as 50,000 feet that can hit within a meter of a target using just enough explosives to disable it—epitomize this trend.[9]

More precise, more proximate.

Defense forces generally aim to address a threat without hurting or damaging people and property nearby, known as creating "collateral damage." Precision enables us to accomplish what the mission requires with little or none of what it doesn't.

Today, digital capabilities, geopolitics, and the changing nature of conflicts catalyze a Proximity revolution in security and defense, from public safety and disaster response through low-burn conflicts and outright warfare. It changes what's possible, what's required, and even who's engaged. As Microsoft's CEO Brad Smith articulated regarding the Russian war in Ukraine, "The front line between Ukraine and Russia actually runs through Redmond, Washington."[10] We'll return to Smith's comment later in this chapter.

RAPID ITERATION, RAPID CHANGE

Rapid military response today generally requires mass-producing and warehousing weapons and other supplies that are *potentially* required to meet potential future challenges. "Just in case" is the traditional military mindset.

While much of the stockpiled equipment might still operate, it's nonetheless often many years old by the time it's called into action. That is, if it's called to action. Forces must make do with what's available even if a particular challenge was not envisioned or addressed by the bureaucratic supply process. Meanwhile, billions of dollars of equipment lie dormant for years, some—fortunately—never seeing action.

While forces will continue to require stockpiles at the ready, this legacy approach alone will not be enough. Digital technologies, many widely available, can translate to more rapid, volatile change in conflict zones as adversaries experiment in real time.

Defense and security challenges are cat-and-mouse games in which advantages shift as adversaries respond to one another's moves. Adversaries respond by exploiting what advantages they have and attacking superior systems at their weakest points.

The U.S. F-117 Stealth Fighter, first fielded in 1988, was a remarkable innovation: a plane nearly invisible to most radars and infrared detectors. Only one F-117 has ever been shot down: in 1999 in Serbia, during the Kosovo war.

It was felled by a combination of (1) spotters on the ground near Aviano Air Base in Italy, who alerted Serbian forces when three F-117s took off unaccompanied by electronic warfare aircraft that could detect enemy radar; (2) use of an operating frequency that would not be identified by a radar detection system (a relatively available technology at the time); (3) loading an anti-aircraft missile vehicle only half full, allowing it to move quickly into the expected path of the F-117s; and (4) a bit of luck. The moment the ill-fated F-117 pilot opened the bomb bay doors, he exposed the plane's very radar-reflective interior. The Serbian anti-aircraft team detected and attacked.

Far weaker adversaries increasingly rely on complex terrain (which long-range systems find challenging) and "asymmetric" approaches (think guerilla warfare) to mitigate the advantages of an army operating at a distance with precision strike capabilities. In mountainous regions and urban warfare, where adversaries may blend in with civilians, long-range imagery cannot identify specific individuals or detect small, concealed weapons.

Improvised explosive devices (IEDs) pose such threats. IEDs were responsible for more than half of U.S. and coalition combat deaths during the Afghanistan and Iraq conflicts.

The U.S. Department of Defense (DOD) moved rapidly—as measured in months[11] rather than years—to develop and field solutions. Small robots represent one of the more innovative responses. The "Fido" PackBot, fitted with a bomb-sniffing device, is an adaptation of a bot from robotics firm iRobot that was originally used in disaster relief efforts. At 42 pounds, it can be carried in a backpack. U.S. Army colonel Bruce Jette, who spearheaded PackBot deployment, went to Afghanistan in 2003 to show warfighters how to use the video-equipped robot, even joining search missions.

iRobot sent an engineer to Iraq to make fixes and improvements on the ground. When soldiers noted that radio signals were not penetrating the walls of deep caves, "Tom Frost, an iRobot engineer at the scene, built a makeshift network of radio repeaters by scavenging old Soviet trucks that littered Bagram Air Base. And when soldiers asked Frost if PackBot could work with the computers integrated into their clothing, he downloaded the necessary code over a satellite. The soldiers also scribbled a drawing of their idea for an extendable neck. The company was already working on that but made it a top priority."[12]

The result, known as BomBot, was effectively a remote-controlled toy-size truck. BomBot would take a 10-pound block of C4 explosive to a suspected IED at up to 35 mph, verify it was an IED, and then blow itself up. "The BomBot was manufactured in only 105 days from the contractual agreement to the first shipment date," said Congressman Alan B. Mollohan, who secured funding for prototyping and testing.

Meanwhile, insurgents quickly adapted by using ready-at-hand technologies such as garage door openers (used as detonators). In a sense, U.S. forces mimicked the rapid innovation cycle of their adversary, adapting commercial off-the-shelf technologies for military use, solutions often emerging from the field. Defined, designed, and delivered proximate to demand.

U.S. forces never fully solved the IED problem. The ongoing threat limited their ability to engage with local inhabitants. Developing rapport and trust with locals was one critical mission that proved additionally difficult as a result.

PRECISION ANYWHERE, ANYTIME

"Situation awareness"—intelligence on enemy and friendly locations and capabilities—used to require sending out scouts who (one hoped) would return in a few days. The information was often imprecise and stale by the time it arrived. Even the relatively sophisticated surveillance aircraft of the 1950s and 1960s had to return to base for their chemical-based film to be developed.

Today, satellites, digital imagery, and connectivity offer real-time surveillance images from nearly anywhere. Sensors, data analytics, AI, and geolocation technologies can unmask highly obfuscated targets and communicate that information to forces on the ground. Where distant systems are ineffective, tiny drones can provide immediate local intelligence.

Lighter precision weapons can be distributed across battlefields, reducing both the distance and delay of an attack or the ability to defend and secure. Some "smart" weapons powerful enough to destroy an armored vehicle are small enough for an individual soldier to carry and operate. They allow troops to successfully attack a target in minutes, rather than waiting up to an hour (or more) for an air or missile strike. Operating in closer proximity also enhances a force's ability to limit collateral damage to people and property. Networks of small units distributed over a large area might be able to hold off large, mechanized armies, as the world witnessed in the opening months of the Russian invasion of Ukraine.

Of course, adversaries might gain access to similar weapons; hence the need for iterative development and production of solutions in the field.

Instead of design, manufacturing, and logistics chains with long lead times, imagine Moment of Use (MoU) production for an ever wider range of military and security applications: converting raw materials and standardized, modular parts into finished products in days or even hours. What if Allied forces in World War II had had rapid development and production on-site for solutions based on real-time learning in the field?

MoU would represent a sea change for defense. Writing about innovation in IEDs—toy drones, for example, adapted to carry and trigger hand grenades—U.S. Navy lieutenant commander Jason Shell prescribes important changes (emphasis added): "To understand the networks that produce these threats and inform innovation and adaptation against them, specialized intelligence *resources will be required close to these new weapons systems* and the friendly forces encountering them. . . . [R]equirements for new countermeasures must be generated close to the battlefield. . . . [T]his may require *engineering, rapid prototyping, and testing capabilities closer to the fight. The U.S. military can no longer afford a homogenously equipped force when fighting localized arms races.*"[13]

The move to greater defense Proximity could engender the use of smaller, cheaper, more easily produced networked systems. Much of the innovation for such systems occurs in software produced in days or weeks by designers aided by low-code or no-code software development platforms and self-coding tools. What to do could be defined on the ground as conditions change.

DISTRIBUTED, PROXIMATE FORCES

The much-publicized U.S. Navy Seal Team 6 that killed Osama bin Laden illustrates the power of a small, local force. Few other small defense groups can execute such operations in complex conditions without heavy casualties. But new technologies have the potential to allow less well-trained forces to wield the flexibility of special operations.

The U.S. Marine Corps is undergoing just such a transformation. As early as 2023, it will no longer field tanks. (Imagine the Marines without tanks!) Lieutenant General Eric Smith explains the threat a small group of seventy-five Marines could pose. These small groups will "change the calculus" as they impede the adversary's ability to track them. "In the past you would think, 'well there's 75 Marines in location X, they're not a threat.' [What] if I can . . . rapidly move using things like our Joint Light Tactical Vehicle and make it incredibly hard for you to find me, both in the electromagnetic spectrum and physically on the ground because of my mobility. You have to respect that very small unit of which we will have dozens and dozens and dozens."[14]

Commanders and analysts have envisioned such proximate models for decades. They're only now becoming practical at scale. Researchers at the Institute for Defense Analyses envisioned twenty years ago how such "small unit precision combat" (SUPC) might operate:

> Prior to deployment, the SUPC cells are fully trained, their equipment containerized for airdrop. The cells can assemble within one hour of notification. Once alerted and enroute to the objective area, the Cell Commander begins mission planning in parallel with the Operational Commander's planning. . . .
>
> Once on the ground, the cell will immediately establish local security by relying upon robust intelligence assets, both in its possession and remotely. . . . It will "plug" into the system of air and ground sensors the Operational Commander established (with input from the Cell Commander). . . . As they develop the situation on the ground, they will adjust . . . as required.[15]

Supported by increasingly accurate battlefield information, command has evolved to instantaneous transmission of instructions and "commander's intent" (the mission, tools, and desired end state for a particular engagement). This readiness permits distributed forces to coordinate actions and adapt plans based on battlefield conditions rather than having to wait to communicate up and down a long chain of command.[16] Command could then migrate to local commanders, proximate to the field of operations. (That is, assuming higher-ups don't apply these technologies to micromanage.)

For distributed forces to understand the commander's broader mission, they need to understand how their commander thinks. The Israeli Defense Forces (IDF) call this "breaking the distance."

The IDF commit much time and effort to creating a psychological closeness—what we might call "psychological proximity" or more narrowly a "proximity of intent"—between soldiers of different ranks to enable autonomous decision-making by troops on the front lines. This closeness includes sometimes contradicting a commander's guidance when an opportunity presents in the moment. "Subordinates often address their officers by their first names—a custom that astonishes representatives of foreign militaries, who are subject to much stricter discipline and wonder how such familiarity can produce such a successful military culture as the IDF."[17]

HEARTS AND MINDS

Psychological Proximity is a pivotal factor for ultimate success: to win the "hearts and minds" of an adversary's population, rather than just their submission—often a more challenging objective.

As noted earlier, MoU capacities might have allowed the United States to more effectively counter IEDs and advance its hearts-and-minds mission. The failure to do so likely prolonged the conflict, allowing the spread of the Islamic State.

Orbiting satellites might reveal something happening on the ground, but that's often not enough for true situation awareness. One typically cannot understand what's going on without close-in observation and direct communication. Militaries call this "human intelligence" or HUMINT.

Going from occupation to peace and prosperity requires understanding context and culture, developing relationships and local human networks. Mobile, point-of-demand capabilities offer solutions to these nuanced, cross-cultural human challenges. For instance, rather than relying on more than fifty thousand local interpreters in the wars in Iraq and Afghanistan— who also put their lives at risk—what if technology had enabled real-time communication across local languages?

In 2001, the U.S. military in Afghanistan field-tested an early version of automated verbal translation called Phraselators. Select a phrase in your language and it speaks the prerecorded phrase in another language you select. At the time, such devices only translated one way and from a limited set of phrases.

By 2021, two-way spoken word translators had become so commonly available that *Rolling Stone* posted an "RS Recommends" for consumer versions.[18] Pocket translators were capable of translating your spoken words into a dozen languages or more, returning the favor for the person with whom you're trying to communicate. As perhaps a sign of human progress from conflict to love, advertisers often touted them as solutions for cross-cultural dating.

This evolution took twenty years. Perhaps a *Star Trek*-style Universal Translator is in our future?

MORE RESILIENT SUPPLY CHAINS, MORE RESPONSIVE SOLUTIONS

The COVID-19 pandemic highlighted the importance of supply chain resilience. Factory shutdowns around the world caused shortages and price increases that in some cases persisted for months. In response, many countries are seeking to relocalize production of critical materials and components.

While an understandable, practical response, doing so with traditional Industrial Age models will prove impractical for many situations or even downright wrongheaded.

MoU production represents a more responsive alternative. Instead of finished products, defense forces could inventory raw materials and standardized components, making only what's needed, responsive to changes in threats and conditions.

Don't expect a 3D-printed aircraft carrier anytime soon, but the DOD is already investing in R&D to eventually enable local, on-demand production of larger and more complex systems, from replacement parts to entire systems.

It's easy to imagine local production of small-scale systems that would enable the SUPC example described earlier. For instance, small, swarming weapon systems (think Alfred Hitchcock's 1963 thriller, *The Birds*) could be produced via AI-enabled 3D printing systems close to a battlefield.

In a warship, physical space is always at a premium, limiting space for storing spare parts. If a ship runs out of a critical part, the part might have to be flown in (at *very* high cost). Running out of critical parts could even compromise an entire operation.[19]

In 2014, the U.S. Navy equipped the USS *Essex* with a 3D printer that produced frames of small drones onto which motors and cameras were attached. These drones could be customized for different missions by simply downloading the design file over a satellite link. As of 2022, the *Essex*'s high-speed printers produced a range of replacement parts. Other ships are equipped to print surgical tools.[20]

More capable MoU production mitigates risks and enables more agile forces prepared for a wider range of challenges.

Beyond weapons systems, DOD's Defense Advanced Research Projects Agency (DARPA) is investing in transportable microreactors that could make food "out of thin air," using electricity to extract carbon, nitrogen, hydrogen, and oxygen from air and water to produce microbes that produce food molecules.[21] (You read that right: food from "thin air.") Telemedicine, combined with point-of-care testing and onsite pharmaceutical production (the effort of a U.S. Army doctor described in chapter 1), could result in dramatically reduced morbidity and mortality due to delays in diagnosis or treatment, such as in remote places or during disaster relief.

TOWARD A CYBER FUTURE

Cyber weapons epitomize Proximity. They can be deployed at the speed of light (literally) and operate, hypothetically, anywhere in the digital sphere. Half a meter or half a world away, physical Proximity is almost irrelevant.[22] They are both everywhere and nowhere.

Nikolai Kuryanovich, a former member of the Russian Duma, claimed in 2008 that "in the very near future, many conflicts will not take place on the open field of battle, but rather in spaces on the Internet, fought with the aid of information soldiers. . . . [A] small force of hackers is stronger than the multi-thousand force of the current armed forces."[23] Unlike traditional weapons and forces, cyber defenses can be raised within days or hours of a new threat being detected. As AI monitoring and response systems engage, responses can become nearly instantaneous. And so can threats.

The speed of cyber evolution and application means that Proximity becomes *essential*. Delay in meeting a threat could mean the difference between continued operations and catastrophic failure. Theft, damage, disruption, and manipulation of data and systems pose increasing risks. For defense forces such risks can be existential. Instantaneous situation awareness and command are useless (or worse) if information is sabotaged or weaponry is directed against unintended targets.

The speed and ubiquitous presence of cyber present new challenges for decision-makers. The need for rapid responses can compress decision-making times in counterproductive, even dangerous, ways.

One analyst makes a comparison with the impact of railroads on diplomatic and military strategy at the turn of the twentieth century. European great powers "placed a premium on deploying their forces before the adversaries did." Large-scale deployments generated ambiguities between nation-states regarding the purpose of the movements—offensive or defensive—potentially escalating tensions even if this had not been the intent.

Unfortunately, the logistics of railway mobilization meant that it was difficult to pause or reverse course. "Once mobilization began, it acquired too much momentum to be stopped in the amount of time that the complicated diplomacy to prevent war would have required."[24] This proved a factor in the months of crisis immediately prior to World War I. Proximity in this case—positioning and mobilizing assets for attack—favored the attacker, creating incentives to strike first.

In the nuclear Cold War standoff between the United States and the Soviet Union, this dangerous game compromised both sides' security. It led to the predelegation of nuclear launch authority to submarine commanders, who could act unilaterally in certain defined situations where a surprise attack might have prevented the president of the United States from giving the order.

Analogous situations arise in cyberwarfare, with grey areas between outright offense or defense, or where cyber teams are unable to be in contact with top commanders.[25] Moreover, the speed in which AI systems become empowered to wage offense and defense means that automated systems will often be *required* to counter an attack. Humans won't be able to respond fast enough.

Given this reality, *how much authority will we cede to software in environments that won't wait for humans to decide?*

Adding to the complexity, cyberwarfare blurs distinctions between military and civilian. Nearly anyone can launch an attack, from a government or corporation to a terrorist cell or individual hacker. Attacks on an adversary's infrastructure such as power plants or airports might be achieved by penetrating civilian information systems. Cyberattacks of this sort have the additional benefit of leaving the assets intact for peacetime operation. You don't have to blow it up to achieve your ends. Throttling a country's financial system could cause capitulation as panicked populations call on their leaders to seek a settlement, yet the infrastructure remains operational following the attack.

Cyber can also make it difficult to know who's attacking. That matters in geopolitics. Identifying the source of an attack is crucial to formulating who should respond and how. If an electric grid is bombed, the utility corporation that owns it is not expected to retaliate. That's accepted as a role for government. However, if a utility's network is hacked, legal authorities and responsibilities are less clear. Could an electric utility corporation launch a cyber counterattack against a foreign government or terrorist group as part of its defense?

Private companies have been critical to Ukraine's defense against Russia. Referring to the fact that Microsoft's Threat Intelligence Center detected Russian cyberattacks on Ukraine a day before the 2022 physical invasion, Microsoft's president Brad Smith commented, "The front line between Ukraine and Russia actually runs through Redmond, Washington."[26] (Microsoft alone reported providing almost a quarter million dollars of technology services as of June 2022.[27]) Cyberwarfare blurs the concept of sovereignty and distinctions between military and civilian.

The Russia-Ukraine war has also seen extensive cyberwarfare proximate to the battle. Smith explains, "What we see is almost potentially an early warning signal. If the Russian military wants to [physically] go into a new site, it may try to take the computers down an hour before the troops start getting close, or the artillery shells start firing."[28]

Moreover, citizens can engage, sending on-the-spot battlefield intelligence reports or broadcasting atrocities to the world as part of the public relations and propaganda front.

One would expect that the potential for limited collateral damage with minimal risk to the attacker would lower the political threshold for use. This is what we've seen thus far. Russia, North Korea, and others employ cyberattacks on a regular basis for a variety of objectives, from financial to geopolitical. The United States and its allies do so as well.

Analogous to "privateering"—government-authorized pirating against adversaries in the sixteenth to eighteenth centuries—some national governments have authorized criminal organizations to conduct cyber espionage.[29] Russia has for years been known to harbor cyber criminals with some version of this understanding: feel free to steal from others as long as you don't harm us—and be ready to act when we require it.

HUMANS OR ROBOTS? SECURITY OR OPPRESSION?

Robotic systems will be of particular relevance for advancing Proximity in security and warfare. Deploying robots in harm's way rather than humans. Doing jobs we don't want to, or can't, fulfill.

Connected, AI-enabled robotics will enable us to monitor, assess, protect, thwart, destroy, and repress nearly anywhere. In the same way that a surgeon halfway across the world can manipulate a robot while using familiar hand motions in an extended-reality environment, a soldier could be driving a tank. Such technologies have massive potential for defense and security—or offense and oppression.

AI and robotics represent the tip of this ethical spear, offering opportunities to remove humans from an expanding range of decisions. Without exploring the vast range of (terrifying) possibilities here, consider the power and threat of swarms of small, autonomous agents capable of deployment anywhere.

Could there be anything with more proximate potential than thousands of insect-sized agents with weapons of their own?

Already today AI systems defeat experienced fighter pilots in simulated "dogfights" (close-in maneuvering among jets in visual range).[30] Many fear that an AI arms race is under way that could pose an existential threat to humanity, akin to nuclear weapons.[31]

In 2018, four thousand Google employees petitioned their company to cease work on Project Maven, which applied AI to identify and track objects based on drone and satellite images. Two months later, Google indicated that it would no longer work on systems that could be weaponized (once its Maven contract commitments were completed).[32]

The Campaign to Stop Killer Robots, founded in 2013 to push counties to enact bans on lethal autonomous weapons, has been organizing tech workers against AI for weapons. Hundreds of technology companies have made a public pledge to "not participate nor support the development, manufacture, trade, or use of lethal autonomous weapons," and an international ban on such weapons is circulating at the United Nations.

Dystopian killer robots illustrate what the campaign terms "digital dehumanization."

Nonetheless, competition is likely to push countries toward greater weapon autonomy. Victory or defeat might depend on it.

Recognizing this pressure, a summit meeting of more than fifty countries—including the United States and China—met at the Hague in February 2023 to discuss, among other things, a U.S. declaration on "responsible military use of artificial intelligence and autonomy."[33] "We ask all parties to join us in adopting international rules as it applies to military research and use of AI," U.S. Assistant Secretary of State for Arms Control Bonnie Jenkins explained at the meeting.

Consider that AI systems, well designed and taught, have the *potential* to make "better" decisions. Robots can react faster than humans, do not fatigue, and do not suffer emotions. Robots can also minimize a force's casualties in battle. Fewer humans at risk.

Urban warfare, now common, is among the most dangerous venues for soldiers. Lieutenant General Jack Shanahan, first director of DoD's Joint Artificial Intelligence Center, forecasts, "We are going to be shocked by the speed, the chaos, the bloodiness and the friction of a future fight in which this will be playing out in microseconds at times."

What decisions—and weapons—will we cede to robots and AI? As General Shanahan suggests, decisions are likely to move so fast that we will become dependent on computational systems to cope.

And how might our perspectives change as we integrate enhanced capabilities with ourselves? Exoskeletons offering superhuman strength, AI and sensor systems amplifying our sensory and cognitive capabilities via direct brain-computer interfaces. These have been under development for years now, from military labs to commercial enterprises such as Elon Musk's Neuralink, advancing ever closer to application.

A future robot apocalypse works great in novels and films, but it's highly unlikely. It won't be us against the robots; it will be us against us, as it has always been.

METAVERSES, METACONFLICTS

While a Zuckerbergian vision of comprehensively virtual lives seems far off, imagine where virtual experiences might be in a generation. Virtual worlds where nearly any experience becomes P = 0.

As these worlds become more immersive, it's likely we'll live more aspects of our lives in them. Anything we come to value in these environments could be stolen, compromised, and even destroyed. Entirely new forms of warfare become possible.

One imaginative marketer created a speculative scenario based on already existing "play-to-earn" games, during which players earn resources to own NFTs (nonfungible tokens) in the form of game characters, weapons, enhanced powers, and so on. NFTs are sellable for actual currency. "Play-to-earn games have economic value in the Metaverse as well as in the real world. . . . If something valuable can be taken away, then there is something worth fighting for. . . . This means that a nation's status would no longer be determined by its resources and manpower, but by the gaming abilities of its people. Today's professional esports players could be tomorrow's cyber soldiers."[34]

The crash in NFT and crypto currency values in 2022 suggests that cyber assets will take time before becoming factors in geopolitical conflict, but how might such a scenario look after many of us have begun experiencing more of life online?

As immersiveness grows, so too will virtual worlds become more essential. We'll come to rely on them for more than meetings and entertainment: careers, resource access, social and community networks, even love. Thus they will also become targets. It's one thing to lose access to a video game, another to find daily life disrupted, even obliterated.

Millions of gamers already take their play versions rather seriously. Future conflicts might become wholly virtual, as mission planning, recruitment, training, and experimentation take place in metaverses. Then perhaps we'll see metaverse-centered warfare itself.

Researchers in the Chinese People's Liberation Army (PLA) have already begun imagining "Battleverses." Quoting an article in the *PLA Daily*,[35] an analyst at the China Aerospace Studies Institute refers to a future metaverse as a "highly developed cognitive world; in essence, a virtual extension of reality." The institute proffers the notion of "cognitive warfare," where opponents can influence, even attack, each other's perception, cognition, and action.[36]

As often paraphrased from Prussian military theorist Carl von Clausewitz, warfare is simply politics by other means. How much more attractive would it be to prevail via virtual reality and AI than by bullets and bombs?

The more immersive the experience, the more insidious the threats. Explosions announce themselves. Manipulation in the metaverse is likely to be camouflaged in moments and interactions of everyday life, potentially even to the extent of regime change.

Societies operate based on shared beliefs or, as anthropologists assert, "myths." Imagine what might become possible in comprehensively immersive virtual worlds. Instead of targeting assets and infrastructure, adversaries could directly target hearts and minds. Consider the following scenario:

> When you put on a headset and sink into the metaverse, you're immersing yourself in an environment that has the potential to act upon you more than you act upon it. . . . [S]ensors will track almost everything you

do and know exactly how you feel while doing it. . . . When processed by AI algorithms, this extensive data could be turned into behavioral and emotional models that enable platforms to accurately predict how users will react when presented with target stimuli. . . . [T]he controller can alter the world around the user, modifying what they see and hear and feel in order to drive that user towards the desired goal. . . .

. . . [T]he target user could easily believe (that avatars are other users) and not realize it's a promotionally altered experience that was targeted specifically at them, injected into their surroundings to achieve a particular agenda. . . . If metaverse platforms are allowed to adopt similar business models as social media, the reference goal will be the agendas of third parties that aim to impart influence over users. . . . Instead of pushing the features of a new car or toy, the third-party agenda could be to influence the target user about a political ideology, extremist propaganda, or outright misinformation or disinformation.[37]

It's one thing to follow media echo chambers. It's another to live within them.

WE'VE SEEN THIS BEFORE

When our ancestors transitioned from hunter-gatherer to farming-centric societies, access to dependable food supported expanding populations. Those populations coalesced around settlements. Once people were dependent on their land, defense of territory and infrastructure became essential.

Hunter-gatherer conflict has been characterized by skirmishes when interests collided. With low population density, small bands of humans could just move on. As populations rose due to agriculture, so did opportunities for conflict.

Migratory cultures dependent on herds of migrating animals presented a particular challenge for agriculture-based societies. If you're tied to the land, you're a ready target for aggressive mobile groups, such as the Huns and Mongols that terrorized the Eurasian continent for centuries.

As our lives evolve into virtual environments, conflict and warfare will change. Are communities in virtual spaces any less vulnerable than those in physical cities and towns?

It's too early to discern the details, but we can define a few ways that virtual worlds will be *differently* vulnerable.

1. Attacking and defending electricity sources and computing infrastructure will rise in priority. Electricity generation, computing infrastructure, and data storage must be designed for resilience and evolvability.
2. While our bodies will remain vulnerable to physical attack, our virtual lives can be more agile and evasive to attack to the extent that we design cloud infrastructure, virtual platforms, and data storage with redundancy and flexibility.
3. Attacking and defending datasets, AI systems, and algorithms will resemble cybercrime more than traditional warfare.
4. Our individual and collective cognitive vulnerabilities will intensify and require new forms of defense.
5. Myths—based to varying extents on "reality"—will become weaponized in proportion to how effectively they can become experienced as real.

Future virtual worlds pose analogous risks, with people being vulnerable to those capable of influencing, assaulting, or even controlling the algorithms that govern life. What new myths might arise that lead our descendants into conflict?

TRANSFORM WARFARE, TRANSFORM SOCIETY

Which future comes to pass may depend in large part on the relationship between civilian society and its militaries. Militaries are social artifacts whose roles go well beyond defending the state and its interests. Elliot Short, an analyst with the ironically named website War Is Boring, notes: "The military, through its actions in war, serves as the main generator of myths in a society, providing the raw material for tales of heroism and sacrifice to be woven into the national narrative, underscoring stereotypes, and offering populations a totem to rally behind in difficult times, all of which inform our notions of national identity. . . . The state offers legitimacy, prestige and privilege, and in return the military offers authority, power, and a means to unify the populations within the state."[38]

In one scenario Short envisions, "replacing human soldiers with robots will have a significant impact on the role which a military fulfills within a society. . . . A battle fought by robots, for example, would not provide the same tales of heroism and sacrifice as one fought by humans. There would be no memorial services, no rousing speeches, no one would say 'they died for their country,' weakening national identity."[39]

Offering counterpoint, Short references researcher Julie Carpenter's book *Culture and Human-Robot Interaction in Militarized Spaces*, which describes the common practice of soldiers to "name their robots, assign them human or animal-like attributes, including gender, and display empathy toward the machines."[40] When a robot soldier was lost, some military personnel even held funerals or wrote letters to the manufacturer, celebrating the machine's bravery. One robot named Boomer, who was lost in battle in Iraq, was given a funeral with a twenty-one-gun salute and awarded a Purple Heart and a Bronze Star.

We may see a time when robot soldiers replace human soldiers in the tales of heroism and sacrifice, offering the script for a new national narrative. Short poses a profound question: *Are we, as humans, able simultaneously to dehumanize our human enemies whilst humanizing the machines we send to kill them?*[41]

Few needs rise to the level of security. Our military and security forces, justice systems, and political institutions define and defend parameters of daily life, hopefully providing space for our pursuits of happiness. In virtual worlds anything will become available at hand, including threats. Thus must defense. Ever ready at P=0.

9

Proximity, Space, Virtual Worlds, and Lives We Desire

- Proximity converges to the limits of imagination.
  - In space, we'll have *nothing but* Proximity.
- Distributed infrastructure to enable anyone-anywhere worlds.
  - Multifold opportunities for "storymaking."
  - The more we're served, the more we risk losing control.
  - Physical inputs no longer required for the generation of sensory experiences.
- If you can generate nearly anything anywhere, who cares about moving anything anywhere?
  - When technology can do nearly anything, what should we do and *why*?

BRAVE NEW WORLDS . . . OR WORLDS WE DESIRE?

In 1949, following the publication of *1984*, George Orwell received a letter from his high school French teacher, Aldous Huxley. Huxley praised Orwell's work as "profoundly important."[1] He also expressed his belief that Orwell's dystopian future, one of oppression by surveillance and force, was less likely in the long run than his own vision published seventeen years earlier in *Brave New World*.

Rather than the "big brother" scenario of *1984*, already under way in Stalin's Russia, Huxley envisioned a World State that genetically engineered human beings for specific purposes within a strictly hierarchical society. The World State encouraged every individual to prioritize sensory fulfillment. Pursuing shallow hedonistic pleasures while avoiding deeper relationships was to be a human being's primary pursuit. Anyone lacking constant "happiness" was prescribed (required) to take doses of soma, a magical pharmaceutical provided gratis.

While describing quite different means, each future achieves similar results: conformity and oppression of individual will. But Huxley's presents a world to which most individuals willingly submit.

Huxley's dystopian future of automated, ever-catered-to desires represents one long-term potential threat of Proximity. Whatever we desire, anywhere, anytime. Orwell's specter of an ever present "big brother" suggests an alternative darkness of always-on monitoring. It's one to which many of us already acquiesce because doing so often leads to convenience and immediate gratification.

But there is another, more uplifting future. How might we wield technology to create worlds we desire rather than just resolving immediate urges? And how might we marshal desires to help us thrive?

Proximity models co-create our lives through constant interaction with our behaviors and desires. As technology becomes more capable of discerning and responding to what moves us, Proximity-enabled products, services, and experiences will shape the world around us. Our desires will result in changes not only from moment to moment, but also within our broader lived environments. Alexa's awkward attentiveness is a harbinger.

This is both inspiring and frightening. It's a path we must navigate if we hope to thrive.

We conclude by exploring two transitions that will characterize our twenty-first century. The multidecade rise of virtual worlds and humanity's aspirations to space ensure that Proximity will prove pivotal. Both have been under way for decades. Only now are they beginning to advance past modest forays beyond Earth and clunky virtual worlds.

Survival in space requires Proximity. Virtual worlds epitomize it. First let's review our Proximity journey thus far, then we'll venture to the future.

PROXIMITY RECAP

Throughout this book, we've explored recent advances and plausible futures. In each "How We" chapter, we can discern our Proximity principles in action.

1. *Moment of Use (MoU) production and provision* of products, services, and experiences: vertical farms, additive manufacturing, and generative AI, to name a few
2. *Data and analytics shared across ecosystems,* such as in "fresh food operating systems" in the food industry, distributed energy resources management (DERM) in power generation and distribution, and a wide range of platforms to support and coordinate remote work
3. *True customer centricity* in terms of deeper, real-time understanding of customer desires and the ability to fulfill them, such as on-demand production of everything from food and apparel to pharmaceuticals and media content
4. *Operating platforms that learn and adapt,* leveraging ever growing databases about more moments of our lives, endowed with increasingly capable AI and analytics: power grids dynamically coordinating between electricity sources and end user needs; manufacturing and distribution systems preempting and adjusting through disruptions; and media streaming platforms that serve us (pander to us, one might say) more effectively with each choice we make

For those of us whose loved ones have faced health emergencies that could have been prevented by early detection, we witness most poignantly these four principles in action. Health-monitoring systems collect data about more moments than ever before, employing analytics to discover threats and propose responses *before* they become an issue. In the process we are learning about each of us as *individuals* instead of as *populations.*

Fundamental will be ubiquitous access to reliable, safe, and sustainably generated electricity. What we've termed the second electricity revolution brings us ever closer to this ideal. *The more proximate our power, the more proximate our lives.* Our conversion of ever more value to digital form—from atoms to bits—requires more electrons where, when, and how we need them. All that we aspire to create in virtual worlds will depend on the widespread availability of two forms of power: computational and electric.

As we learned in chapter 4, "How We Eat," distributed power is *the* key to distributed agriculture. This in turn is a solution for accessible, resilient supplies of nutrition as humanity approaches 10 billion souls by midcentury (even, potentially, nutrition from thin air).

We've also seen how *changing where changes how.* We don't have to be physically proximate to add proximate value, though we must reenvision how we work, collaborate, and manage. We must bring decisions to each moment, supported by widely distributed and increasingly capable computing at the edges. Bringing care to patients rather than patients to the care means changing incentives, protocols, business models, and delivery platforms.

Proximity advises us to *produce when a customer's ready to buy—and not before.* Often this isn't yet possible. Over time, via widespread experimentation, the limits of Proximity will converge to the limits of imagination.

Nowhere will imaginations be more active than in virtual worlds and space. Let's extrapolate each to discover paths toward P = 0.

BEYOND EARTH: "WE'LL HAVE NOTHING BUT PROXIMITY"

On a ship for eight months on the way to Mars, anything and everything you might need must be on board. As Dorit Donoviel explained in chapter 2, en route "we'll have *nothing but* Proximity."

Proximity will be required for humans beyond Earth, at least until we're able to plant viable long-term settlements. We can envision in the far future settlements on Mars or elsewhere, with complex economies and supply chains. They'll be far different from what we have *today* on Earth.

The first settlements are likely to depend on what can be installed and operated at hand. Imagine you're building the first settlement on Mars. You'll only have what you've brought from Earth and resources accessible on your new planet. You and your compatriots will need to be self-reliant. Even if robots and machines build settlements prior to human arrival, they'll still depend on whatever they bring or source nearby.

Space movement pioneer Rick Tumlinson, founder of venture investor SpaceFund and the nonprofit Earthlight Foundation, imagines: "You're on a ship for months. After you leave Earth's bubble, if anything goes wrong, it will be up to you and your crew members to deal with it. With *anything.* Since no one can anticipate everything that could go wrong, expect the unexpected. Proximity on Earth might be for convenience. Proximity on a long space flight would be about life or death."

While Tumlinson sees the value of doctors, physicists, and Olympic-fit astronauts, he reasons that you'd also want people who can just figure things out and work with their hands. "You'll have the most advanced technology in human history, but if something goes wrong, you might need to know how to solder. Or signal in Morse code if your comms systems fail.

The early ships will be more like survivalist missions than luxury cruises. It won't be a billionaire's brief jaunt past the Kármán line."[2]

Tumlinson reasons that Proximity will be visceral, as the feedback loops between your actions and your environment will be immediate. "You'll appreciate Proximity every time you drink your own purified urine."

Even after interplanetary supply lines become possible, settlements on the moon and Mars will have benefited from decades of developing solutions that work on-site at great distance from Earth. Proximate solutions by definition.

Satisfying nutritional needs offers an essential example. It's unlikely that sufficient nutrition will come from the near void of space. Everything space travelers consume will need to be present, or grown, cultured, or created in some manner on board ship or on settlements. Even after we have successfully planted communities on Mars, nutrition will likely need to be generated on-site. If the Roanoke colonists, settlers of the ill-fated first English colony in the New World, had trouble managing through a couple of North Carolina winters, imagine doing so on Mars.

While this sounds like far future stuff—and it is—visionary researchers, technologists, and entrepreneurs are already developing solutions for these off-Earth needs. Some of them, like Interstellar Labs founder and CEO Barbara Belvisi, recognize that the solutions we develop for space are likely to have even more impact here on Earth.

At Slush in Helsinki, Finland, in 2019, Belvisi announced the construction of EBIOS, or experimental BIOregenerative stations, here on Earth. "Those are closed loop systems, completely sealed and environmentally controlled. . . . Inside the station, we recreate an ecological system for humans to live, to have access to food, water and to recycle all the waste."

Combining architecture, engineering, and life sciences with research partners from around the world, Interstellar Labs endeavors to discover how to operate habitats capable of supporting humans within self-sustaining ecosystems. Belvisi's vision is to "be the first ones who are going to put a little bit of life on the Red Planet" and to discover "how to use space technology back on Earth so we can learn how to live more sustainably."[3]

This multicentury journey will catalyze Proximity. Even IF science discovers mechanisms for nearly free transportation of physical goods over vast distances, our descendants will likely rely on proximate models as immediate needs change. Proximity is about anticipating, sensing, and responding with ever greater precision.

Besides, if one day we can generate nearly anything anywhere, who cares about moving anything anywhere? Especially if we can, eventually, find nearly anything in virtual worlds.

NO GOGGLES OR CLUNKY CARTOONS

Recall early video games. Blocks of pixels shooting blocks of pixels, yet people loved them. They've since become dramatically more realistic, even immersive.

Even so, metaverses are still clunky. You stand blindfolded and disconnected from the RL ("real life") around you as you slice Watermelons or battle ogres. (And you look rather silly.) In a generation, we'll consider what we have today as Paleolithic.

Ceyeber suggests our far-more-foresighted future. The ophthalmologic technology company invented the first implantable interocular lens, in its parlance a "smart lens."[4] The lens includes a camera, display, and communications module, designed to be implanted in a patient's eyes. The operation is a simple, tried-and-tested procedure known as a lens exchange. Such procedures have been around for over twenty years to resolve conditions such as cataracts.

Ceyeber founder Robert Edward Grant's long-term vision is to "develop ground-breaking, medical grade smart ocular implantables that . . . enhance human intelligence, augment perceived reality, and digitally capture experiences and individual memories." Potentially life-transformative, inspiring, *and* disquieting capabilities.

Yet the results needn't be dystopian. Imagine access to any information, anywhere, potentially one day replacing other mobile devices. You might never again worry about losing your smartphone.

Whether or not Ceyeber prevails, a range of similar technologies will one day offer immersive access to virtual worlds—and without goggles.

NEW WORLDS AT SCALE

Given the dazzling advancements in gaming—more immersive, realistic, and emergent—we might be tempted to believe virtual RL to be just over the horizon. Several constraints remain, some of which are wickedly hard. In his book *The Metaverse: And How It Will Revolutionize Everything*, Matthew Ball summarizes existing bandwidth, latency, and compute constraints using an example from the game Fortnite: "When a player sees their friend in Fortnite today they can interact using only a limited set of pre-loaded animations (or 'emotes'), such as a wave or a moonwalk. Many users, however, imagine a future where their live facial and body movements are re-created in a virtual world. To greet a friend, they won't pick Wave 17 of the 20 waves pre-loaded onto their device, but will wave uniquely articulated fingers in a unique way."[5]

Developers have used workarounds to resolve bandwidth and latency issues, such as preloading as much as possible onto a user's device and using hybrid local/cloud streaming to keep interactions up to date. The worlds we see are not like the "real world," our experience of which changes by the microsecond.

Current computational platforms aren't sufficient to render updates of too many users in the same virtual spaces in real time. Game companies avoid this problem by spreading users around virtual worlds and accounting for latency delays. While a platform like *Eve Online*, described in chapter 3, "How We Work," boasts over three hundred thousand players, they don't find themselves fully, *simultaneously* active in the same virtual environments, making decisions, interacting, and colliding. It's a hard technology constraint that might soon be overcome.

MetaGravity is one company on the trail of enabling *truly* scalable virtual worlds. Cofounder and CEO Rashid Mansoor's last company, metaverse infrastructure company Hadean, broke multiple records for hyperscale distributed computing. With MetaGravity, he and his partners are building a distributed computing infrastructure capable of overcoming the capacity limitations of large-scale, realistic virtual worlds. As the company describes it, this is "concurrency not limited by mathematics": distributed infrastructure to enable anyone, anywhere worlds.

FROM STORYTELLING TO STORYMAKING

Stories power culture. Collective myths provide structure and texture to our lives, organize us in ways that are varyingly functional (some work, others don't, and this changes over time). They also help us generate meaning in our lives.

The more users become *part* of the story, the more storytelling becomes "storymaking." Whereas theater, film, and other formats evolved to more effectively convey stories designed by their creators, we'll increasingly experience environments within which users and stories evolve together. Participants' decisions will impact the evolution and experiences of the "stories" they live. Different users might discover different experiences within the same "storyworld."

We can already see this in gaming, another storymaking industry. Compare 1980s gaming de riguer PacMan—essentially, move four directions and chomp—to the immersive, interactive experiences of multiplayer games such as Minecraft or Fortnite. Developments in gaming impact the evolution of virtual reality, film, and other storymaking industries.

Media content production is in the midst of a revolution, converging film, gaming, virtual reality, and even AI-generated deep fakes. For instance, "virtual production" studios allow nearly any scene to be filmed nearly anywhere. Sten-Kristian Saluveer, film innovator and head of Cannes Next for the Cannes Film Festival, remarks: "New, immersive experiences capable of being created with superb quality faster and, if done right, at lower cost. The best quality tech, like top virtual production studios, can still be super-expensive, and it takes serious work to figure out how to get the most out of virtual production. Many technologies and capabilities, though, are becoming available at lower cost to more people, meaning more content, more ideas, from anywhere."

As technology offers more comprehensive experiences, we'll all become storymakers. Experiences and plotlines will emerge around us from the aggregation of, and collisions between, our decisions as agents within complex virtual, or virtually augmented, environments. Stories will become shared experiences and evolve via social interactions.

One needn't replace the other. While we cannot know for sure, we believe humans will still value being *told* stories, allowing well-conveyed tales to wash over us. We'll also have new opportunities to co-create.

ONWARD TO P = 0: THE COMING POST-VIRTUAL WORLD

Where might we be on our Proximity journey a generation or two from now? *Our children and grandchildren will be empowered to generate comprehensive lived experiences from whole cloth.* Comprehensively experienced virtual worlds indistinguishable from "real life." This isn't even close to possible yet, but it's the direction we're heading.

Since 2016 Rob has been exploring this concept with neuroscientist Moran Cerf. We call this not-too-distant future age *post-virtual*.[6]

How far and fast virtual reality might advance will be the concerns of the next decade or so. Anyone living for a couple more decades will encounter a world where virtual reality and its cousins, augmented and mixed reality, become commonplace. Virtual reality will become capable of generating experiences that are experienced as comprehensively as what we've traditionally known as "real."

While today virtual and real are easy to distinguish, what happens as these distinctions fade? As this occurs, they are likely to become considered as alternative, complementary versions of experience. Reality from a wider palette.

We can already identify technologies that will enable this journey. We'll address two here: *invisible interfaces* and *intelligence-to-intelligence* (i2i) communications.

How do you move your arm? Do you remark, "Siri, move my arm," or punch a keyboard? Of course not. The interface exists and you're blissfully unaware. The same will occur with respect to our interactions with computing systems and eventually with one another: through invisible interfaces.

Human-computer interactions are rapidly moving beyond screens and keystrokes. Voice-activated human-computer interfaces (HCIs) that use natural language capabilities in smartphones are becoming common. As impressive as voice interfaces are, technologists have already surpassed these with direct mind-activated systems, or brain-machine interfaces (BMIs).

Currently BMIs are either not accurate enough to replace traditional methods or too invasive for widespread practical use. Nonetheless, thought activation of technology has already been demonstrated for applications such as the direct control of artificial limbs, illustrated by the work of John Donoghue's team at Brown University. In the long term this trend extrapolates to disappearing interfaces between brains and technologies.

Such interfaces could lead us to bypassing some established modes of communication. People might still desire keystrokes or voice interfaces, similar to how some people prefer a handwritten letter to an email. Nonetheless, as BMI technologies become more capable, they are more likely to become mechanisms of choice for a wider range of applications.

If brains can interface directly with machines, then two or more brains could potentially interact directly as well. In 2013, Miguel Nicolelis and his team at Duke University electronically connected the brains of two rats, perhaps the first demonstrated brain-to-brain interface.[7] Transmission and translation across invisible interfaces will enable seamless communications between humans, or between various forms of intelligence. This will be true *intelligence-to-intelligence* communications, or *i2i*—metaphorically, *eye-to-eye*.

As our understanding of language advances, the ability to parse content generated in the brain, deriving and conveying meaning, could enable us to overcome the spoken language barrier, to transfer a thought from one brain—human, artificial, or cybernetic—to another without the need for *verbal* communication. Verbal communication will likely remain essential for humans, but we have no way of knowing the choices our descendants will make after they have assimilated i2i capabilities.

Sensory and cognitive systems seamlessly supplementing the biological brain could support a range of activities without conscious thought, analogous to the autonomic nervous system controlling basic living functions. A genius of such systems would be the continuous operation of essential functions in the absence of conscious intervention.

TOWARD A WIDER DEFINITION OF REALITY

As we and virtual reality adapt to each other, the notion of virtuality will change, perhaps fading altogether. (Again, long run.) What we generate and experience, with increasingly subtle, disappearing interfaces, will in this scenario become recognized as additional aspects of reality—wider and more diverse, yet no less "real."

Consider the experience of dreaming. During sleep the brain generates a rich environment with realistic, if sometimes bizarre, encounters. Only upon waking do we realize it was a dream world. Current virtual reality systems fail to generate such comprehensive experiences. We know we can remove the goggles and exit. In most dream states, the choice to exit does not seem operative. Since we trust our senses more than we might recognize (e.g., we rarely question what our eyes present), an interface capable of thwarting cognitive disbelief might support experiences interpreted as real, generating emotions and thoughts.

One of the first examples of a filmed scene presented to a live audience, *L'Arrivée d'un train en gare de La Ciotat* (August and Louis Lumière, 1896), showed the arrival of a train into a station. As the steam locomotive approached, more realistically than ever before, journalist Hellmuth Karasek commented in *Der Spiegel* that "it caused fear, terror, even panic." While historians debate the intensity of the reaction, many who experience recent virtual reality technologies report dissonance, even fear. Walking off a simulated cliff creates a notoriously uncomfortable, even frightening emotional response—even while you're "in reality" standing on solid ground. You know you'll not plummet, but reflexes overtake rationality.

The only way we experience what we know as reality is through stimuli collected by our senses, converted into electric signals that are interpreted by our brains. The only way we'll know that a well-simulated reality is simulated is that we'll know it's a simulation. Absent another frame of reference or qualifying information, simulated stimuli could one day generate experiences identical to reality.

If we can simulate the experience of "real," we can invent new experiences such as the feeling of flying unaided: no longer simply pale simulacra, but fully lived experiences. Our dimensionality of "real" will expand and diversify, subsuming what we today consider virtual.

The post-virtual world is coming. Our concept of reality will need to evolve. When virtual environments become indistinguishable *experientially* from RL, we'll be in a post-virtual world. No one will ask a stupid question like "Should we meet in the 'real' café or a virtual one?" This distinction won't make sense (especially when you'll eventually have the physical *experience* of eating cake and drinking coffee). We will develop a dimensionality of experience, rather than a binary concept of real versus virtual.

Nothing could be more proximate. In the post-virtual world, any experience becomes possible, for most purposes regardless of your physical location. Whatever, wherever, whenever. We will have arrived for most of our lived experiences at P = 0, with experiences created, produced, and provided in real time in response to our behaviors and desires, implicit or explicit, productive or destructive.

To be clear, we are *not* making date predictions. But with a rest-of-the-century horizon, post-virtual is where we're heading.

NOT HAVE YOUR CAKE—AND EAT IT, TOO

Fantasize the meal you would enjoy with no constraints—the most fat-filled, sugar-fortified buffet you can imagine. Now imagine you could enjoy this meal without any calories. *The holistic, visceral experience without ingesting any food.*[8]

Consider eating a chocolate cake. Eating feeds data to our cognitive apparatus. The enjoyment isn't in the cake per se, but in our neural processing of it. Decoupling our sensory desire (the experience of cake) from the underlying survival purpose (nutrition) will soon be within our reach: being able to *not have our cake and eat it, too.*

Physical diets released from the tyranny of desire. In such a world, we'll be able to fulfill nutritional requirements with a narrower supply of inputs. Think Soylent Green, but far more advanced (and not made of people).[9] Nutrition customized for each person based on genomes, microbiomes, or other factors. The social, sensory, and culinary aspects of food delivered via computational systems. (Again, we're extrapolating across the *century.*)

Think of the sustainability implications. Thousands of ingredients currently grown and shipped around the world to fulfill culinary demand—spices, exotic ingredients, meats, fruits, anything that generates culinary enjoyment—would no longer be required for the sensory encounter. Some of us will decide to seek the "real thing," but this will be a *choice* and likely far more expensive (though who knows?).

OVERCOMING TRADE-OFFS

Decoupling provides the prospect of transforming our ecological and ethical impact. Appealing to rationality and compassion to change human behavior has not worked especially well. Smoking and unhealthy diets kill, yet millions still indulge. Even among populations convinced of human-influenced climate change, behavior change has often required government edicts.

One ethical and environmental dilemma we all face is the scale production of meat. Animal husbandry is a potent contributor to climate change. Most people recoil in disgust or shame when presented with how the animals are treated. Despite the ethical predicament, most people continue to consume. Desire rationalized by cultural norms overwhelms ethics for otherwise compassionate, well-meaning people. Decoupling offers a palatable way out.

In such a "decoupled" world—physical inputs no longer required for the generation of sensory experiences—material inputs would be relevant only for survival benefits, such as the mechanistic purposes of survival: feeding, fighting, fleeing, and mating.

SEXUALITY AND RELATIONSHIPS IN A DECOUPLED WORLD

Virtual sexuality solutions have existed for thousands of years, such as pornography, but are caricatures of the real thing. In a world of comprehensively experienced virtual reality, sexual, social interactions between humans and/or simulations will beget new forms of sexuality. Technology-mediated sexuality will complement and might even eventually replace the original for some people. Imagine an AI system designed to respond optimally to individual preferences. Now imagine the prospect of finding a bona fide human companion able to compete sexually. No longer science fiction, our understanding of the mechanisms governing sensation and cognition will later this century likely enable such simulations.

This proposition feels disquieting. It presents a world quite different from our own, though we have a precedent. Pornography can already create unrealistic expectations between human partners. Studies show that three repeated exposures to a specific pornographic flavor often shape the viewers' taste. Extrapolate this to a world where intense, diverse sexual experiences are widely available. While such abundant access to stimulation might cause people to retreat from one another, it is also possible that the role of sexuality in human relationships will change. How will we seek relationships, feel human connections, and build trust in such a future?

Note that sexual compatibility between individuals often fails to correlate with other factors that constitute healthy relationships. Might decoupling liberate the complex interplay between sexuality and relationships? A wide range of sexual encounters might be possible with or without other human beings. Some individuals might be encouraged to engage more often in nonsexual yet intimate relationships without concern for physical compatibility. "He (or she) has a great personality" might acquire new meaning.

Might some of us become victims of seeking ever more intense experiences, like addicts seeking ever larger doses? It will be essential to better understand mechanisms of dependency. Alternatively, widespread availability might *decrease* desire. The experience will always be available, thus less dear. Economist Thorstein Veblen's concept of conspicuous consumption might unravel in a world of experiential abundance.[10]

CAUTIOUSLY TO THE FUTURE

Humans have always sought satisfaction divorced from consequences. It just hasn't worked that well. Diet soft drinks and pornography promise flavor without calories. Neither provides an experience identical to the original. Each generates new problems.

Virtual existence could negatively impact physical activity, yet we will remain (at least for some time) physical beings. We will require new approaches to physical and psychological wellness—already enormous business opportunities.

Decoupling could even threaten our survival. Our brains have not evolved to distinguish between the *sensations* of consuming food or having sex from the *actual* activities. Experiments with rats pitting the need for food against the desire for direct stimulation of neural pleasure centers resulted in what must have been a bleary, euphoric death. *Some of us might choose oblivion.* The hopeful extension of this experiment expanded the mice's options to include social interactions. For most of the mice, their desire for engaging with other mice mattered more than quick hits.[11]

THE MORE WE'RE SERVED, THE MORE WE LOSE CONTROL

The customer as king is a tired metaphor. It's also increasingly accurate.[12]

In childhood stories, we read of kings and queens as benevolent, grandparently sorts or malevolent tyrants. Either way they wield a seductive power. We aspire to be the prince despite the burdens and risks of kingship. Prince Hamlet met an unhappy ending due to forces conspiring from within and without. Death arrived *before* the invading armies.

How would you cope with a constant entourage? Guess what? Like monarchs of old, we've each acquired one, though most of us haven't noticed. Companies, governments, and their systems seek insights into our locations, preferences, and even needs we didn't know we had. We have more choice and access due to competition to serve us at increasingly granular levels.

This situation leads to a consumer conundrum. The more we're served, the more we lose control.

Efforts to serve will become increasingly invasive, deeply personalized, even personal. Today, various players know our browser histories. Tomorrow, what more will be visible with both scale and specificity? How much better will you be served based on your fully mapped genome?

David Krakauer, president of the Santa Fe Institute, likens the data analytical capabilities applied by internet platforms like Google, Amazon, and Alibaba to "brain scanning a billion people."[13] How far will we allow, even encourage, this to go? Regulatory regimes regarding personal data will evolve, but the more we restrict, the less responsive companies can be—and we love convenience.

Regardless of our preferences, like monarchs we are often unaware of machinations under way to understand, influence, leverage, serve, or exploit us. Legions of systems, some we know and most we don't, are seeking to serve, manipulate, and even sabotage us. If you'd prefer to disengage to protect your privacy and sense of control, consider what conveniences and opportunities you'd forego.

Don't begrudge the companies alone. We're building this difficult-to-satisfy society together. As colleague and serial entrepreneur Howard Tullman often quips, "What's WOW today becomes 'so what?' tomorrow." The war for customers intensifies. We are both commanders and victims.

It's not all bad news. Imagine our lives without the efficient, intrusive services of Amazon, Uber, and thousands of yet-to-be-envisioned startups. As we give up control, we're serviced in return.

Consider counsel from one of history's philosopher kings, Marcus Aurelius. "You have power over your mind—not outside events. Realize this, and you will find strength." Aurelius underscores the power and responsibility of *attention*. King customers wield the thumbs up or thumbs down at the Colosseum. Meanwhile, who might be conspiring back at the palace?

ATTENTION AS OUR ESSENTIAL QUESTION

The post-virtual vision of the future underscores how real and pervasive Proximity could become. Any experience, wherever, whenever, requiring only electricity, interfaces, and computational power. The prospect of living $P = 0$ lives.

As increasingly adroit systems—and the companies and interests behind them—advance, each of us will face the essential question of attention, our most limited resource. Automation frees our attention for activities of choice rather than necessity. The Agricultural Revolution released much of humanity from subsistence-level food production. To the extent that necessities of life become more widely available—a critical "if"—more of us will have the option to seek intellectually, emotionally, and experientially engaging activities, or to wallow in sensory surplus.

On what to attend becomes an imperative question for each of us. This is our challenge when faced with anything, anywhere, all the time. One person's distraction could be another's transcendent ritual. The postmodern world deconstructs traditional definitions of value, opening new horizons while fermenting confusion, anxiety, and discord. Unlimited options can paralyze.

The philosopher and a founder of the field of psychology William James asserted in the late nineteenth century that *"attention equals belief." Equals* belief through an iterative process. To what we attend stirs and sways our beliefs, which in turn bias our attentions, moving ever closer to equivalence. The impact of social media on our social-political institutions offers a poignant example.

WHAT SHOULD WE DO?

Over time, AI and robotic systems will overtake more of what humans have traditionally done. What decisions will we cede to AI? How will our roles evolve to not just survive, but to thrive?

In 2018 in the *Harvard Business Review*, Rob asked, *"When technology can increasingly do anything, what should human beings do, and why?"* This question will define our century.

Over decades, automated systems will become more capable than we humans at nearly everything. Even our humans-remain-special safety blankets like creativity and empathy will succumb to technology, at least from a *pragmatic* perspective. Perhaps AI systems will not "feel" empathy as we do, though this distinction hardly matters if they are capable of *using* empathy to accomplish objectives—including to manipulate us. Ethical and metaphysical questions abound.

The market mechanism, driven by efficiency, ensures that we will be best suited to *stop* doing many things. Actuaries hold high-prestige, high-paying jobs. In the near future, AI systems will outperform any human's ability to execute standard actuarial tasks. The mission of actuarial science will remain. How it's accomplished will transform.

As in past transitions, humans will discover new roles, solve problems in new ways, and solve new problems. But this time change will happen faster. Electrification of manufacturing in the late nineteenth century took twenty years to diffuse to *half* of all relevant facilities in the United States. From its consumer launch in November 2022, generative AI system ChatGPT reached 100 million users by January 2023, making it likely the fastest-diffusing nongame application in history.[14]

We're heading toward an elusive search for relevance. Fortunately, AI won't simply lead to an "us-versus-them" robot apocalypse. These technologies will be integrated with our cognitive, living, social systems. As ever, our greatest challenges will remain us versus us.

WHAT LIVES DO WE DESIRE?

Environmental, economic, and geopolitical factors accelerate our path to P = 0. Ambitions in space require proximate solutions, while automation and virtual worlds make more possible anywhere.

When anything becomes possible, we must question what we desire. Sensor and surveillance technologies (à la Orwell) invade our lives, enabling stunning responsiveness via systems that sometimes know more about us than we know ourselves. On-demand designer drugs (though not yet mainstream) and encompassing virtual experiences (à la Huxley) covet our attentions.

What futures will we create? Which will we seek to avoid?

Answers to these questions will be both under our command *and* out of our control. Early twentieth-century philosopher and mathematician Alfred North Whitehead observed, "Society progresses by increasing the number of things we can do without thinking." Both an admonition and an invitation as our lives advance toward P = 0.

To what will we turn our attentions? A defining question, indeed.

Appendix

A Proximity Strategy Workbook

ADVANTAGE SHIFTS TO PROXIMITY

Throughout *Proximity*, we've explored the evolution of industries toward P = 0, our conceptual North Star for where things are heading, and met people and organizations leading the way. Here we offer a workbook to help you and your colleagues convert Proximity to competitive advantage.

Proximity offers foresight and a framework for reenvisioning business models, building new capabilities, and even redefining industries.

We're not asserting that Proximity, as a competitive advantage, is entirely new. Rather, we argue that digital technologies expand the frontiers of Proximity, removing constraints and trade-offs, advancing ever closer to P = 0.

Any company that wants to remain competitive in the long run should seek to understand and translate Proximity into its contexts.

We propose that this process involves two steps:

1. *Make the Proximity leap*: Discover and advance near-term opportunities.
2. *Lead the trend*: Move ever onward to P = 0.

Make the Proximity Leap: Discover and Advance Near-Term Opportunities

Several companies have already been seizing the advantages of Proximity. For example, if in 2016 you decided to bet $10,000 on Domino's

Pizza's focus on Proximity, your investment would have been worth nearly $40,000 by the close of 2021. The same wager of $10,000 on Pizza Hut's owner, Yum Brands, would have been worth just under $15,000. Your investment in Domino's Pizza would have outperformed the same bet on Google ($26,530) or the S&P 500 ($20,863).

This performance was very much due to the old-school pizza franchise's decision to lean into Proximity around 2008. Leaders realized that the value it delivered could be about far more than the right pizza delivered hot and on time. Easy online customization and dependable, transparent delivery became reasons to buy—customizing orders and then tracking them from assembly through delivery.

Domino's created an industry-leading customer digital experience. Given its years of building digital capabilities, Domino's outflanked most competitors during the COVID-19 pandemic. Recognizing that information travels faster than pizza, Domino's collapsed the distance between its consumers and the experience of ordering, delivering, and enjoying its products. Domino's is not alone. History shows us that companies that embrace the potential of Proximity early can create an enormous advantage. Across numerous sectors (e.g., retail, mobility, pharmaceuticals, financial services), fortune favors the proximate. Companies such as Amazon, Alibaba, BMW, CVS, Nike, Porsche, Takeda Pharmaceuticals, Tesla, and Zara all offer examples of producing and providing what customers want in new ways closer to actual demands, and the payoff of doing so.

Behind the lines, we find a cohort of companies arming these Proximity competitors with the technologies that will enable us to reach new levels of Proximity. We looked at 580 companies in the portfolio of exchange traded funds (ETFs) that are focused on key Proximity technologies, such as 3D printing, the metaverse, robotics, AI, IoT, and space, and found 27 companies betting on three or more of these, including NVIDIA, UiPath, Unity Software, Velo3D, Trimble, PTC, Ansys, Microsoft, Qualcomm, Intel, and Teradyn.

The provision side of the equation is ripe with examples worth considering. Amazon's fulfillment strategy is an example. It has invested tens of billions of dollars—as of this writing, close to 10 percent of its sales—to establish fulfillment capabilities closer to consumers. As of 2021, 77 percent of the U.S. population was within an hour's drive of an Amazon delivery station, up from 50 percent in 2018.[1] By contrast, Amazon's attempts to win in China failed. One factor appears to be that Alibaba and other local competitors had already achieved significant coverage of customers across the vast country.

While Proximity advances have been more visible in the *provision* of products, services and experiences (from video streaming to rapid product delivery), technological advances, and digitalization are advancing Proximity in *production* as well (no-sew garments and laser-finished jeans, pharmaceuticals, leafy greens, and automotive replacement parts, for instance).

Automaker Porsche, for example, took an unconventional approach in designing its next generation of production capabilities. It launched a 50–50 joint venture with Schuler, a press manufacturer, to create the Smart Press Shop (SPS).[2] This flexible press shop specializes in efficiently producing small lot sizes via advances like fully automated tool change-over, camera-based tool monitoring, and laser blanking lines.[3] This approach provides Porsche with greater customization capabilities, which it can use to produce parts for other VW Group auto manufacturers, as well as to service external manufacturers. "We made production-as-a-service tangible in the Smart Press Shop and proof that PaaS [Production as a Service] can be realized today, even on a larger scale," says Christian Hoedicke, the operation's managing director.[4]

Amazon and Porsche illustrate that Proximity models are evolving fast. Research and experience recommend four steps for identifying and prioritizing opportunities to generate Proximity-based advantages:

1. Envision P = 0 in your domain. What might your industry look like if the value that industry players create could be produced and provided *immediate* with demand?
2. For each production and provision of value (product, service, and/or experience), brainstorm all the barriers (e.g., technical, social, regulatory) preventing production from approaching P = 0 (e.g., MoU production). Likewise, identify all the barriers that limit the provision of some value (product, service, and/or experience) as close to P = 0 as possible. Then narrow this list to the priority barriers that, if solved, could make the biggest impact.
3. For each production and provision, brainstorm trends that might enable advances toward P = 0 (things like technologies, social change, and regulation). Narrow this list to the priority trends that, if leveraged, you think are likely to have the most significant impact.
4. Leverage the barriers and trends generated in steps 2 and 3 to brainstorm a list of opportunities, combining and redefining them as appropriate. Prioritize this list while considering each opportunity's potential impact for

your business, the effort you imagine it might require to implement, and the likelihood of eventual success.

Step 1: Envision P = 0

P = 0 is a hypothetical state that in most cases is not physically possible. It can be represented visually as shown in figure A.1.

When production appears in the upper left corner of this graph, you're *producing* at great distance well in advance of demand, perhaps manufacturing a ladder months in advance of a consumer eventually purchasing it from a Home Depot store. On the upper right side of chart, you might be *delivering* (a component of "provision") that ladder to a customer only after they've placed an order from a warehouse many miles away. The plots at the bottom center of the chart represent a product, service, or experience produced *and* provided immediately close to demand: P = 0 in our parlance. An example would be a 3D printer generating physical products on demand at your home. Of course, the printer will require raw materials in usable form, perhaps a powder in a cartridge, and that cartridge will be produced and provided much earlier. Nonetheless, the kitchen utensil you print at home is produced and provided at P = 0.

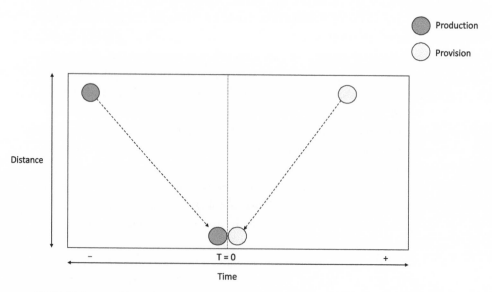

FIGURE A.1 Envisioning P = 0.

Here is an exercise we call "twenty years from now." (Don't worry about the specific time frame. We recommend a twenty-year horizon to release thinking from current paradigms. Chose whatever horizon works for your situation.)

Imagine you grow and process plantains (as one of our clients does) into packaged food goods sold in grocery stores and schools. It's an efficient model by traditional standards (and the product is great), but it's not a "proximate" model.

Now imagine how in twenty years this same product could reach P = 0. (For this exercise, do NOT let reality get in the way! It's an exercise.)

For instance, at the point of demand an AI system operating a middle-school cafeteria decides to offer fried plantains for lunch, just as the first wave of students line up. At that moment, somehow (don't worry about how, for this exercise), plantains are grown from a seed, ripened, cut, fried, and placed on the plates of students who, perhaps through a predictive algorithm, are known to desire plantains for lunch.

Each element of this hypothetical vision can be characterized by one of the following: (a) currently feasible and in operation (e.g., the placing of fried plantains on a plate), (b) currently feasible but not practiced (e.g., predicting which children will want to eat plantains), or (c) currently not feasible (e.g., growing a plantain from a seed within the time it takes a student to step to the front of the line).

The goal in this exercise is to exercise your mind to envision how Proximity could look in future worlds. Be bold and creative. The more audacious your ideas, the more effectively you can identify barriers and, through the process, generate compelling ideas that *could* be pursued within the near to medium term.

And these visioning exercises help you consider ideas for the longer-term future. As breakthroughs launch into your industry via visioning exercises like this (there are many others), you'll have a higher likelihood of seeing them coming. This also means that you and your colleagues will have the opportunity to consider implications and prepare before it's a marketplace scramble.

The goal is to practice "mental time travel," envisioning futures not yet realized from which you might be able to collect relevant ideas for experimentation, prototyping, and in some cases eventual market launch.

Here's an approach we love to get big ideas moving. We call it "no need for focus groups." All we'll need is a customer's desire.

As you explore paths to P = 0, pose a critical question: What value can we have *great* confidence that customers would desire if someone could provide it? The Netflix founders didn't wonder whether humans would want to have any video they want, anywhere, anytime. OF COURSE THEY WOULD. How and what to do so, at what cost, on what equipment—those were uncertainties, but the *desire* to have any video anytime was pretty darn clear.

While most customer desires aren't so obvious, there are many more than you might at first imagine. Mobile phones: What if you could have a phone anywhere, anytime, without a wire to a wall socket? Duh.

Here's an example for the future (at least as of this writing). How about mobile devices that don't require recharging for weeks or months? Crazy? Just wait. In any case, this is an example of what we're saying: IF someone could provide this economically, safely, and reliably, everyone would want it.

Step 2: Brainstorm Barriers

Creating a vision of this ideal, but not yet possible, future will naturally uncover barriers that would have to be overcome to reach this ideal state. The key in this stage is to frame these barriers not as reasons why P = 0 will never work, but rather as problems to solve. If someone complains, "You can't gestate a seed into a ripened fruit in seconds," you want to rephrase this truth as something like "To reach P = 0 we would need to be able to generate a fruit, or some *version* of a fruit, in seconds." Perhaps not a fruit, but instead a food with all of the eating-like properties of a fruit? For instance, a "real" fruit includes seeds that can blossom into new plants. For eating purposes, that's not necessary. Get to the essence of the value being created. In the case of a fruit for consumption by a middle-schooler, it would be for energy, nutrition, and, one hopes, enjoying a satisfying lunch.

At this stage don't adopt an "assessment" mindset (asking, "is this possible?"). Rather, maintain a problem-solving mindset (asking, "what could we do or change to make this, or something sufficiently similar, possible?").

Barriers will naturally fall into four buckets. They will relate to production, provision, time, or space, as illustrated in figure A.2.

Here is a worksheet (figure A.3) to organize your work.

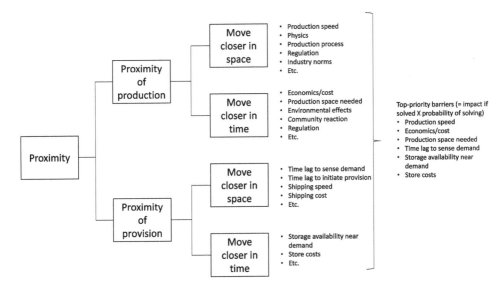

FIGURE A.2 Barriers to overcome for Proximity.

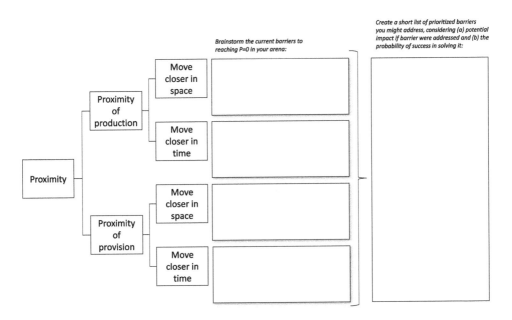

FIGURE A.3 Barriers worksheet.

Step 3: Brainstorm Trends

Barriers change. Over time, some become more daunting while others fade. Shifts in technology, regulation, economics, and sociodemographics make challenges that were once critical trivial to overcome. This is why it's important to consider barriers, as they might change over time.

All sorts of trends can contribute to an exploration such as this, but technology trends should play a critical role in your brainstorm. They change, and we can often see where they are likely heading. Microprocessor power? For decades, faster. Battery life? Longer (per volume). AI? More accurate and relevant to task. Select technologies that you believe are likely to impact your industry and project them to the future. What barriers might fall when you do so?

Sometimes you can see things coming. When the Netflix founders envisioned video streaming in the mid-1990s, streaming full movie files in real time was impossible for nearly everyone. They recognized that compression technologies and internet bandwidth would continue to improve. One day video streaming would become not just possible, but ubiquitous. They committed to being ready.

What barriers might fall soon in your industry? What development paths are likely to advance over the longer term about which you can have deep conviction? You might not be able to predict now, by when, or by whom, but you can discover reasons to believe that technology will advance to make relevant capabilities possible in the medium to long term.

Here is a way to organize your exploration of trends relevant to Proximity (figure A.4). Again, by production or provision, time or space.

Here is a worksheet (figure A.5) to organize your work.

Step 4: Brainstorm Opportunities Suggested by the Barriers and Trends

The best near-term Proximity opportunities address barriers that are (a) valuable if taken down, and (b) closer to being overcome. Map the import of the barriers to the closeness of their resolution. Ideally, we focus on highly valuable barriers that are close to a breakthrough. These will give us the greatest advantage for our effort.

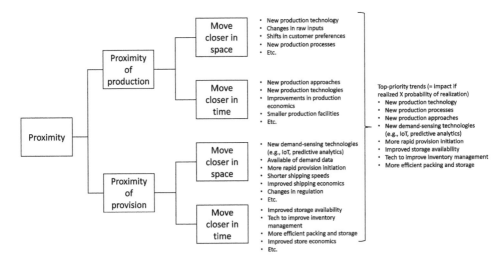

FIGURE A.4 Trends relevant to Proximity.

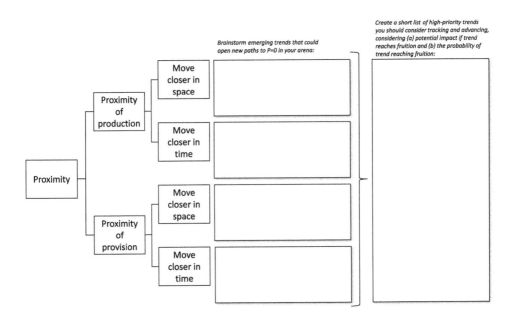

FIGURE A.5 Trends worksheet.

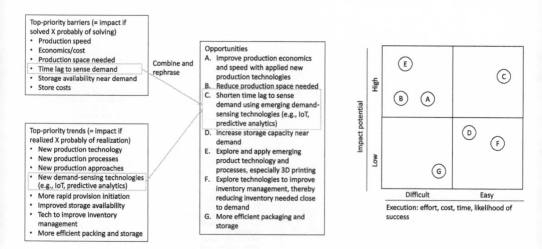

FIGURE A.6 Proximity opportunities posed by barriers and trends.

You can accomplish this process via three steps:

1. Mine the lists of barriers and trends to brainstorm opportunities to advance Proximity. These could be quick wins, medium-term opportunities, or concepts requiring long-term commitment.

2. Map these opportunities onto a matrix according to ease of implementation (effort, cost, time, and likelihood of success) and potential impact if successful (customer satisfaction, revenue growth, strategic differentiation, sustainability enhancement—whatever metrics by which you'd define success).

3. Based on steps 1 and 2, select opportunities to pursue, whether for near-term implementation, longer-term development, or tracking for possible future action.

The process looks like that shown in figure A.6.

Here is a worksheet (figure A.7) to walk through the process.

Use these exercises to catalyze your Proximity thinking. Once you've got things moving, commit to staying ahead in the long run.

Lead the Trend: Move Ever Onward to P = 0

Having catalyzed your Proximity journey, it's time to set yourself up to continually discover, define, and pursue paths to serving customers wherever, whenever. Let's keep two premises in mind:

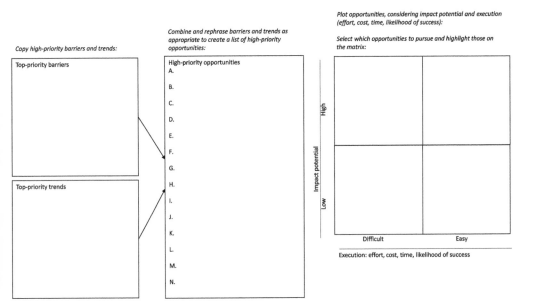

FIGURE A.7 Opportunities worksheet.

1. Ongoing Proximity leadership requires peripheral vision.
2. Winning in the long run requires an ecosystem of partners.

ONGOING PROXIMITY LEADERSHIP REQUIRES PERIPHERAL VISION

Companies, investors, NGO leaders, and policymakers must constantly renew their awareness of what's possible, because what's possible changes. An essential way to discover what's possible is to cultivate peripheral vision. What's percolating on the edges—before it incurs into your markets and changes the game.

The big threats and opportunities start on your peripheries. With rare exceptions, they don't come from your direct competitors. Even if you and your competitors are forward-thinking, innovative companies, most of the big opportunities start somewhere else: research labs, start-ups, new technologies not yet diffused across your industry. Besides, you already know everything your competitors are doing (especially if it's potentially groundbreaking), and they know everything you're doing.

It's not our purview to address this in detail here, but to consistently lead the Proximity trend (or any other significantly new directions, for that matter), you'll need the capability to track developments outside the core of your industry. Peripheries include, but aren't limited to, new technologies, other industries with analogous conditions or needs, start-ups pursuing visions potentially relevant to your customers' future, and other markets in the world that are navigating different realities.

No company can know everything. You'll need to be strategic about which peripheries you select to monitor for opportunities and threats. Here is a simple approach to start building your ongoing peripheral vision or to enhance the sensing mechanisms you already have.

1. *Identify peripheries* you believe could be relevant in the future (technologies, industries, investor and start-up communities, geographies). Prioritize those to actively track.
2. *Monitor them.* You'll need to define mechanisms within your company to do so on an ongoing basis. This isn't a one-and-done effort.
3. Continually ask *who is advancing Proximity*, and how are they doing it? *What might this mean for your company and your customers?*
4. *Share the insights with the right people.* Make sure people know where to take insights from the periphery, or they'll get lost. Who within your company is responsible and empowered to act on these insights?

Peripheral vision transcends Proximity, but it will be difficult to become and remain a leader in this regard without insights from outside business-as-usual.

WINNING IN THE LONG RUN REQUIRES AN ECOSYSTEM OF PARTNERS

No company can be great at everything when so many factors are in flux. Recall how flummoxed Google appeared after Microsoft's announcement of the integration of generative AI platform ChatGPT into its Bing search engine. At the time, Google was one of the top AI players on the planet. It was a leaders, even a pioneer, in AI application, research, and investment, and yet it appeared to be caught flat-footed. Change can challenge anyone.

Given the volatility of change and the diversity of relevant technologies, assets, and capabilities, it is unlikely that any one company will be able to lead Proximity over time. Even companies like Google, Microsoft, and Amazon, some of the largest and best-resourced companies in history, cultivate a wide range of partners in addition to their direct customers. And their ecosystem configurations evolve over time.

Ecosystems play many roles, from market intelligence to competitive moats (for instance, if being part of one universe restricts participants from another, such as with the global airline alliances like Star Alliance and One World). With respect to Proximity, the primary role for ecosystems will be to access capabilities and expertise as competitive requirements change.

CONCLUSION

Proximity has represented an important source of advantage for decades. Indeed, responding to customers where, when, and how they prefer has long been an organizing objective for business.

But Proximity—creating, generating, and providing what customers want, wherever, whenever they want it—is at the onset of an evolutionary leap. Across sectors, it is becoming a pivotal source of advantage, even a competitive requirement. Leading the transformation is the best way to avoid being left behind.

Notes

1. PROXIMITY RISING

1. Unsourced quotes throughout the book are from interviews conducted by the authors.
2. Klaus Schwab, "The Fourth Industrial Revolution: What It Means, How to Respond," World Economic Forum, last modified January 14, 2016, https://www.weforum.org/agenda/2016/01/the-fourth-industrial-revolution-what-it-means-and-how-to-respond/.
3. John P. Banks and Charles K. Ebinger, "The Electricity Revolution," Brookings, last modified November 8, 2013, https://www.brookings.edu/research/the-electricity-revolution/.
4. Roger Ekirch, *At Day's Close: Night in Times Past* (New York: Norton, 2005).
5. Paul A. David, "The Dynamo and the Computer: An Historical Perspective on the Modern Productivity Paradox," *American Economic Review* 80, no. 2 (1990): 355–361.
6. GE Additive, "Additive 101," accessed February 23, 2023, https://www.ge.com/additive/additive-manufacturing.

2. ACCELERATING TOWARD P = 0

1. Rain Noe, "How Arrival Designed Their Vehicles to Sidestep the Most Expensive Parts of Automobile Mass Production," Core77, last modified April 22, 2021, https://www.core77.com/posts/108548/How-Arrival-Designed-Their-Vehicles-to-Sidestep-the-Most-Expensive-Parts-of-Automobile-Mass-Production.
2. Robert C. Wolcott, "EVs Catch Fire. How to Pick Winners: Arrival Channels Henry Ford's Ghost," *Forbes*, last modified December 9, 2020, https://www.forbes.com/sites/robertwolcott/2020/12/09/evs-catch-fire-how-to-pick-winners-arrival-channels-henry-fords-ghost/.
3. "Parameters" are variables in a machine learning system whose values are developed during training of the model to allow the model to convert inputs to desired types of outputs, such as generate text in response to prompts.
4. Ahmed Awadallah et al., "Orca 2: Teaching Small Language Models How to Reason," *Microsoft Research Blog*, November 20, 2023, https://www.microsoft

.com/en-us/research/blog/orca-2-teaching-small-language-models-how-to
-reason/.

5. Awadallah et al., "Orca 2."

6. Remi Lam, "GraphCast: AI Model for Faster and More Accurate Global Weather Forecasting," *Google DeepMind Blog*, November 14, 2023, https://deepmind .google/discover/blog/graphcast-ai-model-for-faster-and-more-accurate-global -weather-forecasting/.

7. Nonetheless, even during the Industrial Revolution, a wider ecosystem view benefited those who were capable of thinking and acting accordingly. For instance, John D. Rockefeller and J. Pierpont Morgan thrived in the Gilded Age partly because they could think and act across multiple industry ecosystems.

3. HOW WE WORK

1. "In First Person: Jos de Blok," SHRM Executive Network, accessed July 1, 2023, https://www.shrm.org/executive/resources/people-strategy-journal/winter2021 /Pages/in-first-person-de-blok.aspx.

2. Bradford Gray and Jako S. Burgers, "Home Care by Self-Governing Nursing Teams: The Netherlands' Buurtzorg Model," The Commonwealth Fund, last modified May 29, 2015, https://www.commonwealthfund.org/publications /case-study/2015/may/home-care-self-governing-nursing-teams-netherlands -buurtzorg-model.

3. Robert C. Wolcott, "Learning to Code Will Eventually Be as Useful as Learning Ancient Greek," *Quartz*, November 22, 2017. The intent was to challenge the misguided belief that teaching people how to code would provide them with long-term job security.

4. Robert C. Wolcott, "2021 Unicorn IPO: Unqork, the No Code Movement & Offending People with the Future," *Forbes*, last modified July 27, 2020, https:// www.forbes.com/sites/robertwolcott/2020/07/27/a-2021-unicorn-ipo-the-no -code-movement—unqork-offending-people-future/.

5. Jason Gale, "Why Doctors Are Using Snapchat Glasses in Operating Rooms," *Time*, last modified January 25, 2018, https://time.com/5118645/shafi-ahmed -snapchat-glasses-medical-training/.

6. Louis Rosenberg, "Huge Milestone as Human Subject Wears Augmented Reality Contact Lens for First Time," Big Think, last modified July 6, 2022, https:// bigthink.com/the-future/augmented-reality-ar-milestone-wearable-contacts/.

7. Rosenberg, "Huge Milestone."

8. "The Future of Micro-Led Technology Is Here," Mojo, accessed July 28, 2022, https://www.mojo.vision/.

9. Founded in 2012, Talkspace gained serious momentum during the first year of the COVID-19 pandemic. After going public in January 2021 at an evaluation of over $1 billion, the company's market value at time of writing has collapsed to around $300 million due to a variety of challenges in managing growth.

10. David Nordfors and Vint Cerf, *The People Centered Economy: The New Ecosystem for Work* (Menlo Park, CA: IIIJ Foundation, 2018).
11. "The Rise of Talent Matching Platforms: Why We Invested in Hyre," Medium,
last modified October 12, 2021, https://medium.com/talent-venture-group/the
-rise-of-talent-matching-platforms-why-we-invested-hyre-492bbc78c35.
12. Find a summary of Erik Brynjolfsson's work at www.brynjolfsson.com.
13. Tom Simonite, "Deepfakes Are Becoming the Hot New Corporate Training
Tool," WIRED, last modified July 7, 2020, https://www.wired.com/story/covid
-drives-real-businesses-deepfake-technology/.
14. Robert Wolcott, "When the Computer Is You," *Forbes*, February 19, 2017, https://
www.forbes.com/sites/robertwolcott/2017/02/19/when-the-computer-is-you
-the-rise-of-proxy-ai/.
15. Michael Schrage, "How Technology-Enabled 'Selves-Improvement' Will Drive
the Future of Personal Productivity," TechCrunch, last modified June 21,
2022, https://techcrunch.com/2017/06/21/how-technology-enabled-selves
-improvement-will-drive-the-future-of-personal-productivity; Robert C. Wolcott,
"How Automation Will Change Work, Purpose, and Meaning," *Harvard Business
Review*, January 11, 2018, https://hbr.org/2018/01/how-automation-will-change
-work-purpose-and-meaning.
16. W. Brian Arthur, "Where Is Technology Taking the Economy?," Quantum
Black, AI by McKinsey, last modified October 5, 2017, https://www.mckinsey
.com/capabilities/quantumblack/our-insights/where-is-technology-taking
-the-economy.

4. HOW WE EAT

1. In a culturally charged aside, the French endured a mustard crisis, as 75 percent of all mustard seed came from Ukraine and Russia.
2. "Obesity Rates by Country 2023," World Population Review, accessed January
7, 2022, https://worldpopulationreview.com/country-rankings/obesity-rates
-by-country.
3. Food and Agriculture Organization, "Global Food Losses and Food Waste,"
2011, https://www.fao.org/3/mb060e/mb060e00.htm.
4. Elle Chang, "International Efforts on Wasted Food Recovery," U.S. Environmental Protection Agency, accessed March 7, 2023, https://www.epa.gov
/international-cooperation/international-efforts-wasted-food-recovery.
5. Kathryn Reid, "10 World Hunger Facts You Need to Know," World Vision,
last modified July 6, 2022, https://www.worldvision.org/hunger-news-stories
/world-hunger-facts.
6. Melisa Gonzalez, "Elzelinde van Doleweerd Fights Food Waste Through 3D
Printed Food," 3Dprint.com, last modified February 20, 2019, https://3dprint
.com/236416/elzelinde-van-doleweerd-fights-food-wastage-through-3d
-printed-food/.

7. Ali Morris, "Elzelinde van Doleweerd Creates 3d-Printed Snacks from Food Waste," Dezeen, last modified October 3, 2018, https://www.dezeen.com/2018/10/03/upprinting-food-elzelinde-van-doleweerd-beijing-design-week-upprinting-food-design/.

8. Linly Ku, "Indoor Vertical Farming: The New Era of Agriculture," Plug and Play, last modified October 6, 2021, https://www.plugandplaytechcenter.com/resources/indoor-vertical-farming-new-era-agriculture/.

9. Eric Wilhelmsen, "Is CEA Being Oversold?," *Food Safety Magazine*, last modified February 1, 2022, https://www.food-safety.com/articles/7522-is-cea-being-oversold.

10. "Our Shared Challenge," Vertical Harvest, accessed July 1, 2023, https://verticalharvestfarms.com/.

11. Peter H. Diamandis, "How 3D Printing, Vertical Farming, and Materials Science Are Overhauling Food," Agritecture, accessed July 1, 2023, https://www.agritecture.com/blog/2019/10/23/how-3d-printing-vertical-farming-and-materials-science-are-overhauling-food.

12. Jennifer Marston, "Farmshelf Unveils Its First Consumer-Facing Vertical Farming Unit," The Spoon, last modified April 21, 2020, https://thespoon.tech/farmshelf-unveils-its-first-consumer-facing-vertical-farming-unit/.

13. "Farmshelf Wants to Take Home Growing Systems from Gimmick to Grocery Store Replacement," AgFunderNews, last modified May 14, 2020, https://agfundernews.com/farmshelf-wants-to-take-home-growing-systems-from-gimmick-to-grocery-store-replacement.html.

14. Simon Harvey, "Plenty Unlimited Plans 'Advanced' R&D Vertical-Farming Facility," Just Food, last modified February 3, 2023, https://www.just-food.com/news/plenty-unlimited-plans-advanced-rd-vertical-farming-facility/.

15. JustAnotherAmerican, "Cost of Raising 1kg of Cricket Meat versus 1kg of Cow Meat," Wikipedia, last modified January 17, 2020, https://en.wikipedia.org/wiki/File:Cricket_diagram_2.png.

16. Jonah van Beijnen and Kyra Hoevenaars, "Dubai's Aquaculture Success Story: Fish Farms LLC," The Fish Site, last modified February 6, 2023, https://thefishsite.com/articles/dubais-aquaculture-success-story-fish-farms-llc.

17. Abigail Abrams, "How Eating Less Meat Could Help Protect the Planet from Climate Change," *Time*, last modified August 8, 2019, https://time.com/5648082/un-climate-report-less-meat/.

18. Jeffrey Klein, "3D Printed Meat: The Most Promising Projects," All3DP, last modified February 19, 2020, https://all3dp.com/2/3d-printed-meat-most-promising-projects/.

19. "The World's First 3D-Printing Restaurant," Food Ink, accessed December 12, 2021, http://foodink.io/.

20. Kishalaya Kundu, "3D-Printed Steak Now Being Served in 30 Restaurants," Screen Rant, last modified December 7, 2021, https://screenrant.com/3d-printed-steak-meat-restaurant/.

21. "Welcome to Biozoon Food Innovations GmbH," Biozoon, accessed December 12, 2021, https://biozoon.de/en/.

22. "What Is the Internet of Things?," IBM, accessed July 1, 2023, https://www
.ibm.com/blogs/internet-of-things/what-is-the-iot/.

23. Annie Petzer, "History of the Internet of Things (IoT)," IT Online Learning, last
modified March 2, 2020, https://www.itonlinelearning.com/blog-history-iot/.

24. "30 by 30," Singapore Food Agency, accessed July 1, 2023, https://www.ourfood
future.gov.sg/30by30.

5. HOW WE PREVENT AND CURE

1. Eve Glicksman, "World First: Drone Delivers Defibrillator That Saves Man
in Cardiac Arrest," Leaps.org, last modified January 5, 2022, https://leaps.org
/drones/particle-3.

2. Rosamond Wayne et al., "Drone Delivery of an Automated External Defibrillator," *New England Journal of Medicine* 383, no. 12 (2020): 1186–1188, https://
doi.org/10.1056/NEJMc1915956.

3. Albert Bourla, *Moonshot: Inside Pfizer's Nine-Month Race to Make the Impossible Possible* (New York: Harper Business, 2022).

4. MedArrive, "Medarrive + Molina Healthcare (Harris County, TX)," YouTube,
last modified March 3, 2022, https://youtu.be/KejiO8nig8U.

5. Michael Schroeder, "Two Firms Team up to Facilitate at-Home Screenings to
Prevent Blindness," MedCity News, last modified January 31, 2022, https://
medcitynews.com/2022/01/two-firms-team-up-to-facilitate-at-home-screenings
-to-prevent-eye-disease/.

6. Emma Tucker, "Artefact's Aim Health Clinic Can Drive Itself to the Patient,"
Dezeen, last modified July 8, 2017, https://www.dezeen.com/2017/07/08/artefact
-aim-health-clinic-drive-itself-to-patient-design-technology/.

7. Nathan Eddy, "What to Know About Autonomous Vehicles in Healthcare,"
HealthTech, last modified December 10, 2020, https://healthtechmagazine.net
/article/2020/12/what-know-about-autonomous-vehicles-healthcare.

8. Nidhi Subbaraman, "Meet the Real-Life Robo-Surgeon Who Fixes Brains in
Ender's Game," NBC News, last modified October 31, 2013, https://www.nbcnews
.com/sciencemain/meet-real-life-robo-surgeon-who-fixes-brains-enders-game
-8c11500771.

9. "Robotic Surgery," Mayo Clinic, last modified May 6, 2022, https://www
.mayoclinic.org/tests-procedures/robotic-surgery/about/pac-20394974.

10. Jessica Miley, "These Tiny Robotic Arms Help Surgeons Perform Life-Saving
Procedures," Interesting Engineering, last modified December 7, 2017, https://
interestingengineering.com/video/these-tiny-robotic-arms-help-surgeons
-perform-life-saving-procedures.

11. James Wright, "Inside Japan's Long Experiment in Automating Elder Care," MIT
Technology Review, last modified January 09, 2023, https://www.technology
review.com/2023/01/09/1065135/japan-automating-eldercare-robots/.

12. Anmol Mohan et al., "Telesurgery and Robotics: An Improved and Efficient
Era," *Cureus* 13, no. 3 (2021).

13. Elise Favis, "New Mobile Games Aim to Help Medical Professionals Treat Coronavirus," *Washington Post*, last modified May 22, 2020, https://www .washingtonpost.com/video-games/2020/05/22/new-mobile-games-provide -unique-approach-medical-professionals-coronavirus-fight/.

14. "10 Internet of Things (IoT) Healthcare Examples," Ordr, accessed July 1, 2023, https://ordr.net/article/iot-healthcare-examples/.

15. "Spire Health Closes $38 Million Financing Round Led by Gilde Healthcare to Advance Respiratory Remote Patient Monitoring," Spire Health, last modified July 14, 2021, https://www.spirehealth.com/news/spire-health-closes-38-million -financing-round-led-by-gilde-healthcare-to-advance-respiratory-remote -patient-monitoring.

16. "Learn About COPD," American Lung Association Scientific, last modified April 28, 2022, https://www.lung.org/lung-health-diseases/lung-disease-lookup/copd /learn-about-copd.

17. "Newsroom," Spire Health, accessed July 1, 2023, https://www.spirehealth.com /newsroom.

18. Associated Press, "Would You Let Your Employer Implant an ID Chip in Your Arm? 150 Employees at Swedish Startup Get Micro-Chipped," *Daily Mail*, last modified April 3, 2017, https://www.dailymail.co.uk/sciencetech /article-4375730/Cyborgs-work-employees-getting-implanted-microchips .html.

19. Bjorn Cyborg, "Why Swedes Are Inserting Microchips into Their Bodies," *The Economist*, last modified August 2, 2018, https://www.economist.com/europe /2018/08/02/why-swedes-are-inserting-microchips-into-their-bodies.

20. Zhanna L. Malekos Smith, "Fear, Uncertainty, and Doubt About Human Microchips," CSIS, last modified June 23, 2020, https://www.csis.org/blogs /technology-policy-blog/fear-uncertainty-and-doubt-about-human-microchips.

21. Robert W. Locke, "Would You Like to Be Microchipped? 3 Questions We Must Ask Ourselves," Medium, last modified December 11, 2019, https://medium .com/swlh/would-you-like-to-be-microchipped-3-questions-we-must-ask -ourselves-e4d1f877ab2e.

22. "No More Needles," Rani Therapeutics, accessed February 12, 2022, https:// www.ranitherapeutics.com/.

23. "Rani Therapeutics Appoints Talat Imran CEO," News Direct, last modified June 22, 2021, https://newsdirect.com/news/rani-therapeutics-appoints-talat -imran-ceo-900202932.

24. "Microscale Wireless Bionauts Reach Deep Locations in the Body, Safely & Precisely," Bionaut, accessed March 9, 2022, https://bionautlabs.com/.

25. Michaela Haas, "Tiny, Injectable Robots Could Be the Future of Brain Treatments," Leaps, last modified August 12, 2021, https://leaps.org/nanobots-brain -tumors/particle-2.

26. Matthew Pava, "Hand Proprioception and Touch Interfaces (HAPTIX)," DARPA, accessed January 7, 2023, https://www.darpa.mil/program/hand -proprioception-and-touch-interfaces.

27. Sean Whooley, "7 Brain-Computer Interface Companies You Need to Know," Mass Device, last modified August 24, 2022, https://www.massdevice.com /brain-computer-interface-bci-companies/.

28. Juon Heggie, "Genomics: A Revolution in Health Care?," *National Geographic*, last modified February 20, 2019, https://www.nationalgeographic.com/science /article/partner-content-genomics-health-care.

29. Jeremy Preston, Ashley Van Zeeland, and Daniel A. Peiffer, "Innovation at Illumina: The Road to the $600 Human Genome," Nature Portfolio, accessed March 8, 2023, https://www.nature.com/articles/d42473-021-00030-9.

30. Some companies already produce small runs of specialized products for so-called orphan conditions—ailments with small patient populations for whom a drug can be a matter of life or death. Even so, the production and delivery model of these orphan drugs won't likely translate well for widespread personalized care. Most orphan drugs carry exceptionally high price tags, often in the tens or hundreds of thousands of dollars, as costs of development must be shared across a small patient population.

31. Kenneth Bonheure and David Schwartz, "How Asia's Largest Pharma Is Leveraging Its Values to Navigate the COVID-19 Crisis," McKinsey & Company, last modified July 30, 2020, https://www.mckinsey.com.br/capabilities/strategy-and -corporate-finance/our-insights/how-asias-largest-pharma-is-leveraging-its -values-to-navigate-the-covid-19-crisis.

32. Gabe Allen, "For These Clinicians, 3D Printers Are Changing Medicine," *Discover*, last modified September 20, 2021, https://www.discovermagazine.com /technology/for-these-clinicians-3d-printers-are-changing-medicine.

33. Allen, "For These Clinicians, 3D Printers Are Changing Medicine."

34. American Friends of Tel Aviv University, "Scientists Print First 3d Heart Using Patient's Biological Materials," Science Daily, last modified April 15, 2019, https://www.sciencedaily.com/releases/2019/04/190415102242.htm.

35. American Friends of Tel Aviv University, "Scientists Print First 3d Heart Using Patient's Biological Materials."

36. Allen, "For These Clinicians, 3D Printers Are Changing Medicine."

37. "Pushing the Boundaries of What's Possible in Children's Health," Boston Children's Hospital, accessed February 24, 2022, http://www.childrenshospital .org/.

38. Heggie, "Genomics: A Revolution in Health Care?"

39. Arthur L. Caplan et al., "No Time to Waste—the Ethical Challenges Created by CRISPR," *EMBO Reports* 16, no. 11 (2015): 1421–1426.

40. "Healthcare Data Breach Statistics," HIPAA Journal, accessed February 23, 2022, https://www.hipaajournal.com/healthcare-data-breach-statistics/.

41. Jenn Francis, "Millennial and Gen Z Consumers Paving the Way for Non-Traditional Care Models, Accenture Study Finds," Accenture, last modified February 12, 2019, https://newsroom.accenture.com/news/millennial-and-gen -z-consumers-paving-the-way-for-non-traditional-care-models-accenture -study-finds.htm.

42. Coindesk, "Designer Drug Markets Get Boost from Crypto," Crypto News, last modified September 2, 2022, https://cryptonews.net/news/other/11706713/.

43. Elham Khatami, "What Is Medical 3D Printing—and How Is It Regulated?," Pew, last modified October 5, 2020, https://www.pewtrusts.org/en/research-and-analysis/issue-briefs/2020/10/what-is-medical-3d-printing-and-how-is-it-regulated.

44. Timothy Gosnear, "Three Big Risks in 3D Printing Pharmaceuticals," Pharma Manufacturing, last modified October 31, 2016, https://www.pharmamanufacturing.com/development/drug-delivery/article/11313444/three-big-risks-in-3d-printing-pharmaceuticals.

45. "Wearables: What Is the Apple Watch?," GCF Global, accessed July 1, 2023, https://edu.gcfglobal.org/en/wearables/what-is-the-apple-watch/1/.

6. HOW WE CREATE AND PRODUCE

1. Raw materials in cartridges might degrade over time due to humidity, temperature, or other factors, and 3D production systems will eventually become obsolete. However, their useful lives will be far longer and more flexible than parts finished for a specific purpose.

2. Find more about transitional business platforms in the Proximity strategy workbook in the appendix and in Rob's article in the *Harvard Business Review* online: Robert C. Wolcott, "Does Your Business Model Look to the Future or Just Defend the Present?," *Harvard Business Review*, last modified March 22, 2016, https://hbr.org/2016/03/does-your-business-model-look-to-the-future-or-just-defend-the-present.

3. NAM News Room, "2.1 Million Manufacturing Jobs Could Go Unfilled by 2030," Workforce, last modified May 4, 2021, https://www.nam.org/2-1-million-manufacturing-jobs-could-go-unfilled-by-2030-13743/.

4. Carl Samson, "Chinese Factory Replaces 90% of Its Workers with Robots, Productivity Increases 250%," NextShark, last modified February 6, 2017, https://nextshark.com/kunshun-factory-robots-replace-humans/.

5. Jonathan Tilley, "Automation, Robotics, and the Factory of the Future," McKinsey & Company, last modified September 7, 2017, https://www.mckinsey.com/capabilities/operations/our-insights/automation-robotics-and-the-factory-of-the-future; "Lights-Out Manufacturing," UpKeep, accessed July 1, 2023, https://www.upkeep.com/learning/lights-out-manufacturing.

6. "5 Reasons for 5G," Bosch, accessed March 12, 2023, https://www.bosch.com/stories/5g-industry-4-0/.

7. Rob Errera, "3D Printing Statistics (2023 Additive Manufacturing Data)," Toner Buzz, last modified June 10, 2022, https://www.tonerbuzz.com/blog/3d-printing-statistics/.

8. Alla Katsnelson, "3D Printed Foods Enter the Kitchen," C&EN, last modified February 2, 2022, https://cen.acs.org/food/food-science/3D-printed-foods-enter-kitchen/100/i5.

9. Kyle Mizokami, "The Navy Is Using 3D Printers to Turn Warships into Weapons Factories," Popular Mechanics, last modified July 12, 2022, https://www.popular mechanics.com/military/a40577952/navy-3d-printing-spares-drone-parts/.

10. See Mizokami, "The Navy Is Using 3D Printers to Turn Warships into Weapons Factories."

11. See Stephen Holmes, "L'Oréal Makes 3D Printing Beautiful," DEVELOP3D, last modified November 15, 2021, https://develop3d.com/profiles/loreal-makes -3d-printing-beautiful/.

12. "Revolutionizing Dermatology with Bioprinting," L'Oréal, accessed July 1, 2023, https://www.loreal.com/en/news/group/revolutionizing-dermatology-with -bioprinting/.

13. This encounter was one of a few that year that catalyzed for the authors what became the notion of Proximity.

14. "Expanding the Possibilities for Human Experience," Relativity, accessed March 13, 2023, https://www.relativityspace.com/mission.

15. Jeff Foust, "Relativity Shelves Terran 1 After One Launch, Redesigns Terran R," Spare News, last modified April 12, 2023, https://spacenews.com/relativity -shelves-terran-1-after-one-launch-redesigns-terran-r/.

16. "What Are the Drawbacks of 3D Printing?," Fonts Arena, last modified December 14, 2022, https://fontsarena.com/blog/what-are-the-drawbacks-of-3d-printing/.

7. HOW WE POWER

1. Aline Eid, Jimmy G. D. Hester, and Manos M. Tentzeris, "5G as a Wireless Power Grid," *Scientific Reports* 11, no. 1 (2021): 636.

2. "Chapter 3: Enabling Modernization of the Electric Power System," U.S. Department of Energy, accessed July 1, 2023, https://www.energy.gov/sites /default/files/2015/09/f26/QTR2015-3D-Flexible-and-Distributed-Energy_0 .pdf.

3. "Extreme Cold Weather Expected to Result in Record Electric Use in ERCOT Region," ERCOT Communications, last modified February 11, 2021, https:// www.ercot.com/news/release?id=1f851612-b1c6-3806-ba84-f192b23083c9.

4. Jaclyn Diaz, "Texas Officials Put the Final Death Toll from Last Year's Winter Storm at 246," NPR, last modified January 3, 2022, https://www.npr.org/2022 /01/03/1069974416/texas-winter-storm-final-death-toll.

5. Briana Zamora-Nipper, "Timeline: Inside the 2021 Winter Storm, Power Crisis," Click2Houston, last modified February 15, 2022, https://www.click2houston .com/features/2022/02/15/timeline-inside-the-2021-winter-storm-power -crisis/.

6. Claire McInerny, "Why Is Texas on Its Own Electric Grid?," KUT 90.5, last modified July 22, 2021, https://www.kut.org/energy-environment/2021-07-22 /texas-electric-grid-february-blackouts-the-disconnect.

7. "Quick Facts TX," U.S. Census Bureau, accessed July 25, 2022, https://www .census.gov/quickfacts/TX.

8. Generac Holdings, "Generac Accelerates Its Energy Technology Capabilities with Acquisition of Enbala Power Networks," Generac Holdings, last modified October 5, 2020, https://investors.generac.com/news-releases/news-release-details/generac-accelerates-its-energy-technology-capabilities.

9. "Systems & Solutions," Toshiba, accessed July 1, 2023, https://www.global.toshiba/ww/products-solutions/renewable-energy/products-technical-services/vpp.html.

10. Andy Colthorpe, "Utility Portland General Electric Launches 4MW Virtual Power Plant Pilot in Oregon," Energy Storage News, last modified July 2, 2020, https://www.energy-storage.news/utility-portland-general-electric-launches-4mw-virtual-power-plant-pilot-in-oregon/.

11. Lisa Cohn, "Here Comes the Future: Bronzeville 'Microgrid Cluster' Set to Begin Operating This Year," Microgrid Knowledge, last modified January 24, 2022, https://microgridknowledge.com/bronzeville-microgrid-cluster-lessons-comed/.

12. Chris Owens, "The 11 Biggest Blackouts of All Time," Blackout Report, last modified December 4, 2020, https://www.theblackoutreport.co.uk/2020/12/07/11-biggest-blackouts/.

13. Abbas Uddin Noyon, Eyamin Sajid, and Reyad Hossain, "Blackouts Return as Bangladesh Feels First Stirrings of Energy Crisis," Business Standard, last modified July 5, 2022, https://www.tbsnews.net/bangladesh/energy/blackouts-return-bangladesh-feels-first-stirrings-energy-crisis-452970.

14. Ann Koh, "Global Gas Crunch Leaves Bangladesh Facing Blackouts Until 2026," Bloomberg, last modified July 31, 2022, https://www.bloomberg.com/news/articles/2022-08-01/global-gas-crunch-leaves-bangladesh-facing-blackouts-until-2026.

15. "A.C. Abdur Rahim," Rahimafrooz, accessed August 26, 2022, https://www.rahimafrooz.com/about-us/.

16. Shahnawaz Khan Chandan, "Niaz Rahim: A Story of Principle Before Profit," *Daily Star*, last modified July 1, 2016, https://www.thedailystar.net/star-weekend/star-people/niaz-rahim-story-principle-profit-1248256.

17. International Energy Agency, "World Energy Outlook 2021: A New Energy Economy Is Emerging," IEA, 2021, https://www.iea.org/reports/world-energy-outlook-2021/a-new-energy-economy-is-emerging.

18. Rusha Shrestha, "Lightyear Focusing on Lightyear 2, Canceling Lightyear 0," *U.S. News*, last modified January 24, 2023, https://www.usnews.com/cars-trucks/features/lightyear-0-production-canceled. https://www.usnews.com/cars-trucks/features/lightyear-0-production-canceled accessed March 11

19. "Sono Motors Commits to Focus Exclusively on Solar Tech Company, and Has Terminated the Sion Program," Sono Motors, last modified February 24, 2023, https://sonomotors.com/en/press/press-releases/sono-motors-commits-to-focus-exclusively-on-solar-tech-company-and-has-terminated-the-sion-program/.

20. Jane Nakano, "South Korea's Hydrogen Industrial Strategy," CSIS, last modified November 5, 2021, https://www.csis.org/analysis/south-koreas-hydrogen-industrial-strategy.

21. "Hyundai Motor Group Reveals 'FCEV Vision 2030,'" Hyundai, last modified November 12, 2018, https://www.hyundai.news/eu/articles/press-releases /hyundai-motor-group-reveals-fcev-vision-2030.html.
22. "H$_2$ Hydrogen Valley Estonia," Vesinkuorg, accessed July 1, 2023, https:// vesinikuorg.ee/.
23. Anmar Frangoul, "'The Most Dumb Thing': Elon Musk Dismisses Hydrogen as Tool for Energy Storage," CNBC, last modified May 12, 2022, https://www .cnbc.com/2022/05/12/tesla-ceo-elon-musk-dismisses-hydrogen-as-tool-for -energy-storage.html.
24. Sven Paulus, "Estonia Is Preparing for a Hydrogen Economy," Invest in Estonia, last modified November, 2022, https://investinestonia.com/estonia-is -preparing-for-a-hydrogen-economy/.
25. Philip Ball, "The Chase for Fusion Energy," *Nature*, last modified November 17, 2021, https://www.nature.com/immersive/d41586-021-03401-w/index.html. (Note that Commonwealth Fusion Systems announced an additional $1.8 billion funding round in December 2021, after this article went to press.)
26. Wal van Lierop, "Net Zero Needs Fusion. What Should Investors Be Asking the Frontrunners?," *Forbes*, last modified November 8, 2022, https://www .forbes.com/sites/walvanlierop/2022/11/08/net-zero-needs-fusion-what -should-investors-be-asking-the-frontrunners/.

8. HOW WE DEFEND

1. Adam Tiffen, "Going Green on the Battlefield Saves Lives," War on the Rocks, last modified May 22, 2014, https://warontherocks.com/2014/05/going-green -on-the-battlefield-saves-lives/.
2. Edward Humes, "Blood and Oil," Sierra, last modified July/August 2011, https:// vault.sierraclub.org/sierra/201107/blood-and-oil.aspx. The 50 percent figure is based on a quote in the article from a single analyst: Bill Browning, a member of the Defense Science Board's Energy Task Force and a founder of an environmental consulting group. The caveat "related to fuel convoys" is a very wide net and is not defined. The number killed or injured in a convoy itself is closer to 15 percent of the total, according to David S. Eady et al., "Sustain the Mission Project: Casualty Factors for Fuel and Water Resupply Convoys: Final Technical Report," Army Environmental Policy Institute, last modified September 2009, https:// apps.dtic.mil/sti/pdfs/ADB356341.pdf. If one counts only soldiers, not contractors, that number increases to about 20 percent. That's still a significant number: more than six thousand soldiers in Iraq and four thousand in Afghanistan.
3. Humes, "Blood and Oil"; Eady et al., "Sustain the Mission Project."
4. In typical fashion, the U.S. Department of Defense has a convoluted acronym for the various elements of a defense force that are key to accomplishing its mission: DOTMLPF, for Doctrine, Organization, Training, Materiel, Leadership and Education, Personnel, and Facilities!

5. Captain A. T. Mahan, *From Sail to Steam, Recollections of Naval Life* (New York: Harper, 1907).

6. Richard H. Van Atta et al., "Transition and Transformation: DARPA's Role in Fostering the Emerging Revolution in Military Affairs," Institute for Defense Analyses, 2003, https://apps.dtic.mil/sti/citations/ADA422835.

7. Quote from Van Atta et al., "Transition and Transformation." Example from Redstone Arsenal, *Redstone Arsenal Complex Chronology: The Redstone Arsenal Era, 1950–1989* (Huntsville, AL: Redstone Arsenal, 2001).

8. George F. Hofmann and Don A. Starry, eds., *Camp Colt to Desert Storm: The History of U.S. Armored Forces* (Lexington: University Press of Kentucky, 1999), 549–553.

9. That human operators are further from harm's way and hence safer from retaliation—*less* proximate in physical distance—is not as important as their ability to achieve military objectives (value creation) quickly and precisely.

10. Chris Daniels, "How Microsoft Was on 'Frontlines' of Russia-Ukraine Conflict Early On," King 5, last modified May 23, 2022, https://www.king5.com/article /tech/microsoft-frontlines-russia-ukraine-conflict/281-f61acb51-7bca-4736 -b83c-5c496ab7e59e.

11. DOD's Mine Resistant Ambush Protected (MRAP) vehicle began to be fielded less than eighteen months from the point that an initial needs statement was released. DOD also developed improved detection technologies and jammers for remote-controlled IEDs in matters of months.

12. Eric Levy-Myers, "Development and Fielding of Semi-Autonomous Mobile Systems (Robotics) in Iraq and Afghanistan," in *S&T Responsiveness in Support of Current Military Operations*, ed. Richard H. Van Atta (Alexandria, VA: Institute for Defense Analyses, 2007).

13. Jason Shell, "How the IED Won: Dispelling the Myth of Tactical Success and Innovation," War on the Rocks, last modified May 1, 2017, https://warontherocks .com/2017/05/how-the-ied-won-dispelling-the-myth-of-tactical-success-and -innovation/.

14. Megan Eckstein, "Early Experiments Are Proving Out Tank-Free Marine Corps Concept," USNI News, last modified February 10, 2021, https://news.usni.org /2021/02/10/early-experiments-are-proving-out-tank-free-marine-corps -concept.

15. Richard H. Van Atta, "Urban Warfare in 2015: The Role of Persistent Assistants in Achieving Capabilities for Small Unit Precision Combat," in *AAAI Spring Symposium: Persistent Assistants: Living and Working with AI*, ed. Daniel Shapiro et al. (Palo Alto, CA: AAAI Press, 2005).

16. In extreme cases, top leaders, who can often see what is happening with a defense force in real time using the same surveillance and reconnaissance assets as the force on the ground, could leave a force waiting for a commander's decision, who's waiting for the lawyer sitting next to him to authorize lethal force, who's waiting for his superior, who's waiting for a White House National Security Council representative. . . .

17. Jerusalem Post Editorial, "Distance Matters," Jerusalem Post, last modified April 4, 2015, https://www.jpost.com/opinion/distance-matters-396167.

18. Oscar Hartzog, "Make Traveling Safer and More Rewarding with These Pocket Translators," Rolling Stone, last modified March 11, 2021, https://www.rolling stone.com/product-recommendations/electronics/best-pocket-translators -1139814/.

19. Hartzog, "Make Traveling Safer."

20. Julian Hanton, "U.S. Navy 3D Prints Custom Drones," Robots.co.uk, last modified October 12, 2015, https://www.robots.co.uk/?p=475. See also Kyle Mizokami, "The Navy Is Using 3D Printers to Turn Warships into Weapons Factories," Popular Mechanics, last modified July 12, 2022, https://www.popularmechanics .com/military/a40577952/navy-3d-printing-spares-drone-parts/.

21. DARPA, "A Cornucopia of Microbial Foods," U.S. Department of Defense, last modified December 12, 2021, https://www.darpa.mil/news-events/2021-12-02.

22. With the rare exception of systems entirely disconnected from the internet with an "air gap." Even then vulnerabilities exist, as illustrated by the Stuxnet example.

23. Brian Krebs, "Report: Russian Hacker Forums Fueled Georgia Cyber Attacks," Washington Post, last modified December 16, 2008, https://seclists.org/isn/2008 /Oct/76.

24. George Perkovich and Ariel Levite, Understanding Cyber Conflict: 14 Analogies (Washington, DC: Georgetown University Press, 2017), 7.

25. Perkovich and Levite, Understanding Cyber Conflict, 12.

26. Daniels, "How Microsoft Was on 'Frontlines.'"

27. Brad Smith, "Defending Ukraine: Early Lessons from the Cyber War," Microsoft, last modified June 22, 2022, https://blogs.microsoft.com/on-the-issues/2022 /06/22/defending-ukraine-early-lessons-from-the-cyber-war/.

28. Smith, "Defending Ukraine."

29. Smith, "Defending Ukraine."

30. DARPA, "AlphaDogfight Trials Foreshadow Future of Human-Machine Symbiosis," U.S. Department of Defense, last modified August 26, 2020, https:// www.darpa.mil/news-events/2020-08-26.

31. Kai-Fu Lee, "The Third Revolution in Warfare," Atlantic, last modified September 11, 2021, https://www.theatlantic.com/technology/archive/2021/09/i-weapons -are-third-revolution-warfare/620013/.

32. "Google Letter," New York Times, accessed July 1, 2023, https://static01.nyt.com /files/2018/technology/googleletter.pdf.

33. Bureau of Arms Control Verification and Compliance, "Political Declaration on Responsible Military Use of Artificial Intelligence and Autonomy," U.S. Department of State, last modified February 16, 2023, https://www.state.gov /political-declaration-on-responsible-military-use-of-artificial-intelligence -and-autonomy/.

34. Aaron Nason, "The Future of War Will Be in the Metaverse," Marketing in Asia, last modified July 29, 2022, https://www.marketinginasia.com/the-future-of -war-will-be-in-the-metaverse/.

35. Chen Dogheng, "Artificial Intelligence: The Winning Blade of Cognitive War," *PLA Daily*, March 3, 2022.
36. John Baughman, "Enter the Battleverse: China's Metaverse War," *Military Cyber Affairs* 5, no. 1 (2022).
37. Louis Rosenberg, "Mind Control: The Metaverse May Be the Ultimate Tool of Persuasion," VentureBeat, last modified October 22, 2022, https://venturebeat.com/virtual/mind-control-the-metaverse-may-be-the-ultimate-tool-of-persuasion/.
38. Elliot Short, "What Happens to Us When Robots Fight Our Wars?," War Is Boring, last modified March 15, 2018, https://warisboring.com/what-happens-to-us-when-robots-fight-our-wars/.
39. Short, "What Happens to Us."
40. Julie Carpenter, *Culture and Human-Robot Interaction in Militarized Spaces* (New York: Routledge, 2016).
41. Short, "What Happens to Us."

9. PROXIMITY, SPACE, VIRTUAL WORLDS, AND LIVES WE DESIRE

1. Jonathan Crow, "Huxley to Orwell: My Hellish Vision of the Future Is Better than Yours (1949)," OpenCulture, last modified March 17, 2015, https://www.openculture.com/2015/03/huxley-to-orwell-my-hellish-vision-of-the-future-is-better-than-yours.html.
2. The "Kármán line" refers to the distance generally recognized as the border between Earth's atmosphere and space, at 100 kilometers above sea level.
3. GIFLondon, "Living in Space | Barbara Belvisi, Interstellar Lab | GIF Virtual 2020," YouTube, last modified April 14, 2020, https://www.youtube.com/watch?v=wKpprkUWOdw.
4. Robert Edward Gordon, interview, January 2023. See also the company's website, https://ceyeber.co/.
5. Matthew Ball, *The Metaverse: And How It Will Revolutionize Everything* (New York: Liveright, 2022).
6. The next few paragraphs originally appeared in Robert C. Wolcott, "The Post-Virtual World: Invisible Interfaces and Our Experience of Reality," Huffpost, last modified January 21, 2017, https://www.huffpost.com/entry/the-post-virtual-world-invisible-interfaces-and-our_b_588392f5e4b08f5134b62118.
7. Miguel Pais-Vieira et al., "Building an Organic Computing Device with Multiple Interconnected Brains," *Scientific Reports* 5, no. 1 (2015).
8. Robert C. Wolcott and Moran Cerf, "Virtual Reality, Sex and Chocolate Cake: Desire in a Post-Virtual World," *Forbes*, last modified March 30, 2017, https://www.forbes.com/sites/robertwolcott/2017/03/30/virtual-reality-sex-and-chocolate-cake-desire-in-a-post-virtual-world/?sh=495aa0673a6c.
9. If this reference is confusing, see the cult science fiction film *Soylent Green* from 1973. Not terribly profound, but super fun to watch.

10. More regarding the post-virtual world is available in Robert C. Wolcott and Moran Cerf, *Foresight* (self-pub., 2017).

11. *Extrapolating decoupling to its logical conclusion suggests obviating the need for our physical bodies.* An entirely cyber existence. When or if this will occur is a matter of speculation, but we are in the early stages of this journey. Increasingly, our human-technology partnership will construct our living realities. To be ready, we must speculate, ponder, debate, and engage. We have the potential to be masters or victims of our emerging universes. Possibly both.

12. Most of this section is adapted from an article Rob published in *Forbes*: Robert C. Wolcott, "The King Customer Paradox: The More Empowered, the More We Lose Control," *Forbes*, last modified April 30, 2017, https://www.forbes .com/sites/robertwolcott/2017/04/10/the-king-customer-paradox-the-more -empowered-the-more-we-lose-control/.

13. Robert C. Wolcott, "Laziness, Technology and Brain Scanning a Billion People: A Conversation with David Krakauer," *Forbes*, last modified July 31, 2017, https://www.forbes.com/sites/robertwolcott/2017/07/31/laziness-technology -and-brain-scanning-a-billion-people-a-conversation-with-david-krakauer/.

14. Benj Edwards, "ChatGPT Sets Record for Fastest-Growing User Base in History, Report Says," Ars Technica, last modified February 1, 2023, https:// arstechnica.com/information-technology/2023/02/chatgpt-sets-record -for-fastest-growing-user-base-in-history-report-says/.

APPENDIX: A PROXIMITY STRATEGY WORKBOOK

1. Matt Leonard, "5 Charts Show Amazon's Growing Logistics Network as It Puts Inventory Closer to Consumers," Supply Chain Dive, last modified August 2, 2021, https://www.supplychaindive.com/news/amazon-ecommerce-warehouse -fulfillment-capital-investment/603731/.

2. "Smart Press Shop Takes Shape at Porsche," Automation, last modified January 15, 2021, https://www.automation.com/en-us/articles/january-2021/smart-press -shop-takes-shape-at-porsche.

3. Simon Scherrenbacher, "Lasers Cutting Blanks for the Smart Press Shop," Schuler, last modified July 23, 2021, https://www.schulergroup.com/major/us /unternehmen/presse/pressemeldungen/archiv/2021/20210723_lbl-sps/index .html.

4. Arnd Huchzermeier and Jan Nordemann, "How Smaller Companies Can Bring Manufacturing Closer to Home," *Harvard Business Review*, last modified December 7, 2022, https://hbr.org/2022/12/how-smaller-companies-can-bring -manufacturing-closer-to-home.

Bibliography

Abrams, Abigail. "How Eating Less Meat Could Help Protect the Planet from Climate Change." *Time*. Last modified August 8, 2019. https://time.com/5648082 /un-climate-report-less-meat/.

AgFunderNews. "Farmshelf Wants to Take Home Growing Systems from Gimmick to Grocery Store Replacement." Last modified May 14, 2020. https:// agfundernews.com/farmshelf-wants-to-take-home-growing-systems-from -gimmick-to-grocery-store-replacement.html.

Allen, Gabe. "For These Clinicians, 3D Printers Are Changing Medicine." *Discover*. Last modified September 20, 2021. https://www.discovermagazine.com /technology/for-these-clinicians-3d-printers-are-changing-medicine.

American Friends of Tel Aviv University. "Scientists Print First 3d Heart Using Patient's Biological Materials." ScienceDaily. Last modified April 15, 2019. https:// www.sciencedaily.com/releases/2019/04/190415102242.htm.

American Lung Association Scientific. "Learn About COPD." Last modified April 28, 2022. https://www.lung.org/lung-health-diseases/lung-disease-lookup/copd/learn -about-copd.

Arthur, W. Brian. "Where Is Technology Taking the Economy?" QuantumBlack, AI by McKinsey. Last modified October 5, 2017. https://www.mckinsey.com /capabilities/quantumblack/our-insights/where-is-technology-taking-the -economy.

Associated Press. "Would You Let Your Employer Implant an ID Chip in Your Arm? 150 Employees at Swedish Startup Get Micro-Chipped." *Daily Mail*. Last modified April 3, 2017. https://www.dailymail.co.uk/sciencetech/article-4375730 /Cyborgs-work-employees-getting-implanted-microchips.html.

Automation.com. "Smart Press Shop Takes Shape at Porsche." Last modified January 15, 2021. https://www.automation.com/en-us/articles/january-2021/smart -press-shop-takes-shape-at-porsche.

Ball, Matthew. *The Metaverse: And How It Will Revolutionize Everything*. New York: Liveright, 2022.

Ball, Philip. "The Chase for Fusion Energy." *Nature*. Last modified November 17, 2021. https://www.nature.com/immersive/d41586-021-03401-w/index.html.

Banks, John P., and Charles K. Ebinger. "The Electricity Revolution." Brookings. Last modified November 8, 2013. https://www.brookings.edu/research/the-electricity-revolution/.

Baughman, John. "Enter the Battleverse: China's Metaverse War." *Military Cyber Affairs* 5, no. 1 (2022): 1–16.

Bionaut. "Microscale Wireless Bionauts Reach Deep Locations in the Body, Safely & Precisely." Accessed March 9, 2022. https://bionautlabs.com/.

Biozoon. "Welcome to Biozoon Food Innovations GmbH." Accessed December 12, 2021. https://biozoon.de/en/.

Bonheure, Kenneth, and David Schwartz. "How Asia's Largest Pharma Is Leveraging Its Values to Navigate the COVID-19 Crisis." McKinsey & Company. Last modified July 30, 2020. https://www.mckinsey.com.br/capabilities/strategy-and-corporate-finance/our-insights/how-asias-largest-pharma-is-leveraging-its-values-to-navigate-the-covid-19-crisis.

Bosch. "5 Reasons for 5G." Accessed March 12, 2023. https://www.bosch.com/stories/5g-industry-4-0/.

Boston Children's Hospital. "Pushing the Boundaries of What's Possible in Children's Health." Accessed February 24, 2022. http://www.childrenshospital.org/.

Bureau of Arms Control Verification and Compliance. "Political Declaration on Responsible Military Use of Artificial Intelligence and Autonomy." U.S. Department of State. Last modified February 16, 2023. https://www.state.gov/political-declaration-on-responsible-military-use-of-artificial-intelligence-and-autonomy/.

Caplan, Arthur L., Brendan Parent, Michael Shen, and Carolyn Plunkett. "No Time to Waste—the Ethical Challenges Created by CRISPR." *EMBO Reports* 16, no. 11 (2015): 1421–1426. https://doi.org/10.15252/embr.201541337.

Chandan, Shahnawaz Khan. "Niaz Rahim: A Story of Principle Before Profit." The Daily Star. Last modified July 1, 2016. https://www.thedailystar.net/star-weekend/star-people/niaz-rahim-story-principle-profit-1248256.

Chang, Elle. "International Efforts on Wasted Food Recovery." EPA. Accessed March 7, 2023. https://www.epa.gov/international-cooperation/international-efforts-wasted-food-recovery.

Cohn, Lisa. "Here Comes the Future: Bronzeville 'Microgrid Cluster' Set to Begin Operating This Year." Microgrid Knowledge. Last modified January 24, 2022. https://microgridknowledge.com/bronzeville-microgrid-cluster-lessons-comed/.

Coindesk. "Designer Drug Markets Get Boost from Crypto." Crypto News. Last modified September 2, 2022. https://cryptonews.net/news/other/11706713/.

Colthorpe, Andy. "Utility Portland General Electric Launches 4MW Virtual Power Plant Pilot in Oregon." Energy Storage News. Last modified July 2, 2020. https://www.energy-storage.news/utility-portland-general-electric-launches-4mw-virtual-power-plant-pilot-in-oregon/.

Crow, Jonathan. "Huxley to Orwell: My Hellish Vision of the Future Is Better than Yours (1949)." OpenCulture. Last modified March 17, 2015. https://www.openculture.com/2015/03/huxley-to-orwell-my-hellish-vision-of-the-future-is-better-than-yours.html.

Cyborg, Bjorn. "Why Swedes Are Inserting Microchips into Their Bodies." The Economist. Last modified August 2, 2018. https://www.economist.com/europe /2018/08/02/why-swedes-are-inserting-microchips-into-their-bodies.

Daniels, Chris. "How Microsoft Was on 'Frontlines' of Russia-Ukraine Conflict Early On." King 5. Last modified May 23, 2022. https://www.king5.com/article/tech /microsoft-frontlines-russia-ukraine-conflict/281-f61acb51-7bca-4736-b83c -5c496ab7e59e.

DARPA. "AlphaDogfight Trials Foreshadow Future of Human-Machine Symbiosis." U.S. Department of Defense. Last modified August 26, 2020. https://www .darpa.mil/news-events/2020-08-26.

——. "A Cornucopia of Microbial Foods." U.S. Department of Defense. Last modified December 12, 2021. https://www.darpa.mil/news-events/2021-12-02.

David, Paul A. "The Dynamo and the Computer: An Historical Perspective on the Modern Productivity Paradox." *American Economic Review* 80, no. 2 (1990): 355–361.

Diamandis, Peter H. "How 3D Printing, Vertical Farming, and Materials Science Are Overhauling Food." Agritecture. Accessed July 1, 2023. https://www.agritecture .com/blog/2019/10/23/how-3d-printing-vertical-farming-and-materials-science -are-overhauling-food.

Diaz, Jaclyn. "Texas Officials Put the Final Death Toll from Last Year's Winter Storm at 246." NPR. Last modified January 3, 2022. https://www.npr.org/2022/01/03 /1069974416/texas-winter-storm-final-death-toll.

Dogheng, Chen. "Artificial Intelligence: The Winning Blade of Cognitive War." *PLA Daily*, March 3, 2022.

Eady, David S., Steven B. Siegel, R. Steven Bell, and Scott H. Dicke. "Sustain the Mission Project: Casualty Factors for Fuel and Water Resupply Convoys: Final Technical Report." Army Environmental Policy Institute. Last modified September, 2009. https://apps.dtic.mil/sti/pdfs/ADB356341.pdf.

Eckstein, Megan. "Early Experiments Are Proving Out Tank-Free Marine Corps Concept." USNI News. Last modified February 10, 2021. https://news.usni.org /2021/02/10/early-experiments-are-proving-out-tank-free-marine-corps-concept.

Eddy, Nathan. "What to Know About Autonomous Vehicles in Healthcare." Health Tech. Last modified December 10, 2020. https://healthtechmagazine.net/article /2020/12/what-know-about-autonomous-vehicles-healthcare.

Edwards, Benj. "ChatGPT Sets Record for Fastest-Growing User Base in History, Report Says." Ars Technica. Last modified February 1, 2023. https://arstechnica .com/information-technology/2023/02/chatgpt-sets-record-for-fastest-growing -user-base-in-history-report-says/.

Eid, Aline, Jimmy G. D. Hester, and Manos M. Tentzeris. "5G as a Wireless Power Grid." *Scientific Reports* 11, no. 1 (2021): 636. https://doi.org/10.1038/s41598-020 -79500-x.

Ekirch, Roger. *At Day's Close: Night in Times Past*. New York: Norton, 2005.

ERCOT Communications. "Extreme Cold Weather Expected to Result in Record Electric Use in ERCOT Region." Last modified February 11, 2021. https://www .ercot.com/news/release?id=1f851612-b1c6-3806-ba84-f192b23083c9.

Errera, Rob. "3D Printing Statistics (2023 Additive Manufacturing Data)." Toner Buzz. Last modified June 10, 2022. https://www.tonerbuzz.com/blog/3d-printing -statistics/.

Favis, Elise. "New Mobile Games Aim to Help Medical Professionals Treat Coronavirus." *Washington Post*. Last modified May 22, 2020. https://www.washingtonpost .com/video-games/2020/05/22/new-mobile-games-provide-unique-approach -medical-professionals-coronavirus-fight/.

Fonts Arena. "What Are the Drawbacks of 3D Printing?" Last modified December 14, 2022. https://fontsarena.com/blog/what-are-the-drawbacks-of-3d-printing/.

Food and Agriculture Organization. "Global Food Losses and Food Waste." FAO, 2011. https://www.fao.org/3/mb060e/mb060e00.htm.

Food Ink. "The World's First 3D-Printing Restaurant." Accessed December 12, 2021. http://foodink.io/.

Foust, Jeff. "Relativity Shelves Terran 1 After One Launch, Redesigns Terran R." Spare News. Last modified April 12, 2023. https://spacenews.com/relativity-shelves -terran-1-after-one-launch-redesigns-terran-r/.

Francis, Jenn. "Millennial and Gen Z Consumers Paving the Way for Non-Traditional Care Models, Accenture Study Finds." Accenture. Last modified February 12, 2019. https://newsroom.accenture.com/news/millennial-and-gen-z-consumers-paving -the-way-for-non-traditional-care-models-accenture-study-finds.htm.

Frangoul, Anmar. "'The Most Dumb Thing': Elon Musk Dismisses Hydrogen as Tool for Energy Storage." CNBC. Last modified May 12, 2022. https://www.cnbc .com/2022/05/12/tesla-ceo-elon-musk-dismisses-hydrogen-as-tool-for-energy -storage.html.

Gale, Jason. "Why Doctors Are Using Snapchat Glasses in Operating Rooms." *Time*. Last modified January 25, 2018. https://time.com/5118645/shafi-ahmed-snapchat -glasses-medical-training/.

GCF Global. "Wearables: What Is the Apple Watch?" Accessed July 1, 2023. https:// edu.gcfglobal.org/en/wearables/what-is-the-apple-watch/1/.

GE Additive. "Additive 101." Accessed February 23, 2023. https://www.ge.com /additive/additive-manufacturing.

Generac Holdings. "Generac Accelerates Its Energy Technology Capabilities with Acquisition of Enbala Power Networks." Generac Holdings. Last modified October 5, 2020. https://investors.generac.com/news-releases/news-release-details /generac-accelerates-its-energy-technology-capabilities.

GIFLondon. "Living in Space | Barbara Belvisi, Interstellar Lab | GIFVirtual 2020." YouTube. Last modified April 14, 2020. https://www.youtube.com/watch?v =wKpprkUWOdw.

Glicksman, Eve. "World First: Drone Delivers Defibrillator That Saves Man in Cardiac Arrest." Leaps.org. Last modified January 5, 2022. https://leaps.org/drones /particle-3.

Gonzalez, Melisa. "Elzelinde Van Doleweerd Fights Food Waste Through 3D Printed Food." 3Dprint.com. Last modified February 20, 2019. https://3dprint.com/236416 /elzelinde-van-doleweerd-fights-food-wastage-through-3d-printed-food/.

Gosnear, Timothy. "Three Big Risks in 3D Printing Pharmaceuticals." Pharma Manufacturing. Last modified October 31, 2016. https://www.pharmamanufacturing.com/development/drug-delivery/article/11313444/three-big-risks-in-3d-printing-pharmaceuticals.

Gray, Bradford, and Jako S. Burgers. "Home Care by Self-Governing Nursing Teams: The Netherlands' Buurtzorg Model." The Commonwealth Fund. Last modified May 29, 2015. https://www.commonwealthfund.org/publications/case-study/2015/may/home-care-self-governing-nursing-teams-netherlands-buurtzorg-model.

Haas, Michaela. "Tiny, Injectable Robots Could Be the Future of Brain Treatments." Leaps. Last modified August 12, 2021. https://leaps.org/nanobots-brain-tumors/particle-2.

Hanton, Julian. "U.S. Navy 3D Prints Custom Drones." Robots.co.uk. Last modified October 12, 2015. https://www.robots.co.uk/?p=475.

Hartzog, Oscar. "Make Traveling Safer and More Rewarding with These Pocket Translators." Rolling Stone. Last modified March 11, 2021. https://www.rollingstone.com/product-recommendations/electronics/best-pocket-translators-1139814/.

Harvey, Simon. "Plenty Unlimited Plans 'Advanced' R&D Vertical-Farming Facility." Just Food. Last modified February 3, 2023. https://www.just-food.com/news/plenty-unlimited-plans-advanced-rd-vertical-farming-facility/.

Heggie, Juon. "Genomics: A Revolution in Health Care?" National Geographic. Last modified February 20, 2019. https://www.nationalgeographic.com/science/article/partner-content-genomics-health-care.

HIPAA Journal. "Healthcare Data Breach Statistics." Accessed February 23, 2022. https://www.hipaajournal.com/healthcare-data-breach-statistics/.

Hofmann, George F., and Donn A. Starry, eds. Camp Colt to Desert Storm: The History of U.S. Armored Forces. Lexington: University Press of Kentucky, 1999.

Holmes, Stephen. "L'Oréal Makes 3D Printing Beautiful." DEVELOP3D. Last modified November 15, 2021. https://develop3d.com/profiles/loreal-makes-3d-printing-beautiful/.

Huchzermeier, Arnd, and Jan Nordemann. "How Smaller Companies Can Bring Manufacturing Closer to Home." Harvard Business Review. Last modified December 7, 2022. https://hbr.org/2022/12/how-smaller-companies-can-bring-manufacturing-closer-to-home.

Humes, Edward. "Blood and Oil." Sierra. Last modified July/August, 2011. https://vault.sierraclub.org/sierra/201107/blood-and-oil.aspx.

Hyundai. "Hyundai Motor Group Reveals 'FCEV Vision 2030.'" Last modified November 12, 2018. https://www.hyundai.news/eu/articles/press-releases/hyundai-motor-group-reveals-fcev-vision-2030.html.

IBM. "What Is the Internet of Things?" Accessed July 1, 2023. https://www.ibm.com/blogs/internet-of-things/what-is-the-iot/.

International Energy Agency. "World Energy Outlook 2021: A New Energy Economy Is Emerging." IEA, 2021. https://www.iea.org/reports/world-energy-outlook-2021/a-new-energy-economy-is-emerging.

Jerusalem Post Editorial. "Distance Matters." Jerusalem Post. Last modified April 4, 2015. https://www.jpost.com/opinion/distance-matters-396167.

JustAnotherAmerican. "Cost of Raising 1kg of Cricket Meat Versus 1kg of Cow Meat." Wikipedia. Last modified January 17, 2020. https://en.wikipedia.org/wiki/File:Cricket_diagram_2.png.

Katsnelson, Alla. "3D Printed Foods Enter the Kitchen." C&EN. Last modified February 2, 2022. https://cen.acs.org/food/food-science/3D-printed-foods-enter-kitchen/100/i5.

Khatami, Elham. "What Is Medical 3D Printing—and How Is It Regulated?" Pew. Last modified October 5, 2020. https://www.pewtrusts.org/en/research-and-analysis/issue-briefs/2020/10/what-is-medical-3d-printing-and-how-is-it-regulated.

Klein, Jeffrey. "3D Printed Meat: The Most Promising Projects." All3DP. Last modified February 19, 2020. https://all3dp.com/2/3d-printed-meat-most-promising-projects/.

Koh, Ann. "Global Gas Crunch Leaves Bangladesh Facing Blackouts Until 2026." Bloomberg. Last modified July 31, 2022. https://www.bloomberg.com/news/articles/2022-08-01/global-gas-crunch-leaves-bangladesh-facing-blackouts-until-2026.

Krebs, Brian. "Report: Russian Hacker Forums Fueled Georgia Cyber Attacks." Washington Post. Last modified December 16, 2008. https://seclists.org/isn/2008/Oct/76.

Ku, Linly. "Indoor Vertical Farming: The New Era of Agriculture." Plug and Play. Last modified October 6, 2021. https://www.plugandplaytechcenter.com/resources/indoor-vertical-farming-new-era-agriculture/.

Kundu, Kishalaya. "3D-Printed Steak Now Being Served in 30 Restaurants." Screen Rant. Last modified December 7, 2021. https://screenrant.com/3d-printed-steak-meat-restaurant/.

L'Oréal. "Revolutionizing Dermatology with Bioprinting." Accessed July 1, 2023. https://www.loreal.com/en/news/group/revolutionizing-dermatology-with-bioprinting/.

Lee, Kai-Fu. "The Third Revolution in Warfare." Atlantic. Last modified September 11, 2021. https://www.theatlantic.com/technology/archive/2021/09/i-weapons-are-third-revolution-warfare/620013/.

Leonard, Matt. "5 Charts Show Amazon's Growing Logistics Network as It Puts Inventory Closer to Consumers." Supply Chain Dive. Last modified August 2, 2021. https://www.supplychaindive.com/news/amazon-ecommerce-warehouse-fulfillment-capital-investment/603731/.

Levy-Myers, Eric. "Development and Fielding of Semi-Autonomous Mobile Systems (Robotics) in Iraq and Afghanistan." In S&T Responsiveness in Support of Current Military Operations, ed. Richard H. Van Atta. Alexandria, VA: Institute for Defense Analyses, 2007.

Locke, Robert W. "Would You Like to Be Microchipped? 3 Questions We Must Ask Ourselves." Medium. Last modified December 11, 2019. https://medium

.com/swlh/would-you-like-to-be-microchipped-3-questions-we-must-ask -ourselves-e4d1f877ab2e.

Mahan, Captain A. T. *From Sail to Steam, Recollections of Naval Life.* New York: Harper, 1907.

Malekos Smith, Zhanna L. "Fear, Uncertainty, and Doubt About Human Microchips." CSIS. Last modified June 23, 2020. https://www.csis.org/blogs/technology -policy-blog/fear-uncertainty-and-doubt-about-human-microchips.

Marston, Jennifer. "Farmshelf Unveils Its First Consumer-Facing Vertical Farming Unit." The Spoon. Last modified April 21, 2020. https://thespoon.tech /farmshelf-unveils-its-first-consumer-facing-vertical-farming-unit/.

Mayo Clinic. "Robotic Surgery." Last modified May 6, 2022. https://www.mayoclinic .org/tests-procedures/robotic-surgery/about/pac-20394974.

McInerny, Claire. "Why Is Texas on Its Own Electric Grid?" KUT 90.5. Last modified July 22, 2021. https://www.kut.org/energy-environment/2021-07-22/texas -electric-grid-february-blackouts-the-disconnect.

MedArrive. "Medarrive + Molina Healthcare (Harris County, TX)." YouTube. Last modified March 3, 2022. https://youtu.be/KejiO8nig8U.

Medium. "The Rise of Talent Matching Platforms: Why We Invested in Hyre." Last modified October 12, 2021. https://medium.com/talent-venture-group/the-rise -of-talent-matching-platforms-why-we-invested-hyre-492bbc78c35.

Miley, Jessica. "These Tiny Robotic Arms Help Surgeons Perform Life-Saving Procedures." Interesting Engineering. Last modified December 7, 2017. https:// interestingengineering.com/video/these-tiny-robotic-arms-help-surgeons -perform-life-saving-procedures.

Mizokami, Kyle. "The Navy Is Using 3D Printers to Turn Warships into Weapons Factories." Popular Mechanics. Last modified July 12, 2022. https://www .popularmechanics.com/military/a40577952/navy-3d-printing-spares-drone -parts/.

Mohan, Anmol, Um Ul Wara, Muhammad Taha Arshad Shaikh, Rahil M. Rahman, and Zain Ali Zaidi. "Telesurgery and Robotics: An Improved and Efficient Era." *Cureus* 13, no. 3 (2021): e14124. https://doi.org/10.7759/cureus.14124

Mojo. "The Future of Micro-Led Technology Is Here." Accessed July 28, 2022. https://www.mojo.vision/.

Morris, Ali. "Elzelinde van Doleweerd Creates 3d-Printed Snacks from Food Waste." Dezeen. Last modified October 3, 2018. https://www.dezeen.com/2018/10/03 /upprinting-food-elzelinde-van-doleweerd-beijing-design-week-upprinting-food -design/.

Nakano, Jane. "South Korea's Hydrogen Industrial Strategy." CSIS. Last modified November 5, 2021. https://www.csis.org/analysis/south-koreas-hydrogen -industrial-strategy.

NAM News Room. "2.1 Million Manufacturing Jobs Could Go Unfilled by 2030." Workforce. Last modified May 4, 2021. https://www.nam.org/2-1-million -manufacturing-jobs-could-go-unfilled-by-2030-13743/.

Nason, Aaron. "The Future of War Will Be in the Metaverse." Marketing in Asia. Last modified July 29, 2022. https://www.marketinginasia.com/the-future-of -war-will-be-in-the-metaverse/.

News Direct. "Rani Therapeutics Appoints Talat Imran CEO." Last modified June 22, 2021. https://newsdirect.com/news/rani-therapeutics-appoints-talat-imran -ceo-900202932.

New York Times. "Google Letter." Accessed July 1, 2023. https://static01.nyt.com/files /2018/technology/googleletter.pdf.

Noe, Rain. "How Arrival Designed Their Vehicles to Sidestep the Most Expensive Parts of Automobile Mass Production." Core77. Last modified April 22, 2021. https://www.core77.com/posts/108548/How-Arrival-Designed-Their-Vehicles -to-Sidestep-the-Most-Expensive-Parts-of-Automobile-Mass-Production.

Nordfors, David, and Vint Cerf. *The People Centered Economy: The New Ecosystem for Work.* Menlo Park, CA: IIIJ Foundation, 2018.

Noyon, Abbas Uddin, Eyamin Sajid, and Reyad Hossain. "Blackouts Return as Bangladesh Feels First Stirrings of Energy Crisis." The Business Standard. Last modified July 5, 2022. https://www.tbsnews.net/bangladesh/energy/blackouts -return-bangladesh-feels-first-stirrings-energy-crisis-452970.

Ordr. "10 Internet of Things (IoT) Healthcare Examples." Accessed July 1, 2023. https://ordr.net/article/iot-healthcare-examples/.

Owens, Chris. "The 11 Biggest Blackouts of All Time." The Blackout Report. Last modified December 4, 2020. https://www.theblackoutreport.co.uk/2020/12/07 /11-biggest-blackouts/.

Pais-Vieira, Miguel, Gabriela Chiuffa, Mikhail Lebedev, Amol Yadav, and Miguel A. L. Nicolelis. "Building an Organic Computing Device with Multiple Interconnected Brains." *Scientific Reports* 5, no. 1 (2015): 11869. https://doi.org/10.1038 /srep11869.

Paulus, Sven. "Estonia Is Preparing for a Hydrogen Economy." Invest in Estonia. Last modified November, 2022. https://investinestonia.com/estonia-is-preparing-for -a-hydrogen-economy/.

Pava, Matthew. "Hand Proprioception and Touch Interfaces (HAPTIX)." DARPA. Accessed January 7, 2023. https://www.darpa.mil/program/hand-proprioception -and-touch-interfaces.

Perkovich, George, and Ariel Levite. *Understanding Cyber Conflict: 14 Analogies.* Washington, DC: Georgetown University Press, 2017.

Petzer, Annie. "History of the Internet of Things (IoT)." IT Online Learning. Last modified March 2, 2020. https://www.itonlinelearning.com/blog-history-iot/.

Preston, Jeremy, Ashley Van Zeeland, and Daniel A. Peiffer. "Innovation at Illumina: The Road to the $600 Human Genome." Nature Portfolio. Accessed March 8, 2023. https://www.nature.com/articles/d42473-021-00030-9.

Rahimafrooz. "A.C. Abdur Rahim." Accessed August 26, 2022. https://www.rahimafrooz .com/about-us/.

Rani Therapeutics. "No More Needles." Accessed February 12, 2022. https://www .ranitherapeutics.com/.

Reid, Kathryn. "10 World Hunger Facts You Need to Know." World Vision. Last modified July 6, 2022. https://www.worldvision.org/hunger-news-stories/world-hunger-facts.

Relativity. "Expanding the Possibilities for Human Experience." Accessed March 13, 2023. https://www.relativityspace.com/mission.

Rosenberg, Louis. "Huge Milestone as Human Subject Wears Augmented Reality Contact Lens for First Time." Big Think. Last modified July 6, 2022. https://bigthink.com/the-future/augmented-reality-ar-milestone-wearable-contacts/.

———. "Mind Control: The Metaverse May Be the Ultimate Tool of Persuasion." VentureBeat. Last modified October 22, 2022. https://venturebeat.com/virtual/mind-control-the-metaverse-may-be-the-ultimate-tool-of-persuasion/.

Samson, Carl. "Chinese Factory Replaces 90% of Its Workers with Robots, Productivity Increases 250%." NextShark. Last modified February 6, 2017. https://nextshark.com/kunshun-factory-robots-replace-humans/.

Scherrenbacher, Simon. "Lasers Cutting Blanks for the Smart Press Shop." Schuler. Last modified July 23, 2021. https://www.schulergroup.com/major/us/unternehmen/presse/pressemeldungen/archiv/2021/20210723_lbl-sps/index.html.

Schrage, Michael. "How Technology-Enabled 'Selves-Improvement' Will Drive the Future of Personal Productivity." TechCrunch. Last modified June 21, 2022. https://techcrunch.com/2017/06/21/how-technology-enabled-selves-improvement-will-drive-the-future-of-personal-productivity.

Schroeder, Michael. "Two Firms Team Up to Facilitate at-Home Screenings to Prevent Blindness." MedCity News. Last modified January 31, 2022. https://medcitynews.com/2022/01/two-firms-team-up-to-facilitate-at-home-screenings-to-prevent-eye-disease/.

Schwab, Klaus. "The Fourth Industrial Revolution: What It Means, How to Respond." World Economic Forum. Last modified January 14, 2016. https://www.weforum.org/agenda/2016/01/the-fourth-industrial-revolution-what-it-means-and-how-to-respond/.

Shell, Jason. "How the IED Won: Dispelling the Myth of Tactical Success and Innovation." War on the Rocks. Last modified May 1, 2017. https://warontherocks.com/2017/05/how-the-ied-won-dispelling-the-myth-of-tactical-success-and-innovation/.

Short, Elliot. "What Happens to Us When Robots Fight Our Wars?" War Is Boring. Last modified March 15, 2018. https://warisboring.com/what-happens-to-us-when-robots-fight-our-wars/.

Shrestha, Rusha. "Lightyear Focusing on Lightyear 2, Canceling Lightyear 0." U.S. News. Last modified January 24, 2023. https://www.usnews.com/cars-trucks/features/lightyear-0-production-canceled.

SHRM Executive Network. "In First Person: Jos de Blok." Accessed July 1, 2023. https://www.shrm.org/executive/resources/people-strategy-journal/winter2021/Pages/in-first-person-de-blok.aspx.

Simonite, Tom. "Deepfakes Are Becoming the Hot New Corporate Training Tool." WIRED. Last modified July 7, 2020. https://www.wired.com/story/covid-drives-real-businesses-deepfake-technology/.

Singapore Food Agency. "30 by 30." Accessed July 1, 2023. https://www.ourfood future.gov.sg/30by30.

Smith, Brad. "Defending Ukraine: Early Lessons from the Cyber War." Microsoft. Last modified June 22, 2022. https://blogs.microsoft.com/on-the-issues/2022/06/22 /defending-ukraine-early-lessons-from-the-cyber-war/.

Sono Motors. "Sono Motors Commits to Focus Exclusively on Solar Tech Company, and Has Terminated the Sion Program." Last modified February 24, 2023. https://sonomotors.com/en/press/press-releases/sono-motors-commits-to -focus-exclusively-on-solar-tech-company-and-has-terminated-the-sion-program/.

Spire Health. "Newsroom." Accessed July 1, 2023. https://www.spirehealth.com /newsroom.

——. "Spire Health Closes $38 Million Financing Round Led by Gilde Healthcare to Advance Respiratory Remote Patient Monitoring." Last modified July 14, 2021. https://www.spirehealth.com/news/spire-health-closes-38-million-financing -round-led-by-gilde-healthcare-to-advance-respiratory-remote-patient-monitoring.

Subbaraman, Nidhi. "Meet the Real-Life Robo-Surgeon Who Fixes Brains in 'Ender's Game.'" NBC News. Last modified October 31, 2013. https://www.nbcnews.com /sciencemain/meet-real-life-robo-surgeon-who-fixes-brains-enders-game -8c11500771.

Tiffen, Adam. "Going Green on the Battlefield Saves Lives." War on the Rocks. Last modified May 22, 2014. https://warontherocks.com/2014/05/going-green -on-the-battlefield-saves-lives/.

Tilley, Jonathan. "Automation, Robotics, and the Factory of the Future." McKinsey & Company. Last modified September 7, 2017. https://www.mckinsey.com/capabilities /operations/our-insights/automation-robotics-and-the-factory-of-the-future.

Toshiba. "Systems & Solutions." Accessed July 1, 2023. https://www.global.toshiba /ww/products-solutions/renewable-energy/products-technical-services/vpp.html.

Tucker, Emma. "Artefact's Aim Health Clinic Can Drive Itself to the Patient." Dezeen. Last modified July 8, 2017. https://www.dezeen.com/2017/07/08/artefact-aim-health -clinic-drive-itself-to-patient-design-technology/.

United States Census Bureau. "Quick Facts TX." Accessed July 25, 2022. https:// www.census.gov/quickfacts/TX.

UpKeep. "Lights-Out Manufacturing." Accessed July 1, 2023. https://www.upkeep .com/learning/lights-out-manufacturing.

U.S. Department of Energy. "Chapter 3: Enabling Modernization of the Electric Power System." Accessed July 1, 2023. https://www.energy.gov/sites/default/files /2015/09/f26/QTR2015-3D-Flexible-and-Distributed-Energy_0.pdf.

Van Atta, Richard H. "Urban Warfare in 2015: The Role of Persistent Assistants in Achieving Capabilities for Small Unit Precision Combat." In *AAAI Spring Symposium: Persistent Assistants: Living and Working with AI*, ed. Daniel Shapiro, Pauline Berry, John Gersh, and Nathan Schurr, 122–128. Palo Alto, CA: AAAI Press, 2005.

Van Atta, Richard H., Alethia Cook, Ivars Gutmanis, Michael J. Lippitz, Jasper Lupo, Rob Mahoney, and Jack H. Nunn. "Transition and Transformation: DARPA's Role in Fostering the Emerging Revolution in Military Affairs." Institute for Defense Analyses, 2003. https://apps.dtic.mil/sti/citations/ADA422835.

van Beijnen, Jonah, and Kyra Hoevenaars. "Dubai's Aquaculture Success Story: Fish Farms LLC." The Fish Site. Last modified February 6, 2023. https://thefishsite.com /articles/dubais-aquaculture-success-story-fish-farms-llc.

van Lierop, Wal. "Net Zero Needs Fusion. What Should Investors Be Asking the Frontrunners?" *Forbes*. Last modified November 8, 2022. https://www.forbes .com/sites/walvanlierop/2022/11/08/net-zero-needs-fusion-what-should -investors-be-asking-the-frontrunners/.

Vertical Harvest. "Our Shared Challenge." Accessed July 1, 2023. https://vertical harvestfarms.com/.

Vesinkuorg. "H2 Hydrogen Valley Estonia." Accessed July 1, 2023. https://vesinikuorg .ee/.

Wayne, Rosamond, Anna M. Johnson, Brittany Bogle, Evan Arnold, Christopher J. Cunningham, Michael Picinich, Billy M. Williams, and Jessica K. Zègre-Hemsey. "Drone Delivery of an Automated External Defibrillator." *New England Journal of Medicine* 383, no. 12 (2020): 1186–1188. https://doi.org/10.1056/NEJMc1915956.

Whooley, Sean. "7 Brain-Computer Interface Companies You Need to Know." Mass Device. Last modified August 24, 2022. https://www.massdevice.com/brain -computer-interface-bci-companies/.

Wilhelmsen, Eric. "Is CEA Being Oversold?" *Food Safety Magazine*. Last modified February 1, 2022. https://www.food-safety.com/articles/7522-is-cea-being-oversold.

Wolcott, Robert C. "Does Your Business Model Look to the Future or Just Defend the Present?" *Harvard Business Review*. March 22, 2016. https://hbr.org/2016/03 /does-your-business-model-look-to-the-future-or-just-defend-the-present.

——. "EVs Catch Fire. How to Pick Winners: Arrival Channels Henry Ford's Ghost." *Forbes*. December 9, 2020. https://www.forbes.com/sites/robertwolcott/2020/12 /09/evs-catch-fire-how-to-pick-winners-arrival-channels-henry-fords-ghost/?.

——. "How Automation Will Change Work, Purpose, and Meaning." *Harvard Business Review*. January 11, 2018. https://hbr.org/2018/01/how-automation-will-change -work-purpose-and-meaning

——. "The King Customer Paradox: The More Empowered, the More We Lose Control." *Forbes*. April 30, 2017. https://www.forbes.com/sites/robertwolcott/2017/04/10 /the-king-customer-paradox-the-more-empowered-the-more-we-lose-control/.

——. "Laziness, Technology and Brain Scanning a Billion People: A Conversation with David Krakauer." *Forbes*. July 31, 2017. https://www.forbes.com/sites /robertwolcott/2017/07/31/laziness-technology-and-brain-scanning-a-billion -people-a-conversation-with-david-krakauer/

——. "The Post-Virtual World: Invisible Interfaces and Our Experience of Reality." Huffpost. January 21, 2017. https://www.huffpost.com/entry/the-post-virtual -world-invisible-interfaces-and-our_b_588392f5e4b08f5134b62118.

——. "2021 Unicorn IPO: Unqork, the No Code Movement & Offending People with the Future." *Forbes*. July 27, 2020. https://www.forbes.com/sites/robertwolcott

/2020/07/27/a-2021-unicorn-ipo-the-no-code-movement—unqork-offending
-people-future/.

Wolcott, Robert C., and Moran Cerf. *Foresight*. Private Publication, 2017.

——. "Virtual Reality, Sex and Chocolate Cake: Desire in a Post-Virtual World." *Forbes*.
March 30, 2017. https://www.forbes.com/sites/robertwolcott/2017/03/30/virtual
-reality-sex-and-chocolate-cake-desire-in-a-post-virtual-world/.

World Population Review. "Obesity Rates by Country 2023." Accessed January 7,
2022. https://worldpopulationreview.com/country-rankings/obesity-rates-by
-country.

Wright, James. "Inside Japan's Long Experiment in Automating Elder Care." MIT
Technology Review. Last modified January 09, 2023. https://www.technology
review.com/2023/01/09/1065135/japan-automating-eldercare-robots/.

Zamora-Nipper, Briana. "Timeline: Inside the 2021 Winter Storm, Power Crisis."
Click2Houston. Last modified February 15, 2022. https://www.click2houston
.com/features/2022/02/15/timeline-inside-the-2021-winter-storm-power-crisis/.

Index